Teaching Grammar

Language in Education
Series Editor
Michael Stubbs

Language is central to education. Yet very little writing about language is presented in a way that is suitable for teachers to help and guide them in their classroom practice. This series aims to explore in a non-technical way, aspects of language immediately relevant to practising and trainee teachers.

Learning about Writing: The Early Years
Pam Czerniewska

Teaching Grammar: A Guide for the National Curriculum
Richard Hudson

Teaching Grammar

A Guide for the National Curriculum

Richard Hudson

BLACKWELL
Oxford UK & Cambridge USA

First published 1992

Blackwell Publishers
108 Cowley Road
Oxford OX4 1JF
UK

Three Cambridge Center
Cambridge, Massachusetts 02142
USA

A CIP catalogue record for this book is available from the British Library.

Library of Congress Cataloging in Publication Data

Hudson, Richard A.
   Teaching grammar: a guide for the national curriculum / Richard Hudson.
      p.   cm. — (Language in education)
   Includes bibliographical references and index.
   ISBN 0–631–16624–6: $49.95. — ISBN 0–631–16625–4 (pbk.): $19.95
   1.   English language—Grammar—Study and teaching—Great Britain.
   I.   Title.   II.   Series.
PE1068.G5H83   1992
ISBN 0–631–166–246
        0–631–166–254 (pbk)

Typeset in 11 on 13pt Palatino
by Photo-graphics, Honiton, Devon
Printed in Great Britain by Biddles Ltd, Guildford

This book is printed on acid-free paper.

Contents

Part II Some grammar lessons

Part III Aims and means

Part IV

Part V Appendix

Editor's foreword

This series contains short books on language in education, on topics where practical knowledge is urgently needed in schools.

The books aim to help with daily practice in schools and classrooms in principled ways. They should be of interest to practising teachers and student teachers, to teacher trainers, advisers and inspectors, and to those involved in educational administration, at the level of head of department or head of school, or in local education authorities.

The books follow several important guidelines:

- their main purpose is to make knowledge about language accessible to those who need it
- they therefore avoid jargon and presuppose no knowledge at all about linguistics
- they are not, in fact, books about linguistics: they are books about language, informed by current linguistic thinking
- they contain large numbers of examples, which, as far as possible, are taken from real data, such as children's written work, transcripts of classroom talk and pupils' school textbooks
- they discuss topics which teachers and parents themselves think are important: What *is* grammar and why doesn't it seem to be taught these days? How do children learn to write? Why can't some children learn to spell? What is normal and abnormal in language

development? Why is there so much debate about English teaching? . . .

A great deal of knowledge has been gained about many linguistic topics which are important in education. For practical purposes, such knowledge can be accepted as widely agreed and factual – at least it is the best we have available in areas where it is badly needed by teachers, advisers and administrators. However, this knowledge is often not in an appropriate form: it is often in journal articles or in relatively technical books. It is therefore the responsibility of linguists to present it to teachers, clearly and in an accessible form. If this is not done, then practical decisions will still be taken, by individual teachers and others – but possibly uninformed by the best in current thinking about language in education.

There have recently been very large changes in the British education system, particularly centred on the Education Reform Act and the National Curriculum. In a longer term perspective, the changes which this legislation has brought about are part of a long struggle around the forms and purposes of education. But debates about teaching English as a mother tongue and teaching foreign languages have certainly been very sharp in recent years. And there is no doubt that 'knowledge about language' has been given particular prominence (and has received a great deal of publicity in the mass media) via the curriculum proposals for English and modern languages. 'Standard English' and related topics carry a heavy symbolic load, and much of the discussion, sometimes fuelled by statements by prominent politicians and other public figures, has been confused and even hysterical. An aim of this series is to encourage considered and rational debate in an area where deeply felt emotions are often at stake.

The books in the series have been written with British teachers in mind, though the issues they discuss are clearly also of relevance in other countries. Due to rapid changes in the school system, British teachers are currently under considerable pressures, and are under particular pressures in areas of the curriculum which concern language.

The aim then, is to provide critical studies of aspects of

language which are important to professional practice: to identify problems and to help to solve them with reference to the best current knowledge about language. The books are not therefore primarily conceived as theoretical contributions. However, if linguists seriously think about language as it is used in schools and classrooms, this inevitably leads to new insights, and such studies of language in use may well raise theoretical problems of fundamental interest to linguists.

This book by Richard Hudson tackles directly a very difficult question which has caused misunderstandings and problems for teachers over many years (at least the last 50 years or so). What is grammar and how should it be taught?

Hudson is very well qualified indeed to discuss this question. He holds a Chair of Linguistics at University College London. He is one of the major linguists in Britain, and has published important books on grammatical theory. But he has also concerned himself over many years with introducing students to linguistics (he has published very readable introductory textbooks). And, through other writing and by organizing conferences, he has encouraged many linguists to think about the practical applications of knowledge about language, both in schools and in students' careers after school and university.

In this book, he presents a large number of central, up-to-date grammatical ideas, and then shows how they can be tackled in lessons. The book should be of great help to teachers who feel that grammar is important, but do not quite know how to teach it. And it should also persuade others that grammar can be a substantial and interesting study for children in schools. (It is unfortunate that many people's rejection of grammar in schools is based on views of grammar which are simply very out-of-date stereotypes.) The topic is especially important for new kinds of teaching needed for the National Curriculum in English.

Michael Stubbs

To Gaynor, Lucy and Alice

Preface

I have written this book with rather specific readers in mind, namely teachers at primary schools, or secondary-school English teachers who are responsible for applying the new National Curriculum for English in England or Wales. This requires teachers, among other things, to teach children about ordinary spoken English, Standard English, and language in general; but it is generally recognised that many teachers of English are not adequately prepared to do this. For various historical reasons entirely beyond their control, most teachers were taught very little about language at school and college, certainly much less than they are now expected to teach their pupils. Somehow this hole has to be plugged, and most of the plugging will probably have to be provided by books.

The National Curriculum defines quite specific objectives, but leaves a great deal to the imagination; for example, when it says that children should be able to talk about 'grammatical differences between Standard English and a non-standard variety' it does not say which particular grammatical differences (there are hundreds of them) or of course which non-standard variety. This gives schools and teachers ample room for exercising their own discretion, but until you know what is on the menu you can't choose from it, so I have made some quite specific decisions in the hope that this will be more helpful than keeping the discussion at a decent level of generality. In particular, part II contains suggestions for ten 'grammar lessons' on different topics and for different ability levels. The intention is to show the kind of thing that can be done with grammar, rather than to lay down a complete syllabus.

I have assumed no technical knowledge about language, and I have tried hard not to frighten readers by unnecessary technicalities. Many of my colleagues in academic linguistics would probably be horrified by some of my simplifications, and by the things I have just not mentioned at all. At the same time, the book is meant for teachers, not for pupils, so I have tried to present a coherent intellectual framework of ideas about language which I would be quite willing to defend on academic grounds. These ideas may be hard to assimilate at first, so I have repeated them in different places, supported with examples; by the time you have been introduced to the same idea from several different directions you may find it is quite easy and natural.

To support the learning process I have collected all the main ideas together and presented them in an 'encyclopedia of grammar', which makes up part IV of the book. I thought this would be more helpful than a brief 'glossary of technical terms'. You may find this useful while reading the book, or afterwards; or you may like just to browse through it.

It should become obvious within the first few pages that grammar 'ain't what it used to be'. I am not trying to reintroduce the bad old ways of teaching grammar that have virtually died in most of our schools. Nor am I offering just a set of general principles about linguistic equality and the like: grammar takes us into the fine details and complexity of language structure, and if we don't get our hands dirty exploring this, we haven't 'done grammar'. I believe that both you and your pupils will find the experience exciting and rewarding.

This is my seventh book, but it has been far harder to write than any of the others. What you see is the fourth attempt, which stands on the ruins of one complete book and two half books. I believe that each version has moved nearer to the kind of book you really want and need, thanks to a very large amount of helpful advice and encouragement from Mike Stubbs, the series editor. However I should also like to acknowledge tactful criticism from Liz Gordon and Theo Manicki, both of whom read all or part of the third version and told me it was still too technical; and to thank Anna Gregory and Sheila Black, who read an earlier version of the present book and gave encouragement and guidance.

The book has been a family affair. I admire the work done by my wife Gaynor and her team of social workers, and wanted to make a contribution, however small, to solving some of the problems that afflict our society; and improbable though this may seem, I believe that grammar has an important part to play in making our society work better. Our daughters have contributed in different ways: Lucy has encouraged me by showing that it is possible to interest an adolescent in grammar; and Alice has kept my feet on the ground by showing that it isn't easy to do so. Finally, my father John went through the whole manuscript with his editorial pencil, and has made it all flow much better. He is a master of good style, and he claims that he learned it through all the sentence analysis and parsing that he did at school in the days before school grammar died. I am grateful to him for all his hard work, and I suspect you will be too.

Part I

Background

Notation

*	=	ungrammatical
( )	=	optional
CAPITALS	=	dictionary-word
(/ . . .)		
/ . . . /	=	phonemes
X–y	=	y-form of X

1

English teaching

The state of grammar in schools

One of the most bizarre facts about British education, when compared with the systems found in most other European countries, is the almost complete absence of grammar (in a narrow sense) from the curriculum of most schools. Most school-leavers don't understand, or even know, terms like 'preposition' and 'subject', and have no idea at all how prepositions and subjects are used in English even if they know a little about their use in foreign languages. This is certainly true of most of the students who join the university department in which I work (a department of linguistics), who are presumably more likely than any to know about such things; and if it is true of them it is even more likely to be true of the bulk of the population. This is true as of 1990, but the new National Curriculum for English looks set to push us into line with the rest of Europe.

It hasn't always been so in Britain, as witness the fact that academically selective secondary schools have been called 'grammar schools' for centuries. But this century has seen the gradual disappearance of grammar even from these schools, and in general one could pronounce grammar well and truly dead in state-maintained schools. (The situation is only marginally different in private schools.) The only exception to this generalisation is in the teaching of foreign languages, but even here the emphasis on communicative efficiency has been at the expense of grammatical knowledge. True, Latin and Greek teachers still tend to talk about grammar, but very few pupils study these languages now. And true, there has recently been a resurgence of interest in language, leading to two A-level syllabuses in English language and the whole 'language awareness' movement, both of which I welcome; but these trends rarely involve central grammatical notions like prepositions and subjects. I shall assume, therefore, that Britain is now a country without school grammar.

This may not be entirely a bad thing, as it gives us a chance to make a new start unhampered by the heavy hand of grammatical tradition.

The version of traditional grammar which was taught in schools is extremely dogmatic, and therefore fits badly into current educational theory. I shall be offering something quite different in this book: a body of discoveries which children can make (in part) for themselves. Grammatical exploration is already found in a few classrooms (so I am told), but it was positively discouraged by traditional grammar. Some parts of traditional grammar are correct, so we all have the chance of rediscovering the grammatical wheel for ourselves; but some parts are wrong, and can now be corrected.

It was in any case time to review the role of grammar teaching, which was traditionally tied closely to teaching of the standard language and of 'good style'. We can now see several other important contributions which grammar teaching could make, ranging from raising the status of non-standard dialects to improving the learning of foreign languages. Ideological conflicts might have made it hard to add these functions to a living tradition of grammar teaching.

On the other hand, there is much to be learned from countries where grammar is still taught and is presented in a comprehensible and attractive way. In Germany, for example, sophisticated grammatical concepts are taught in first-language German lessons to pupils across the entire ability range (Hauptschule, Realschule and Gymnasium). So, contrary to what has often been claimed, it certainly is not true that grammar is inherently too hard for all but the most academic pupils. Grammar plays a part in these lessons along with the study of literature and the development of writing skills, and all three parts feed one another. It would be silly to ignore the experience of such countries.

How did Britain get into the present situation? I have to admit that I am guessing, but I have the impression that we stand at the end of a long period, perhaps extending back to the late nineteenth century, during which school grammar lost its academic roots, and just shrivelled and died. In the eighteenth century school grammar-books were written by serious scholars – for example, one was written by Joseph Priestley, who is more famous for having discovered oxygen. During the nineteenth century school grammars fed on the linguistic scholarship of the day, which was primarily historical, so we find school books full of rather dry facts about the history of the Indo-European languages; but for grammar itself there was an increasing tendency for one generation of school books to be based solely on the previous generation of school books, without any serious input from the universities.

The training of teachers showed a similar trend: as far as grammar was concerned, teachers were only passing on what they themselves had learned at school, without any 'boost' from their college or university years. When this happens only one consequence is possible: pedagogical disaster. Ignorant, dogmatic teachers try to teach trivial skills and false facts which aren't worth teaching, and (to their credit) many children fail to learn them. At that point the only sensible thing to do was to stop, but what was stopped was not just *bad* teaching of grammar, but *all* teaching of grammar. In retrospect this is a clear case of an important baby being thrown out with some rather dirty bathwater.

The National Curriculum for English

This situation has been changed (in England and Wales) by Act of Parliament. The Government has decided, after consulting all sorts of experts (including the teaching profession), that it is time we had a National Curriculum for English; and that grammar should play a part in that curriculum. (I have picked out all the relevant sections in the National Curriculum and listed them in part V; I hope you will find this helpful.)

How important is grammar in the National Curriculum? If measured by the number of direct references in the National Curriculum, it isn't very important; and there is no question of children having to pass examinations in grammar for its own sake. But grammar pops up all over the place – under speaking, listening, reading and (of course) writing, under standard and non-standard dialects, under accuracy and appropriateness, under the spelling of single words and the punctuation of whole paragraphs, and in connection with literature, with the media and with jokes. The intention of the National Curriculum is very clear: that grammatical ideas should be available to teachers and to pupils for use as tools. Without those tools, a great many of the other jobs which the English teacher has to do will be very, very much harder. So the part assigned to grammar is important, even though it keeps a low profile.

Unfortunately it is also important in another respect, as a source of problems. You who are reading this book are doubtless keenly aware of these problems: if you are a teacher, then it is up to you not only to teach these tools, but also to acquire them for yourself. It is one thing to accept general principles and attitudes, such as a respect for the pupils' own language. But it is quite a different undertaking to come to terms with concepts such as 'subject', 'tense' and 'pronoun' to the extent of being absolutely confident in applying them, in understanding their relations, and in explaining them in a suitably simple way to your pupils. You may or may not have learned a few bits and pieces of grammar at school, but you're unlikely to have studied it at a higher level; and the chances are that you didn't learn any even at school (unless you are sufficiently old to have forgotten most of it by now).

My aim in this book is to help by providing what you need in order to start 'doing grammar' with your classes. What I shall tell you is based on the latest and best in theoretical and descriptive linguistics; and I hope that by the end of the book you may see that linguistics does not (entirely) deserve the negative image it has acquired among school-teachers. However I shall try not to deserve the review that one small boy wrote about a book on penguins: that it told him a lot more about penguins than he really wanted to know.

It would have been easy to write an outline of what modern linguists think about grammar; but I doubt if that is really what you need. (There are in any case plenty of books like that on the market, many much better than I could have written; the chapter on 'Useful books' includes some suggestions.) Instead I have tried to do something much harder: to pick out ideas that you can apply straight away. Moreover, I have related my suggestions directly and explicitly to the requirements of the National Curriculum, in the belief that this will be of most help. Fortunately I like most of the 'grammatical' bits of the National Curriculum, so applying my ideas to it has been quite an exciting challenge.

At the same time I have tried to give a basic framework of ideas within which you can locate the details. This is the start of a 'linguistic theory', and it has the advantage of any theory: that it allows one to understand things better, in the same way that a map allows one to understand better than a set of instructions for following particular routes. Some parts of this theory are just common sense – the idea, for example, that a word has both a pronunciation and a meaning, and that these are different. Other bits will take a little more explaining, and may at first strike you as strange; for example that a sentence has a 'syntactic' structure which is distinct from its 'semantic' structure, and which may even conflict with the latter. (If you don't know what I mean by terms like 'syntactic' and 'semantic', you will find them explained in the encyclopedia in part IV; equally you can be sure that if I use technical terms without explaining them this is because they don't really matter at that point.)

This book therefore offers a collection of rather concrete applications held together by a web of very general ideas. In the applications I have tried to cover all age ranges (from 5 to 16) and all the main grammatical topics mentioned by the National Curriculum, in order to show that grammarians have something for everybody. But of course there are plenty of other facts and ideas in linguistics, many of which could be applied to classroom teaching, so my ten applications are obviously not the end of the story. Similarly the web of general ideas offers such a rudimentary introduction to linguistic theory that I think even my argumentative colleagues would accept it! A teacher of English really needs a much more sophisticated theory of language than the one I offer here, but you have to start somewhere, and my little web will do until you can find something better.

Discovery-learning and the National Curriculum

How should grammar be taught? The National Curriculum itself says very little about this, but it is based on the Cox report (see the references in part V), which takes a very clear and consistent stand in favour of 'discovery-learning'. The pupils discover general patterns for themselves in material which is presented by the teacher. This is exactly the opposite of the traditional approach to grammar teaching, as I can show with a very simple example.

Take the following words: *dung, clung, hung*. How many two-word sentences can you make out of them? If we treat it just as a mathematical problem all the following pairs qualify:

Dung clung.	Dung hung.
*Clung hung.	*Clung dung.
*Hung dung.	*Hung clung.
*Dung dung.	*Clung clung.
*Hung hung.	

But only the top two examples are in any way acceptable as examples of 'English'; the remainder are ungrammatical, as shown by the star before them (a standard bit of notation used by linguists). This doesn't of course mean that they can't be used, since part of the fun of using language is finding excuses for breaking the rules. The poet in you may rise to the challenge of composing a little poem containing one or two of the starred pairs. The fact remains that every English speaker would agree that the starred ones aren't English in the same sense that the top two examples are, for all their oddity.

Why? As a first approximation we can say that there are two positions, and only *dung* can occur in the first position and only *hung* and *clung* in the second. We seem, then, to have discovered that English words are of at least two different kinds: those like *dung* and those like *hung* and *clung*. Suppose I say *Thung clung*; then you can guess that, whatever *thung* may mean, it is a word of the same type as *dung*. We have started to discover some word-classes.

Contrast this discovery-learning approach with the traditional one. I start by telling you that English has nouns and verbs, and I give you some examples of each: *dung* is a noun, and *clung* and *hung* are verbs. Then I tell you that nouns can occur in various places, one of which is before a verb. From this information you can work out that *Dung clung* is allowed, but that (in the absence of further information) **Dung dung* is not. This seems a much more efficient teaching method, compared with the hard work you had to do in the discovery-learning approach; but many educationalists believe that it is much less effective because it leaves the learner as a passive recipient of second-hand knowledge. It may allow the teacher to cover a great deal more territory in a lesson; but does the learner cover the same ground by actually learning it?

The general arguments for discovery-learning are quite familiar, and the method is already applied by many teachers; but it is particularly well suited for teaching grammar. This is because the primary aim is to make pupils aware of what they know already, namely the grammar of their own language. The ideas, concepts and terminology that emerge from the exploration of their ordinary spoken English can then be used as tools for helping them to expand their knowledge and to learn to apply it in 'schoolroom' contexts (for example in writing essays).

We assume, then, that children already know (unconsciously) a great deal of grammar before they reach school; for instance they already know that *Dung clung* is allowed but that *Clung dung* is not, though they couldn't explain this difference. This means that most of the data needed for a grammar lesson are already in the children's heads, so the teacher's role is mainly to guide them in exploring the patterns in the data and in gradually expanding their linguistic horizons. It is emphatically not to teach them 'the rules of English grammar' as though English were a foreign language. (Of course a different approach is needed for the minority of pupils who don't know English well enough to take part in this kind of activity; but in their case it is equally important to recognise that they already know a great deal of grammar, even if it is not the grammar of English.)

One of the consequences of the discovery-learning approach to grammar is that questions of terminology become less important; what matters is the word-classes (or other categories) that the pupils discover, rather than the names that we give them. Let me quote the part of the Cox report which deals with discovery-learning in the teaching of grammar, to reinforce what I have just said and to give it pedagogical respectability.

Questions of pedagogy are crucial in discussion of linguistic terminology. It is often assumed that to argue for the value of linguistic terminology is also to argue for the learning and testing of such terms in exercises and drills. But these things by no means necessarily go together.

In an article on discovery-learning, Bruner discusses the learning of grammar. He starts from the process of leading children to discover what is in their own heads, and describes a lesson on sentence structure. This involved writing a sentence on the board, and getting the children to form similar sentences:

The	man	ate	his	lunch.
A	boy	stole	a	bike.
The	dog	chased	my	cat.

| My | father | skidded | the | car. |

| A | wind | blew | his | hat. |

Usually, he says, they use their intuitive knowledge of the language to form sentences with the same structure. It is then possible to ask how different combinations of the words are possible, such as:

| A | man | stole | the | car. |

| My | father | chased | his | hat. |

Other questions can also be introduced: how is it possible to go on forming such sentences for ever? What columns are emerging in the sentences? Can other columns be added? Bruner writes:

[The children] talked about the family of words which would fit [in the various columns] ... Only then did we introduce some terminology. We talked about *type* and *order* ... We were soon building up the idea of productivity ... Once the children break into an idea in language, once they get a sense of distinction, they quickly 'turn around' on their own usage and make remarkable strides towards linguistic understanding. The only point I would make is that you must wait until *they* are willing reflectively to turn around before you start operating with the abstractions.

Terms are needed to allow teachers and pupils to discuss many aspects of language. But it is important that the terms are introduced as they are needed, in order to focus attention on important distinctions or similarities. Their meaning will be apparent because they relate to an immediate context. They should be introduced to initiate linguistic understanding, serving as a focus for wider discussion, when the teacher judges that an intervention to make something explicit will help the pupil. ... Indeed they must be introduced on occasions, if discussion is not to remain unformed, vague and inexplicit. However, terms should not be introduced through drills. (Cox Report, 5, 12–16; the quotation is from Jerome Bruner, 'Some elements of discovery', 1965, see the list of references on p. 280 below)

These principles strike me as admirable, but they raise a serious practical problem: how to cope with the 'debris' that any act of discovery-learning throws up. For example, how would Bruner have reacted if one of his pupils had contributed the sentence *The boy ate his quickly*? (A perfectly good sentence, incidentally, as in *The man ate his lunch slowly, and the boy ate his quickly*.) In some respects this continues the pattern of *The man ate his lunch*, but in other respects it is obviously different: *his quickly* does not parallel *his lunch*.

Unfortunately we can't trust children to do the decent thing and keep their examples within the desired pattern, but we have to be able to say something a bit more helpful and encouraging than 'No, that's not relevant; has anyone got any better ideas than that one?' A teacher who knows quite a lot of grammar could say something like this:

Yes, that looks as though it fits in, but in fact it's different in interesting ways; for example try adding *sandwiches* after *his*; you'll find it works before *quickly* but not before *lunch*; also, try shifting the last word before *ate*; this works with *quickly*, but not with *lunch*. So do you see that there are some big differences between your example and mine in the ways the words fit together?

Hopefully by that point the pupil will have been persuaded that the example is different, and in the process will have become more sensitive to sentence structures.

But what about a teacher who doesn't yet know enough about grammar to be able to work out little tests like that in the middle of a lesson? One answer is that maybe it doesn't matter if the odd misfit creeps into an exercise like this; as the exploration progresses the dross will drop out at the bottom, so to speak. For example, if you were to build on Bruner's examples in order to work on the way in which words like *his* and *the* are used, examples like *his lunch* will quickly squeeze out those like *his quickly*.

Another answer is that the teacher would at least realise that the example didn't fit, and could say something like: 'Well, that looks OK, but I feel somehow it's not the same pattern – *his quickly* feels very different from *his lunch*. Can anyone help me by thinking of a way to bring out the difference?' With luck some bright pupil might get to the answer before the teacher, and it would at least give the teacher time to think.

But a third, and more optimistic, answer is that by the time you have finished this book you should have learned enough grammar to cope with problems of this kind. Moreover, to be even more optimistic, every hour of discovery-learning experienced by the pupils is also one that you experience yourself, and since you probably have far more hours of it per week than any one child you are likely to discover a very large amount of grammar indeed, very fast. Not that you will ever 'discover' the whole of English grammar in this way; there is far too much of it for anyone to become aware of, whatever method they use. But you will certainly find that problems recur, and that this year's discoveries can be recycled in next year's teaching.

This, then, is what I mean by 'grammar teaching'. It probably isn't what you expected me to mean, and it almost certainly isn't what Prince Charles had in mind when he made his famous plea for grammar teaching in January 1990:

In the last two decades we have witnessed a situation where our education has no longer been centred on the idea that the English language is an enormously precious legacy to be handed on carefully. We have seen the abandonment of learning the rules of grammar and the parts of speech as boring and irrelevant. Learning poetry by heart has been abandoned, together with the idea of English as something really to be *learnt* [his emphasis], by effort and application, by long and careful familiarity with those who had shown how to clothe their thought in the most precise, vivid and memorable language. . . . But there is now, I think, a growing consensus on what needs to be taught and it is heartening to witness the widespread recognition of this in the new national curriculum for English. (Guardian Weekly, 7 January 1990)

I share his wish for an improvement in the standards of literacy among our citizens, but I disagree fundamentally with his prescription for a cure. A return to the bad old days of 'the grammar grind' would, in my opinion, be of little use to anyone. It would be equally futile to believe that an improvement in performance would follow immediately from intense immersion in great literature.

What the National Curriculum actually calls for is a completely new approach – one which, incidentally, has not been used anywhere in the world, so far as I can tell, though it has some similarities to grammar teaching in Europe. (As I put the last touches to this manuscript I heard of apparently similar initiatives in Norway.) This is based on discovery-learning of grammar in which the child's own non-standard spoken language is just as relevant as written Standard English, and the aim is just as much to deepen the child's awareness of what it already knows and does as to help the child to learn Standard English. It combines liberal respect for the child's values with the hard-nosed aim of raising standards, in the belief that the former will in fact support the latter.

2

What grammarians do

This chapter provides some important background information about academic grammar, which will help you to understand my approach. But you may prefer to skip both this chapter and the next one, at least on a first reading, in order to get straight into my practical suggestions for teaching grammar which start in part II.

Who are the grammarians?

Grammar is one of the most ancient intellectual pursuits. In the West we place the start of grammar in ancient Greece, in about 300 BC, though Socrates, Plato and Aristotle had all made incidental contributions to its foundations before then. Our word *grammar* comes (indirectly) from the Greek *téchne grammatiké*, which simply meant the art of using letters (*grammata*). As any English teacher knows, there is no clear boundary between learning to spell (use letters) and learning to put words together to make effective sentences; consider for example the use of *'s* in *He's nice* and *Mary's book*, and the use of capital letters to start sentences. The Greeks studied grammar partly for practical reasons, because Greek children needed to learn to read Homer and to write, but partly for intellectual reasons, because Greek thinkers were intrigued by the structures of their language and wanted to understand it. These dual aims still drive grammarians over two thousand years later.

Interestingly, somewhat similar developments had taken

place a few centuries earlier in ancient India, in connection with the then current language, Sanskrit; and about the fifth century AD grammatical scholarship was born in China, another apparently independent development. At least in the Indian case, the blend of applied and theoretical work was much the same as in Greece.

The history of grammar between ancient Greece and our days is interesting, and although I shall say little more about that history it is vital to be aware that it exists. This is because what can loosely be called 'traditional grammar' is the direct product of this tradition, and what we can (equally loosely) call 'modern grammar' builds on traditional grammar; so ultimately modern grammar too can be traced back to the ancient Greeks.

If grammar has already been being studied for so long, we should by now have solved most of the problems; but we haven't. How is this? Putting the same doubt in another form, what hope have we of solving now problems that are still outstanding after over two thousand years of work?

Certainly part of the answer is that there is far more to grammar than most people realise. Any language contains a very large number of facts which are relevant to grammar, however this term is defined (we shall consider some definitions later in this chapter); the total number of facts for each language must surely run into thousands. And since there are around five or six thousand languages in the world, it is not surprising if some facts can't yet be fitted neatly into a total integrated grammar.

However, the main reason for our under-achievement is that the goal-posts have been moved from time to time, which makes a lot of earlier work irrelevant to the present. Very roughly, we can divide the history of grammar into two phases, bounded by the fourth century BC and 1957.

300 BC to 1957

Some very important general facts were discovered and applied to the grammar of various European languages during this first long phase. Word-classes like 'verb' and 'noun' were discovered quite quickly, and 'grammatical functions' such as 'subject' and 'object' came to light somewhat later.

A particularly important example of progress in this period is the discovery that some languages could best be described in terms of abstract categories like 'number', 'gender' and 'case', which link the internal structure of a word to the rules for using it, rather than by linking internal structure directly to use. For example, English *ducks* and *geese* are both plural (for instance, both occur with *these* rather than with *this*) although this plurality is signalled by a suffix -*s* in one case and by a vowel-change in the other. It is much easier to express the rules for choosing between *this* and *these* (or between *is* and *are*) in terms of the simple category 'plural' than to refer directly to suffixes, vowel-changes and so on.

This may seem obvious to us now, but it is only because the Greeks discovered it. It is comparable to the discovery that different visible symptoms can be manifestations of the same disease, and conversely that a single symptom (such as a fever) can be linked to various different diseases. The abstract category 'malaria' allows us to link a complex of causes (involving mosquito bites and the like) to a complex of symptoms, some of which overlap with symptoms of other diseases; and in just the same way, 'plural' provides a link between a complex of rules of use (for instance, after *these*, before *are*) and a complex of visible 'symptoms', such as ending in -*s*.

A great many of the analytical categories discovered in this period are still with us. In addition to those just described we still use most of the word-classes (so-called 'parts of speech' – noun, verb, adjective and so on) in any modern grammar of English, and also the functions like 'subject' and 'object'. On the whole the tradition survived on the basis of authority ('X is so because that's what my grammar book/teacher says'), and during most of these centuries there was little debate about alternatives. The product of this long tradition is what I have been calling 'traditional grammar', and my main criticism is not so much that it is wrong, but rather that it is dogmatic (hence the 'dead hand of tradition' that I referred to earlier). If our goal is to encourage children to explore their language and to discover things for themselves, then traditional grammar will certainly not do as a basis. This is why I said that the death of traditional grammar in British schools may have been in some respects a blessing as it gives us a chance to make a clean break with the past.

1957 to now

In 1957 Noam Chomsky (of the Massachussets Institute of Technology) showed how grammar could be studied in a scientific way, by building completely explicit formal models of grammars and testing them against the facts. Such grammars are called 'generative grammars' because they 'generate' structures in a technical sense of this term, meaning that the grammar makes a precise distinction between the structures that it allows and those that it does not. A grammar 'generates' any sentence that it allows.

Most generative grammars use some kind of technical notation, but this is not essential as long as there is no uncertainty about what the grammar allows. Here is a tiny generative grammar which uses prose; let's call it Grammar 1. You will notice, incidentally, that it contains 'rules', but that unlike traditional grammar rules these are simply statements about what is normal, rather than edicts about what we ought to do (but presumably would not do without the edict).

GRAMMAR 1

A sentence is allowed if every word in it fits one of the following rules:

1 The word is *I* and it is followed immediately by *like*.
2 The word is *like* and it is followed (not necessarily immediately) by *sentences*.
3 The word is *sentences*.
4 The word is *short* and the next word is *sentences*.
5 The word is *very* and the next word is either *short* or *very*.

You can probably see that (and how) this little grammar generates the following sentences.

(1) I like sentences.
(2) I like short sentences.

Sentence (1) is allowed because *I* fits the pattern in rule 1, *like* fits the one in rule 2 and *sentences* fits the one in rule 3. Sentence (2) is just the same except that it contains *short*, which is allowed by rule 4.

Things get slightly more exciting when we add *very*, as in (3):

(3) I like very short sentences.

Very is allowed by rule 5 to occur before *short*, so since all the other words are allowed by the other rules the sentence as a whole is allowed. But rule 5 also allows *very* to occur before itself – more precisely, it allows one occurrence of *very* to occur before another one. This means that *very very* is allowed, as in (4):

(4) I like very very short sentences.

But it also allows *very very very*, and *very very very very*:

(5) I like very very very short sentences.
(6) I like very very very very short sentences.

And so on; in fact the grammar generates an infinite number of sentences because it is always possible to make one more just by adding another *very*. So just five rules generate an infinite number of sentences.

Now the point of this example is that we can compare the range of sentences that Grammar 1 generates with the range that a native speaker of English accepts as grammatical. If the two turn out to be the same, then maybe we can take Grammar 1 as a formal description of English grammar; but if they are different, we certainly cannot. So how does Grammar 1 fare as a factual claim about English? As far as it goes, Grammar 1 does well: every sentence that it generates seems fine to any native speaker of English, though they get pretty boring as the number of *very*'s rises. But there are plenty of perfectly good English sentences that Grammar 1 does not generate, such as *I live in London* and *The cat sat on the computer*. So we can reject Grammar 1 as a factual claim about English, and return to the drawing-board.

This, then, is generative grammar, the basis for what I call 'modern grammar'. It is true that the rules in Grammar 1 are not the kind of rule that Chomsky himself uses, but this is not important to the main point: a generative grammar is totally explicit about what structures it allows and what it doesn't. The adoption of generative grammar has completely changed the character of grammar (and of the typical grammarian). Generative grammars can be forbiddingly technical, which is one reason why it is important for professional grammarians to interpret their work to language teachers.

So who are the modern grammarians? Some of them would call themselves generative grammarians (or generative linguists), and write complex formal grammars somewhat like our Grammar 1 (but much more complex and formal). A generative grammarian needs a general theory of grammar (just as a physicist needs a theory of matter), and we now have a number of competing theories with names such as 'transformational grammar', 'lexical-functional grammar', 'generalised phrase-structure grammar', 'systemic grammar' and 'categorial grammar'. This wealth of theories is the last thing the language teacher wants to find, so again a guide is needed. If you want to explore theoretical linguistics you will find some of the books listed in the 'Useful books' chapter helpful. You should at least know that Noam Chomsky is without doubt still the dominant generative grammarian, since even those who disagree strongly with his theoretical conclusions tend to define their positions in relation to his work.

However, in addition to the generative grammarians there are a lot of modern grammarians whom we might call 'descriptive grammarians', who are less concerned with general theorising and more with sorting out the facts in a more or less rough-and-ready way. Some descriptive grammarians concentrate on a single language, and probably the most important name for an English teacher to know is that of Sir Randolph Quirk (of University College London, I'm proud to say), who coordinated the writing of an enormous 1,700-page grammar of modern English. Other descriptive grammarians study vast numbers of languages – often several hundred languages – in order to discover general patterns which may be shared by all languages. We shall consider some examples of this kind of work later on.

These, then, are the 'modern grammarians' to whom I shall refer. What unites us, and separates us from 'traditional grammarians', is the principle of debate rather than dogma: that what counts in deciding between alternative analyses is facts, rather than the weight of authority. (I should admit that this description of traditional grammar is very unfair to some of its greatest exponents, who argued their case just as energetically as any modern linguist; and conversely even modern linguists can be disappointingly dogmatic.) The debates are lively, and sometimes bloody, but they have undoubtedly produced progress. It seems fair to compare the change since 1957 to the change from alchemy to chemistry – a change to fewer certainties, but more truth.

What is grammar?

Where sociology is the study of society, and biology is the study of living organisms, grammar is the study of grammar. This ambiguity is shared by the names of most academic disciplines (for example, 'English' is the name both of the language and of its academic study) and causes very few problems because the context usually makes it clear whether we are referring to the phenomenon or to its study.

A somewhat more dangerous ambiguity involves generality: are we talking about grammar in general, as found in all languages, or just about the grammar of a single language? Where it matters we must mark this distinction.

What is much more frustrating, for both experts and novices, is the vagueness of the boundary around grammar, when this term applies to the phenomenon. Does grammar include vocabulary? And what about meaning? And pronunciation? The only help I can give here is to issue a warning: if you read around, you may well find that the meaning of this term varies from page to page even within the same book in a way that can only be described as sloppy.

Demarcation disputes are of little interest to outsiders, but even as an insider I find it hard to raise enthusiasm for arguing about where, precisely, the boundaries of grammar 'really' lie.

For example the grammar of a language has traditionally been distinguished from its vocabulary, the idea being that the grammar fixed the general patterns of sentence structure, and the vocabulary filled in the details. But how general is general? Let's apply Bruner's technique (discussed in chapter 1) to the patterns described in our Grammar 1. Here are some representative examples of sentences that all seem to illustrate the same combination of patterns.

1	2	3	4	5	6
I	like	any	very	short	sentences.
We	discussed	some	rather	tricky	problems.
People	hated	my	awfully	boring	example.
He	wore	his	somewhat	expensive	coat.
She	wrote	the	most	amazing	book.

The patterns found in these sentences are very general, in the sense that they are available to a lot of different words. Subject to a few other restrictions, such as those imposed by the need to make sense, any word in column 1 can be followed by any word in column 2, and so on across all the columns. (A generative grammar for these words would allow $5 \times 5 \times 5 \times 5 \times 5 \times 5 = 15,625$ sentences!) It is easy to see how the facts can best be shared between a grammar book and a dictionary: the grammar book should define the patterns common to all five sentences, referring only to general word-classes like 'noun', and the dictionary should list the words and tell us in which word-classes they each belong. (I shall now use capital letters for the words that are listed in dictionaries, to contrast them with the forms and uses found in particular sentences.)

But what about the word TOO? In general terms this belongs with the words in column 4: VERY, RATHER, AWFULLY, SOMEWHAT, MOST. This is because it can occur freely before the words in column 5: *too short, too tricky, too expensive*, etc. (as in, for example, *This is too short*). But it has the peculiarity of not occurring freely after all the words in column 3; for example, consider the effect of putting TOO in the fourth position in the first two sentences:

(7) *I like any too short sentences.
(8) *We discussed some too tricky problems.

I have taken the liberty of starring these examples because I think you will agree that they are decidedly odd. Instead of occurring, like VERY, RATHER and so on, between a column 3 word (ANY, SOME, . . .) and a column 5 one (SHORT, TRICKY, ...), TOO is used before a column 5 word which has to be followed in turn by the word A (or AN), and then by a column 6 word: *too short a dress, too tricky a problem*. This is a very strange pattern which is not available to any of the other column 4 words (*very short a dress, *rather tricky a problem*). So where do the facts about TOO belong? They aren't just details about patterns that are otherwise allowed by the grammar, so they ought to be included in the grammar; but they apply only to TOO (and a handful of other words like SO and HOW), so they are hardly general at all.

The answer is surely that they should be mentioned in any self-respecting grammar book about English, and *also* in any dictionary; and in recognition of this fact publishers nowadays tend to blur the distinction between these two kinds of book. In particular, a modern dictionary can be expected to include a lot of apparently 'grammatical' information.

You may have noticed that I followed Bruner's advice in

starting from the categories (as in 'column 4 word') rather than from the standard terminology. However, if you already knew some terms it would have been easier to follow the discussion if I had used the standard names for our word-classes. Here they are, for your convenience:

1	2	3	4	5	6
I	*like*	*any*	*very*	*short*	*sentences.*
noun	verb	determiner	adverb	adjective	noun

All these names are quite traditional with the exception of 'determiner', which linguists have invented. It includes the traditional 'article' and various kinds of traditional adjective.

Returning to the boundaries of grammar, it would be easy to make similar points about the supposed boundaries between grammar and other kinds of facts about words. Just to survey the territory briefly, we might consider the following boundaries:

Grammar versus meaning Should the grammar define the meanings of the patterns that it describes? For example, suppose it distinguishes words like *walked, came* and *was* from those like *walks, comes* and *is*, calling the first set 'past tense' and the second 'present tense'. Should it describe the differences in meaning between past-tense verbs and present-tense ones? Some linguists consider meaning to be outside grammar, while others see it as the very heart of grammar; but, frankly, who cares? The undisputed fact is that words are used to express meanings, so someone, somewhere, should be studying the meanings that different words and word-patterns convey; and life is too short to worry about whether or not their work should be classified as part of grammar.

Grammar versus encyclopedias Furthermore, if the grammar does cover the meaning of a word, how much of this meaning does it include? For example, does the fact that TOOTH refers to something found in the mouth belong in the grammar? This is where the publisher's distinction between dictionaries and encyclopedias becomes relevant, and it is interesting to notice that many publishers have now officially abandoned this distinction as well.

Grammar versus pronunciation If grammar includes vocabulary, then presumably it includes what we know about the pronunciations of words, in addition to the more general information which most people would expect in a grammar, for instance about affixes (pointing out perhaps that the *-ing* suffix is often pronounced as though it were written *-in*) and about intonation (yes–no questions tend to have a rising intonation).

Grammar versus register If the grammar tells us that sentences like *Here comes your dad* and *In the corner of the field stood an old oak tree* are possible, it presumably also has to tell us that they belong to different registers (informal spoken versus literary written), and similarly for vocabulary differences like DAD versus FATHER and TRY versus ATTEMPT. (A 'Register' is like a dialect, but is reserved for use on a particular kind of occasion rather than by a particular kind of speaker.)

Grammar versus discourse It is uncontroversial that a grammar should show that both KNOW and THINK can be followed by a subordinate clause (a little sentence inside the bigger one), and that this clause is optional:

(9) I know (she likes me).
(10) I think (she likes me).

Brackets are a standard way of showing that part of an example is optional. But the grammar should surely go further, to distinguish these two cases of optionality. When the subordinate clause is missing, the two verbs are understood very differently, as you can see from the following examples.

(11) A: She likes you.
     B: Yes, I know.
(12) A. She likes you.
     B: Yes, I think.

The missing subordinate clause is reconstructed on the basis of a preceding sentence after KNOW, but not after THINK. (If this meaning had been intended, B should have answered *Yes, I think so* in (12).) When THINK is used without a subordinate clause, it refers generally to the act of thinking, with a meaning rather like that of MEDITATE (as in *I have to think hard when I'm doing grammar*). The links between the sentences in (11) belong to the study of discourse. (Roughly speaking, a discourse is a sensible sequence of sentences, and the phenomenon called 'discourse' comprises the patterns which are found in such sequences.)

My conclusion, then, is that there are no natural boundaries around 'grammar', so in principle I shall allow the term to embrace any kind of information about words. However, having said this I must emphasise the 'in principle', to explain why in practice I shall use the term more narrowly. For purely practical reasons I shall make the following exclusions:

(a)   I shall exclude most of pronunciation because, as the National Curriculum stresses, it is not the school's business to teach children to use standard pronunciation (the so-called 'received pronunciation' or 'RP accent') although the school should certainly teach the standard 'dialect' – that is, all other parts of the grammar of Standard English. It's true that a study of the local accent (pronunciation) is just as legitimate as a study of the local dialect, but any study of English pronunciation is liable to fall into the trap of taking RP as its reference point so I have decided to play safe and ignore pronunciation altogether.

(b)   I shall exclude most of word-meaning because this is often recognised in schools as a separate matter from 'grammar', and in a short book like this I can't afford to give space to what many readers will consider irrelevant. I should like to stress, though, that in my view the study of word-meanings is one of the most important things children can do in the English lesson, or even in school. For instance, they could explore the semantic relations among little sets of words such as the following:

OTHER	ELSE		
DESPISE	CONTEMPT	(cf HATE: HATRED)	
WHILE	DURING	MEANWHILE	
ALTHOUGH	IN SPITE OF	THOUGH	
IF	UNLESS		
BUY	SELL	COST	CHARGE
INVENT	DISCOVER		
FLOWER	ROSE	BRAMBLE	

(c)   In order to minimise the risk of offending my colleagues I shall try to concentrate on the bits of grammar which everyone recognises as 'grammar'. Hopefully this will also increase the chances of the ideas still being academically respectable in ten years' time. It is in this rather narrow sense of grammar that I claimed in the first chapter that the teaching of grammar is virtually dead in British schools. Grammar, as I am using the term, should include *at least* ideas like 'preposition' and 'subject', which are universally accepted as part of grammar.

What, then, is 'grammar' going to mean in this book? It will refer to the following kinds of facts about words:

1   about the classes to which they belong (e.g. 'noun');
2   about the structures of words that can be described in terms of notions like 'suffix' (e.g. *dogs* = stem + suffix);
3   about the abstract distinctions that are sometimes signalled by these word-structure differences (e.g. 'singular' versus 'plural');
4   about the abstract relations among words in sentences, which I have called their 'grammatical function' (e.g. 'subject');
5   about the order in which words occur (e.g. 'TOO + adjective' precedes A);
6   about certain parts of word-meaning, when these can be related to other matters listed earlier (e.g. the difference in meaning between *dog* and *dogs*);

7   about the relations between the meanings of words
    in a sentence (e.g. the different roles of *dogs* and *cats*
    in *Dogs chase cats*);
8   about the 'informational' structures signalled for
    instance by differences in word order (e.g. the differ-
    ence between *I can't stand cats* and *Cats I can't stand*);
9   about register differences between word-patterns (e.g.
    This is Dick Hudson here, used only on the telephone,
    versus the synonymous *I'm Dick Hudson,* which is
    used elsewhere).

Even with the limitations that I have imposed on grammar,
it is still a vast field. This is why teachers, in an ideal world,
need so much training if they are to be able to deal with every
grammatical problem as it comes up in class.

Some basic principles

Modern linguistics rests on various principles, of which I shall
discuss just two: descriptivism and mentalism. I shall explain
these principles, and then discuss their relevance to teaching.
We shall see that some quite complex questions arise.

Descriptivism   This is the principle that when we study a
language we should accept it as it is, without trying to change
it. For example, the sentence *It is me* is normal English, much
more normal than the alternative *It is I* which some traditional
grammars recommend. When we apply the principle to non-
standard varieties it means that we must accept them too; so
for many non-standard varieties of English *I done it* is right,
i.e. grammatical.

What we are *not* claiming is that 'anything goes', though
this was certainly the implication of some of the wilder things
that linguists said in the 1950s and 1960s. Any linguistic
variety, whether it is a standard language (what linguists like
to call a 'standard dialect') or a local dialect, consists of rules
which allow some sentences but not others; so when we

say that some sentence is 'grammatical' this really means 'grammatical according to variety X'. So even if *I done it* is right in a non-standard dialect, it will not do as an attempt at standard dialect. And conversely, *I did it* is simply wrong in that non-standard dialect! These conclusions are inescapable once we accept the principle of descriptivism.

For the historical record, descriptivism is not part of the Chomskyan revolution of 1957, which changed linguistics into a science. It was already very firmly established in linguistics by then, and indeed it is important to recognise that a great deal of traditional grammar, from its earliest origins, was pure description, even if it was applied exclusively to a standard language. It would be quite unfair to traditional grammar to label it all prescriptive.

Mentalism If a language is not contained in prescriptive grammar-books, where is it? The obvious answer, which linguists accept, is that it is contained in the heads of its speakers, as a rather special part of their knowledge. Even a dead language (such as Latin) once had speakers, and our descriptions of its grammar are attempts to capture the linguistic knowledge of native speakers. Mentalism, then, is the principle that what we are trying to study when we study a language is a mental phenomenon, the native speaker's knowledge of the language.

Acceptance of mentalism has two different consequences for a linguist's work. The first is a matter of methodology: if the object of study is in people's heads, how can we get at it? The easy answer is: 'Ask them!', and this is in fact the main tool in the linguist's kit. Suppose you have found a native speaker of the language you want to study. Of course it's no good asking your speaker simply to tell you about the language, because the question is too general. But you can ask specific questions such as 'What do you call ...?', 'What do you say when you want to . . .?' or even 'What's the past tense of . . .?' (Imagine you were the native speaker in question, and I asked you what the past tense of GO was; provided I had already explained to you what I meant by 'past tense', and given some examples with other verbs, you would have no difficulty in giving the answer, even though it may surprise you.) And of course there's no reason why linguists shouldn't study their own language, supplying both the questions and their answers.

This easy method of exploring linguistic knowledge has some serious weaknesses as well as some strengths. In particular, the speaker's answers may be unreliable, especially if there is a conflict between a 'respectable' (standard) answer and a less respectable one. Suppose the speaker regularly uses *done* as the past tense of DO (as in *I done it*). If you ask for the past tense of DO, you may nevertheless be given *did* on the grounds that this is the form that the speaker has been told is 'correct'. The speaker may even deny ever using *done* in the sincere belief that this is the case. However less direct questioning usually shows that the speaker at least knows the non-standard form, and knows the kind of person who typically uses it – questions like 'Do any of your friends/family ever say . . .?' or 'What kind of person says . . .?' will generally elicit this information.

Apart from direct and indirect questioning, there is of course another obvious source of relevant data: speakers' own behaviour, that is, what they themselves say or write. Written material is easy to collect in large quantities, and speech is almost as easy thanks to tape recorders. We can call these materials 'performance'. This is a standard linguistic term, and is contrasted with 'competence', which means linguistic knowledge. Some linguists make a great deal of use of performance data, but, like answers to questions, such data do not provide direct evidence for competence. This is because competence is only one of the many elements that are involved in planning and executing a piece of speech or writing. For example, if I type *thep roblem* instead of *the problem* you can't use this as evidence that I think *thep* is an alternative to *the*; and more generally you can never use an extract of my performance as irrefutable evidence for my competence. This evidence always has to be corroborated in some way.

The second consequence of mentalism in linguistics is a radical change in the nature of grammar writing compared with most of traditional grammar. We are used to the idea that a grammar book describes some 'language', which belongs to some 'community'; so we can buy books about the grammar of English, or French, or Swahili. We know that communities can vary enormously in size, from the community to which English belongs, numbered in hundreds of millions, to a tribal community on the edge of extinction with only a handful of members. But how does this familiar idea square with mentalism? If language is a kind of knowledge, it is found in minds, but where is the mind of a community? And for that matter, where does one community end and the next begin? There are no obvious boundaries round the communities that speak any of the following languages or dialects:

- English (what about people in, say, Malaysia who regularly speak English but also speak Malay, Chinese and perhaps Tamil?);
- standard English (do you belong?);
- non-standard London English (only if you were born within hearing range of Bow Bells?).

Worse still, we all know that when every detail is taken into account, each speaker is in fact unique (thanks to local words or expressions, family words, technical terminology acquired through business or hobbies, and so on). So if we want to write a grammar for some 'language', we must write a different grammar for every person who might claim to speak it.

Fortunately, this problem need not worry us a great deal because the idea of writing a 'complete grammar' is only a fantasy which no linguist really believes in. What we all do is to work on partial grammars, where the problems of defining the community of speakers aren't particularly important. We are mostly aware of differences among speakers with respect to the facts we are analysing, but we generally relegate these differences to footnotes because nothing much depends on them. Indeed what often strikes me, as a working grammarian, is the extraordinary degree of similarity among speakers who apparently belong to widely separated communities. For example, many of the fine details of ordinary spoken English are the same wherever English is spoken as a native language (without a pidgin/creole basis), even after centuries of separation from their shared origin in Britain.

My conclusion is that although mentalism locates grammars firmly in the heads of individuals, it is still possible to make valid generalisations which apply to whole communities because individuals build their own grammars on the model of the people around them, and generally follow their models faithfully down to the finest details. Nevertheless the perspective of mentalism is quite different from that of the more traditional descriptions of standard languages, because what we are trying to model in our grammars is the contents of an individual mind, and not that of the community's standard language.

How do our two principles of descriptivism and mentalism relate to each other and to teaching? It should be clear that they are both highly relevant, and complementary, as background to the proposal that children should be encouraged to investigate their own grammars, which makes discovery-learning a possible teaching method. Descriptivism is relevant because non-standard and standard dialects can be accepted as equally valid objects of study; *I done it* is as good an answer to the question, 'What is the past form of *I do it?*' as is *I did it*. And mentalism is relevant because all the data children need is in their own heads, and can be elicited by the standard questioning methods.

I believe this answer is both true and useful; but it is not complete, as any language teacher knows. The problem is obvious: if every speaker's linguistic knowledge is as good as every other's, then every child's must be as good as every adult's, so who needs a language teacher?

Well, *do* we really need language teachers? More specifically, do English-speaking children need an English teacher? One of the excesses of which linguists have been guilty during the last few decades has been to imply that the first-language teacher has no role to play in the child's language development, on the grounds that a child neither needs nor uses explicit teaching in order to learn its first language. Though this claim is certainly true of the early stages of language acquisition, it is unhelpful to generalise it to all stages and strands of the acquisition process.

The most obvious contribution of the English teacher (in an English-speaking class) is that of teaching literacy and the standard written language. If children were left to their own devices (by parents as well as by the school) then the vast majority of them would never learn to read and write, still less to do so in Standard English. But the teaching of standard literacy is diametrically opposed to the principles of descriptivism and mentalism. There are objective, external, standards of correctness to which the child has to aspire – for example it is not the case that everyone's spelling of a word is as good as anyone else's (descriptivism), or that spellings are located exclusively in people's heads (mentalism). Society has codified the standard language (more precisely, it has allowed publishers to do this on its behalf), and an important part of a child's education is to learn this codified language.

This very traditional role of English teachers does not worry me, as a linguist, in the slightest, and I believe the same is true of most of my colleagues. However there is a problem of reconciling the English teacher's new dual roles with each other. On the one hand we are asking the English teacher to arrange discovery-learning lessons in which the children can explore their own language and learn about grammar in the spirit of modern linguistics; but at the same time we are asking for instruction in the traditional literacy skills, in which the child is treated as an empty vessel waiting to be filled up (by, one hopes, humane and sensible methods); or in a more modern vein, the child is a novice or 'apprentice' who learns how to 'search for meaning' at the feet of an expert, the teacher. And in between these two extremes we are asking for a combination of discovery and instruction as methods for improving children's communicative skills – the skills needed for structuring information, taking account of the addressee's needs, and so on.

Broadening our perspectives somewhat, the recent 'language awareness' movement has shown how the foreign-language teacher can be asked to ride the same two horses, though with less weight on the discovery-learning one. The assumption in this case is that although British children don't know any French, they do know a lot of 'language' which the French teacher can build on. And of course the same is true of teachers of English as a second language, if they have the skills needed to explore the learner's first language.

As I shall explain in the following chapters the two strands of language teaching ought to support each other if skillfully woven together, precisely because the new language is presented as an addition to the child's existing language. As children become more aware of their own (non-standard) grammar the task of learning the grammar of the standard language should become easier and more rewarding, and similarly for learning foreign languages. And as they learn more of the standard dialect, or of the foreign language, they will not only become more aware of their own grammar (because of the contrast), but they will also learn to use the other language as a quarry from which they can borrow material to expand their own grammar.

Some achievements of grammarians

In this final section I should like to boast a little about some of the things that have been achieved, worldwide, by grammarians (that is, by linguists working on grammar). If I could claim that they have all been achieved since 1957, I would, because this would be very impressive indeed. However I can't, because as I explained in the first section modern linguists are building on firm foundations laid over the past two thousand years; if we had been really starting from scratch in 1957 we might not yet have got round to discovering nouns and verbs.

My intention is not only to polish the image of grammar, but also to give a realistic idea of what linguistics has to offer. The following is a list of areas of research in linguistics, with an evaluation of our achievements. In some cases the work has led to solid bodies of knowledge, but in others we still have little more than programmatic statements about what could or should be investigated.

Standard English grammar Standard English has been studied far more than any other language, and all academic bookshops are full of books about English grammar. Standard English has been the test-bed for every general theory of grammar, for the obvious reason that this is the native language of most academic grammarians (modern linguistics having been largely an American development until fairly recently). The focus on Standard English has also been encouraged by the vast demand for EFL ('English as a Foreign Language') materials. By far the most impressive compendium of facts about Standard English is the gigantic *Comprehensive Grammar of the English Language* by Quirk and his colleagues, which I mentioned earlier, but even this does not include everything that is known about the grammar of Standard English, scattered among the more technical books and journals. Although we are still a long way from a 'complete grammar', we are certainly a lot nearer to it than 30 years ago.

Non-standard English grammar We know far less about non-standard grammar, which is a great pity in the present context. Moreover what we do know has been analysed less thoroughly than the corresponding facts about Standard English. For example, we know that some dialects of British English allow sentences like *No I never* (corresponding to Standard *No I didn't*), but we don't understand the system of rules which allow such sentences. (In other words, precisely what are the rules that allow these sentences while, presumably, excluding sentences like *Yes I always* and *He washed up because I never*?)

Grammar of other languages I have been unable to find any estimate of the number of languages for which usable grammars exist, but they must certainly be counted in hundreds, and possibly even in thousands (especially if we distinguish between different dialects of the same language). A great deal of work has been done on the standard versions of most of the European languages (including Welsh), so there are reasonably accessible grammars of all the languages that are taught in British schools, and it should be possible to find some information about most of the languages of communities recently arrived from Asia and Africa. Because of the dominant position of English in modern linguistics, some of these grammars can be accused of imposing the structure of English on languages for which it is not appropriate. This is ironical, because one of the main complaints of modern linguists about traditional grammar is that it tended to force all languages into the mould of Latin.

General grammatical categories   The work on English and other languages has added to the list of general grammatical categories which we inherited from traditional grammar; terms like 'determiner', 'adjunct' and 'tensed' are now part of the stock in trade of any working grammarian, in addition to the more traditional terms like 'noun', 'subject' and 'singular'. Some linguists believe that the same basic list of analytical categories can be expected to apply to every language, while others disagree strongly, arguing that if every language is analysed correctly a lot of categories will turn out to be peculiar to individual languages. What is undoubtedly good about these developments is that much of the terminology is very widely accepted, which makes the debate a good deal more meaningful.

General grammatical phenomena   We have built up a list of patterns which are very widespread across languages, and which again can be identified by fairly standard terms. Some of these terms are quite traditional (such as 'coordination', 'passives', 'relative clauses') while others are more recent. Typical examples are 'extraction', 'gapping' and 'island constraints'. This list of patterns allows one to ask very general questions about a language, such as 'Does it allow extraction?', or 'What island constraints does it have?'

Grammatical universals   The hundreds or thousands of grammars that I mentioned earlier constitute a vast database which has been used for testing a wide variety of generalisations that may be true of all languages. For example, it seems that every language has a series of words meaning, respectively, 'I', 'you' and 'neither I nor you' (for instance, 'he/she/it'); but some languages have just a single word, translatable as 'self', which covers 'myself', 'yourself', and 'him/her/itself'.

One of the most interesting kinds of generalisation links patterns pairwise in 'if – then' statements: 'If a language has X, then it will also have Y.' For example, some languages have prepositions (like English OF, IN, WITH), which are 'preposed' to their accompanying noun (such as (*a pint*) *of beer, in London, with Mary*), whereas other languages have postpositions, which are like prepositions except that they follow the noun. This is true of Japanese, in which for example the translation for 'in London' is *Rondon ni*. Similarly, in some languages the verb follows the subject but precedes the object (as in English), but in others (such as Welsh) the verb precedes both of them. An example from Welsh is (13).

(13)   Lladdodd   y   ddraig   y   dyn.

      killed   the   dragon   the   man

      'The dragon killed the man.'

When these two dimensions of variation are compared with one another, however, they turn out to be related: if a language normally has both the subject and object after the verb, then it will also have prepositions. This is interesting because it immediately raises a question: Why? We already have a number of interesting candidates for an answer, but it is too soon to announce The Answer.

Theoretical frameworks   I have already mentioned that grammarians have invented a rich assortment of general theories. It may now be easier to understand why this has happened – because we know a lot of facts about a lot of languages, and each fact has required us to think hard about a lot of other facts (since grammatical facts don't grow on trees, but have to be discovered). Partly for practical reasons, and partly out of simple curiosity, we all long for a general theory which will allow us to see exactly how all these facts fit together – and if possible one which will also show how they mesh with all the other things we know (about how our minds work, about the world, and so on). Needless to say we are nowhere near finding a well-worked-out and comprehensive theory of the kind I have just described, but our theory builders are working on it, and we can already offer a dozen or so incomplete alternatives.

This list of achievements does not include all the areas where grammarians have been active, but I think it does include those areas where the most solid achievements have been made. There has also been a lot of activity on the acquisition of first and second languages, and on the mental processes that are involved in speaking, hearing and reading. In principle this work is of great potential interest to language teachers, but we are still at an earlier stage than in the other areas.

So much, then, for what grammarians do. At least one simple generalisation is justified: a lot is known about grammar. All that remains is for me to show you how it could be applied in teaching English.

3

What is Standard English?

Standard English as a dialect

One of the main requirements of the National Curriculum is for pupils to leave school competent in Standard English. According to the report of the Kingman committee (1988), which laid the ground for the National Curriculum, this requirement turned out to be completely uncontroversial ('No item of evidence received by the Committee contained disagreement with this point', para. 2.31). In a sense we all know what the requirement means, but as soon as we try to make it precise the meaning seems to slip away through our fingers.

The trouble is that very few of us have a clear idea of precisely what we mean by 'Standard English'. When I started to write this book I became aware that the notion was almost as vague in my mind as 'slang' and 'guttural'. I dare say most teachers share my confusion, which bodes ill for their chances of being able to plan their teaching efficiently; and since the term 'Standard English' is among those which need to be explained to pupils, the clearer it is the better.

The simplest answer is that Standard English is just one *dialect* among many, similar for instance to Yorkshire English, London English, etc. The only thing which makes Standard English stand out from all the others is its social status – the fact that it is used by the rich and powerful, by publishers and so on. This answer is the one given by most linguists and sociolinguists, and is certainly a better starting point for any discussion than the popular alternative, according to which Standard English *is* English and all the alternatives are simply unsuccessful attempts to speak 'proper' English. One of the great achievements of the last few decades is that this view is now officially recognised as misleading, unhelpful and wrong.

It is true that the view of Standard English as 'just' a dialect is also one-sided and needs to be balanced by another view, as I shall explain in the section on Standard English as a collection of registers below. However it is near enough to the truth to be worth developing here.

If a dialect is a way of speaking that is characteristic of a particular group of speakers, then Standard English is a dialect, because it is used by a particular group of people (those I referred to above, very crudely, as 'the rich and powerful'; we might define them more abstractly and perhaps more accurately as members of the 'upper middle class'). Contrary to the popular misconception, it isn't the only dialect that has a grammar; they all do (otherwise they wouldn't be recognisable as a particular 'way of speaking'). The grammar you learn as a child is (more or less) the same as the grammar of the people you interact with, so if you grow up in London, you normally learn London dialect, and if in Cornwall, Cornish dialect; and if you grow up in a household where (exceptionally) Standard English is spoken then your grammar will be that of Standard English. It is in order to show this similarity to other dialects that linguists often call Standard English 'the standard dialect' (probably with a small 's' in *standard*, to cut it down to size!).

Linguists also like to make a clear distinction between the notions 'dialect' and 'accent'. An accent is a particular way of pronouncing a dialect. The sentence *We weren't saying anything* is an example of Standard English (unlike for instance *We wasn't saying anything* or *We weren't saying nothing*), but it can be pronounced in many different ways; for example the -*r*- in the middle of *weren't* may or may not be pronounced as a consonant, and all sorts of vowel sounds can be used for *say*-. The distinction between dialect and accent allows us to ignore these differences of pronunciation in discussing dialect.

Roughly speaking, then, dialect involves differences which would appear in a transcription using ordinary (that is, non-phonetic) spelling – differences like those between *weren't* and *wasn't*, or between *anything* and *nothing*. Accent, in contrast, involves differences of pronunciation which the ordinary orthography conceals; we spell *weren't* in the same way whether we pronounce the *-r-* or not.

The most important consequence of this distinction is to allow Standard English to be separated conceptually from the accent that linguists call 'received pronunciation' (RP, also known more popularly as BBC English or Oxford English or talking posh or a plummy accent or . . .). Most speakers of Standard English use an accent that shows where they come from, but there is a 'pure' variety of received pronunciation which is genuinely non-regional. Standard English is spoken at home only by a minority of people, but the number who speak it with received pronunciation is even smaller. Sociolinguists tell us that perhaps 10 per cent of the population use Standard English at home, while a mere 1-2 per cent use received pronunciation. The distinction between standard dialect and received pronunciation is vitally important for all teachers, because the National Curriculum explicitly denies the need for the school to teach received pronunciation as part of Standard English. This is surely correct, and uncontroversial.

When seen as one dialect among many, Standard English is fairly easy to define as the dialect that can't be pinned down to a particular region within the English-speaking world. If we concentrate on its spoken form, then we can say it is also the kind of English that is spoken by (among others) members of the upper middle class. The second definition is meant as a rider to the first, in order to exclude some non-standard forms (such as double negatives like *I didn't say nothing*) which are very widely used and therefore as non-regional as Standard English. If you are a native speaker of English and are a teacher, then the standard dialect is probably the kind of English that you speak. If that is true, then your duty according to the National Curriculum is to help your pupils to learn to speak your dialect (but *not* with your accent).

This, of course, is the pedagogical crunch. What if the pupils don't want to learn to speak like you? Indeed, it is almost certain that they won't want to because they have very powerful (and sensible) reasons for wanting to go on speaking non-standard dialect – the need to be respected and accepted by their peers and by their families. For instance, how can they start saying *We were* while all these important people say *we was*? The following quotation from a Birmingham child is probably typical:

> You always try to be the same as everyone else. You don't sort of want to be made fun of . . . sort of posher than everyone else. Then you get sort of picked on. But then if you use a lot of slang and that, people don't think much of you. (Romaine 1984)

The last sentence about people not thinking much of you presumably refers to the evaluation by the Powers That Be – teachers, examiners, employers and so forth; and 'slang' must refer to non-standard features. This child confronts a conflict between the school's demand for Standard English, and the neighbourhood's demand for non-standard.

The National Curriculum recognises this perceived conflict, but (rightly) denies that it is real. Instead it builds on a great deal of research in sociolinguistics which has confirmed what we all know: that different varieties can be reserved for use on different occasions. We all have different ways of speaking according to whether we are telling a joke to our friends, addressing a conference audience, or talking to small children. In many communities complete languages coexist on this basis – one language for use at home and another for public occasions – and even more commonly different dialects share the social world between them.

This is what the National Curriculum envisages for Britain: peaceful and non-competitive coexistence between Standard English and other language varieties (whether non-standard dialects of English or languages other than English). It asks all pupils to learn Standard English so that eventually they can use it in school and later in other areas of life such as work; but it leaves them free to use whatever language they want at home and with their friends.

This aim seems to be very widely accepted so there is no need to argue the case against the policy which it replaces, which was a wholesale replacement of ('corrupt') non-standard dialects by ('correct') Standard English. The view of the National Curriculum is unambiguous: 'Pupils should be encouraged to respect their own language(s) or dialect(s) and those of others.' Unfortunately this revolution in English teaching leaves the teacher with a serious problem: precisely how should the standard dialect be taught?

How to teach the standard dialect

As soon as we abandon the view that non-standard English is a corruption of Standard English we also have to give up trying to teach it by exhorting pupils to pull up their socks and try harder. Teaching Standard English is a content subject, just like teaching French, and until children know some Standard English they can't be expected to use it. But how do you teach the rights and wrongs of Standard English without threatening non-standard dialects – for example, how do you teach that *we was* is wrong in Standard English without implying that it must therefore be wrong in all dialects?

More seriously still, how do you stop the prestige of schools, books, etc., from rubbing off onto Standard English and making it *de facto* superior to non-standard dialects? The mere fact of being taught in school is enough to give any language or dialect a higher profile than those that are not taught. If it's worth all this time and effort to study Standard English, it really must be important – and by implication, non-standard dialects can't be important if they're not taught or studied.

In my opinion the best solution is to devote a large proportion of class time to the study of the children's own language. (This view is completely in accord with the spirit of the National Curriculum as I read it, though it isn't spelled out in so many words.)

This need not be at the expense of the study of Standard English, for the simple reason that most of the differences between Standard English and non-standard dialects are quite specific, and rather trivial, which means that most things which are true of the English of any fluent native speaker will also be true of Standard English. For example, the rules for forming and using plural nouns are virtually the same in non-standard dialects and in Standard English. For most parts of grammar, therefore, studying the children's own English is the same as studying Standard English. This will be true of most of the lessons I shall describe in the next chapter. But where there is a difference between the two, it should be confronted head-on by an investigation of *both*, rather than simply by an account of the standard forms.

An example may help here, so let's look at the double-negative pattern found in *We weren't doing nothing*. We shall imagine a lesson in which you and your class explore the non-standard rules for using *nothing*, starting with a comparison of sentences like (1) and (2).

(1)   We weren't doing nothing.
(2)   We were doing nothing.

Which of these would they use when talking to their friends? Or which would their friends use when talking to them? Let's assume the most likely answer: (1).

You now ask why that is; why can *nothing* be used after *weren't* but not after *were*? Finding the answer to this question should take you through a range of other verbs, testing their negative forms against their positive forms, with appropriate changes elsewhere in the sentence. For example to compare *can't* with *can*, you offer them (3).

(3a)   We can't see nothing.
(3b)   We can see nothing.

Unfortunately, you will find that most verbs don't have a negative form, but need a negative form of DO; for instance *don't want* is the negative equivalent of *want*:

(4a)   We don't want nothing.
(4b)   We want nothing.

If you haven't already discussed these things with the class you can earmark them for future attention. The class should by this time have discovered the following rule for their dialect:

RULE: *Nothing* is fine after a negative verb, but not after a positive one.

You then generalise to other words like *nobody* or *no* (as in *no sweets*), to show that the same rule applies to these words as well. What can you call these words? How about 'N-words'? Let's update our rule to make it more general.

RULE: N-words are fine after a negative verb, but not after a positive one.

If the class are already studying French, you can point out to them that their dialect is just like French: words like *pas* and *rien* are (basically) used only after verbs containing *ne*, as in (5).

(5a) Nous ne faisions rien. 'We weren't doing nothing.'
(5b) *Nous faisions rien.

Now you can turn to Standard English. One way to make the comparison would be to write up some non-standard sentences containing N-words, and to write against each one its standard translation. Let's assume that you have decided to call the children's language by the name of the local town, rather than 'non-standard' (which sounds too similar to 'substandard'). I shall call the local dialect just 'Town', and 'Standard English' reduces naturally to 'Standard'.

TOWN	STANDARD
We weren't doing nothing.	We weren't doing anything.
We don't want nothing	We don't want anything.
We didn't buy no sweets.	We didn't buy any sweets.

You can draw up the Standard list yourself, or you can elicit it from the class if you think they know the forms.   After some exploration, an easy generalisation will emerge: where Town uses an N-word, Standard uses what you might call an A-word – a word like *anything, any, anyone*. (A-words don't all start with *any*, or even with *a*; one of them is *ever*. I don't in fact know whether this corresponds to *never* in Town, or whether Town follows the same rules as Standard for this word.) In other words you can write another rule for Standard which is just like the one for Town except for mentioning 'A-word' where the latter mentions 'N-word'.

RULE FOR S: A-words are fine after a negative verb, but not after a positive one.

RULE FOR T: N-words are fine after a negative verb, but not after a positive one.

This example could be developed into a major research project to be conducted by the class, because we have only uncovered a small part of the relevant rules. What about N-words before the verb?

(6a)   Nothing didn't happen.
(6b)   Nothing happened.

Here their judgements will almost certainly be reversed, preferring (6b) over (6a). In fact, I think you will find that Town grammar is precisely the same as Standard in this area, so any discoveries they make about Town apply directly to Standard as well.

Another question: how many N-words are possible after a negative verb? Give them the words *We didn't give* and ask them to continue, using nothing but N-words. They may stick at (7a), but they may offer (7b) too.

(7a)   We didn't give nobody nothing.
(7b)   We didn't give nobody nothing nowhere.

And how does our translation rule work in such cases? You can assure them that it works just fine.

(8a)   We didn't give anybody anything.
(8b)   We didn't give anybody anything anywhere.

And another: does Town allow A-words in any other kinds of sentence? What about the sentence I have just written, for example? Try pairs like the following.

(9a)   You bought anything.
(9b)   Did you buy anything?

Here too their judgements will probably be the same as for Standard: *anything* is fine in a question like (9b), but not in (9a); and more generally, the same is true for all A-words. So Town has A-words, just as Standard does, but uses them only in questions, whereas Standard uses them both in questions and after negative words.

Notice that at no point have we said anything about 'double negatives', or about illogicality ('two negatives make a positive'). You will also notice that grammar is taught primarily by discovery-learning, as explained in chapter 1. The pupils are exploring what they know already, which is probably a non-standard dialect, so it is merely a matter of terminology whether or not we say that you have been 'teaching them non-standard English'. You have certainly not taught them to use non-standard English; there is no need for this, since they already use it. What you have done is to teach them *about* non-standard, by making them aware of its structure; and by studying this structure in school you should have given it the seal of educational respectability, along with volcanoes, feudal agriculture and Standard English.

This approach should have a number of benefits. It should make pupils feel more positive about their own language (and perhaps even about the social background from which this language came). Secondly it should help them to see that Standard English is not a rival to their non-standard dialect, but an addition to it (just as French is a supplement to English and not a substitute for it). The two systems are simply different, and needed for different occasions, but neither is better than the other. Thirdly they should understand the new facts about Standard English more easily if they already understand their own grammar.

The distinctive characteristics of the standard dialect

One practical problem remains for the teacher: how to plan teaching in such a way that this kind of systematic study follows an orderly pattern, rather than simply reacting to problems as they arise in the lesson. This is an important problem because the data are quite complex and an unprepared exploration could easily dissolve into chaos. What would be very helpful for any teacher is a checklist of the main non-standard features to be expected in the children's language.

I can't provide such a list for the simple reason that most non-standard features are restricted to a particular region. What I can offer, however, is a useful research instrument which you could use either on your own or with a class. This is a questionnaire prepared by Jenny Cheshire and Viv Edwards for use in schools, in order to study the distribution of the main non-standard features that dialectologists are aware of. It comprises nearly two hundred sentences each of which contains one non-standard item. All these items are grammatical somewhere, but most of them are ungrammatical in most areas, so by working through the list you should be able to assemble a list of the main distinguishing characteristics (other than vocabulary) of your local non-standard dialect. The questionnaire is given in chapter 5 in part III below.

This completes my discussion of Standard English as a dialect. I have deliberately cut a number of corners in order to avoid getting sidetracked into irrelevant details, but it is now time to acknowledge some of the simplifications. First of all we have the fact that there are regional standards in spoken English, notably the difference between the Standard English recognised in Scotland (and Northern Ireland) and the one recognised in England and Wales. For example *My hair needs washed* is grammatical in Standard Scots English but not in Standard English English; and conversely for *My hair needs washing*.

And secondly we have the rather obvious fact that Standard English is less clearly defined than I have implied. Those of us who try to analyse the details of its grammar are constantly reminded of this by the difficulty of getting all our colleagues to agree with our judgements. For example, would you accept the following as sentences of Standard English?

(10) Who did you give a prize?
(11) That book was given Bill by his aunt.

Whatever your answers, some linguist somewhere has at some time agreed with them – and other linguists have disagreed! It is important to be aware of this problem, but I very much doubt if it will cause serious difficulties in an English lesson, as the disagreements are rather minor.

Standard English as a collection of registers

In the discussion so far I have taken the position which most linguists adopt: the differences between Standard English and other dialects are just arbitrary differences, like the differences which distinguish the regional non-standard dialects from one another. This view is in line with the more general belief shared by linguists about the relations among linguistic variet-ies (languages or dialects): that they are all equal as far as their grammars are concerned, though some have more social status than others. Linguists developed the slogan 'All langu-ages are equal' in reaction to uninformed claims about primi-tive languages or non-standard dialects which contained no grammar and precious little vocabulary, leaving their speakers to communicate mainly by grunts and gestures. In this context, of course, I fully accept the slogan.

However, in the context of educational discussions of Standard English I think the slogan is unhelpful and has had some negative effects. The problem is that what most people refer to as Standard English is not, in fact, on all fours with non-standard dialects. The difference isn't just a matter of social status, but also involves the grammars of the varieties concerned. To simplify a little, Standard English is much 'bigger', as well as being different. In other words, a grammar of Standard English would be much longer than one for any non-standard dialect, and similarly (but more so) for a dictionary. This is because Standard English is generally taken to include not only 'ordinary' casual speech – chatting about holidays or the weather, joking, controlling children, and so on – but also a number of other kinds of language for which non-standard dialects are not used by anybody. For 'kinds of language' linked to 'kinds of use' linguists often use the term 'register', so I can express the same idea by saying that Standard English contains far more registers than does any non-standard dialect.

First, and most obviously, Standard English is used in writing, and especially in commercial publications; it has a set of written registers. This means that all the paraphernalia of writing is part of Standard English, so Standard English has a standard spelling for each word, a standard system of punctuation, and so on, whereas non-standard dialects do not. It is true that non-standard varieties can be written down, and sometimes are, but this written output is tiny compared with Standard English.

This fact about Standard English is hard to reconcile with the claim that Standard English is just one dialect among many. One could object that I am just playing with words in using 'Standard English' to refer to two fundamentally different things: the dialect spoken natively by a certain section of our society, and the written version of their dialect. One could point out, for example, that it is perfectly possible to know Standard English in the first sense without knowing it in the second sense – as is indeed the case for all Standard-speaking children before they learn to read and write. You could even go so far as to say that written Standard English isn't really a proper human language because speech is primary and writing is secondary; therefore the written language cannot be part of the dialect Standard English.

All these arguments carry some weight in an academic argument, but they are basically irrelevant in the educational context because the fact is that Standard English *does* include written English in the terminology of all the important participants: HM Government, the National Curriculum, and teachers. In fact, for these people Standard English is *primarily* written, because of the dominant part that literacy plays in school. In the National Curriculum only one attainment target out of three (or five, according to how you count them) is concerned with speech, so it is even more important for children to learn to read and write in Standard English than it is for them to learn to speak it. To a great extent written Standard English is the same in its grammar as spoken Standard English, with the addition of punctuation (and spelling, of course). However there are some features of speech that are not normally permitted in writing. They include examples like the following (based on Williams 1990).

(12) *Well*, I bought it.
(13) My dog, *it* was just about to come down.
(14) There was *this* frog sitting on a pond, *a china frog*.
(15) We were checked *and stuff*.
(16) I went up to get my *sort of* ribbon thing.
(17) It was quite a thing, *it was*.
(18) He woke up *ever so* suddenly.

Conversely, structures which are common in writing can be extremely rare in (unscripted) speech:

(19) In the far corner stands a marble statue.
(20) The students were playing tennis, and the teachers cricket.
(21) The above arguments lead to the following conclusion:
 . . .
(22) An ardent nationalist, he rejoiced at every victory.

Standard English, then, includes a written register while

the non-standard dialects don't; we have written and spoken Standard English, but (to all intents and purposes) only spoken non-standard. This is one big difference between standard and non-standard dialects which makes the former much bigger than the latter.

Another such difference is that Standard English contains a range of stylistic alternatives for use on different occasions which is not matched in non-standard dialects. All dialects have a wide range of styles for different occasions – for joking with friends, talking to small children, playing games, and so on. But Standard English is different in being favoured on official and public occasions: in interviews, in dealing with government, in speeches, etc.

This means that in Standard English we find a range of styles related to formality. At the casual end of this spectrum the non-standard dialects are an alternative to Standard English, but at the formal end there is no alternative. For example, alongside the casual GET we have RECEIVE and OBTAIN; alongside TRY we have ATTEMPT; and so on and on. These alternatives are basically different ways of saying precisely the same thing; for instance, compare (23) and (24).

(23)   I regret to inform you that you received no prize.
(24)   I'm afraid you didn't get a prize.

These mean precisely the same; if one is true then the other must also be true. The difference between them is a matter of formality, impersonality, pretentiousness or pomposity rather than of meaning (in at least the ordinary sense of this word).

Discussing stylistic differences such as these is presumably the bread-and-butter work of secondary English teachers, so it is important to recognise their existence in Standard English. A speaker or writer who controls a wide range of different styles is at a great advantage, as it makes all the difference to social relations and success or failure in communication; and the official and public styles are especially important in employment.

On the other hand it is also important to be clear that knowing a lot of different ways of saying the same thing is not in itself a sign of intellectual superiority. A child with a large vocabulary consisting mainly of synonyms like TRY and ATTEMPT need not have any more to say, or have a richer set of concepts, than one who has just one word for each set of synonyms and therefore a smaller vocabulary. The same is true for technical terms; if I learn the technical name for a concept that I already know (say, that drying out is dehydration) then I have not learned anything except another word.

The third way in which Standard English is bigger than non-standard dialects is in the existence of a range of vocabulary and constructions which have no non-standard equivalent, and which express meanings that aren't otherwise available. We can call these parts of Standard English its 'technical' registers.

As far as vocabulary is concerned we can illustrate the technical registers from any academic discipline. The specialist vocabulary is part of Standard English and not part of any non-standard dialect – words like METAPHOR, BISECT, FEMUR, TITHE, LATITUDE, SUBJUNCTIVE, CODA or MOLECULE. In schools most of these words are the responsibility of some specialist teacher other than the English teacher, but there are a lot of other more general 'academic' words which the latter might take responsibility for: words like MINIMISE, EVOLVE, ANTICIPATION, DEDUCE, RELATIONSHIP, RECONCILE and STRATEGY. Unlike the words discussed in the previous paragraph, these terms (whether specialist or general) are not just alternative names for commonplace concepts. They denote concepts which are typically acquired through education and/or reading, and a firm control of them presumably indicates an ability to use the corresponding concepts.

A serious question arises at this point: are these words really exclusive to Standard English? Unfortunately, I can't give an answer based on hard research evidence because of our lack of information about non-standard dialects. The fact is, of course, that Standard English is now available to all through education and dictionaries as a source of new vocabulary, so there is nothing to stop a speaker who knows a word such as MINIMISE from using it as part of an otherwise non-standard sentence: *We wasn't minimising the side-effects enough.* We simply don't know to what extent this happens, but we can be sure that at least some people who have passed through our schools do it with some words.

This fluidity at the border between Standard English and non-standard dialects is conceptually troublesome, but from an educational point of view it seems to me to be entirely desirable. The kind of words we are concerned with here are both a symptom and a means of conceptual growth; on balance conceptual growth is a good thing, so the more such words a person knows, the better. They are not in competition with existing non-standard words so a non-standard speaker can treat them as part of non-standard vocabulary, and use them in combination with ordinary non-standard words and forms. My guess is that this doesn't happen a great deal at present because of the way in which Standard English and 'schoolish' vocabulary are taught, but if the National Curriculum is applied successfully it should become commonplace.

For simplicity I have been concentrating on vocabulary in this discussion of the technical registers of Standard English, but there are also sentence patterns which have no equivalent in non-standard dialects. Once again the easiest examples are provided by academic specialities:

(25)   Three and five makes eight.
(26)   Three plus five makes eight.
(27)   The slope varies as one on r.

These structures allow one to express ideas that would be difficult, if not impossible, to express in ordinary conversational English.

A rather different sort of sentence pattern, of particular interest to English teachers, is the kind that allows the user – especially the writer – to package complex information in a variety of ways which are not generally available in casual registers (and therefore not available in non-standard dialects). The need for this kind of construction is especially clear where complexity in the ideas involves some kind of 'parallelism' between two ideas. Here are some examples, in which I have tried to make the parallels explicit by the layout:

(28) Alan and Bill invited
Anna and Beth respectively.
(29) Alan did well in physics and
Bill   in geography.
(30) Alan likes physics more than
Bill   geography.
(31) Alan will invite Anna and
Bill will   Beth.
(32) Alan loves, but
Bill detests,   the music they play in assembly.

At least some of these structures are useful tools in any language-user's kit, and are worth teaching and learning as ways of compressing relatively complex ideas into a smaller number of words. Any literate person ought at least to be able to understand them, but it is fairly certain that children will not encounter constructions like these in their everyday experience of speech – chatting with friends, watching television, arguing with parents or shopping. The English teacher is the obvious person to broaden their experience.

The point of this discussion has been to recognise that Standard English is understood by most people to include not only the everyday 'dialect' of a social elite but also virtually everything that is written in English, plus speech that is closely related to this writing – lectures, speeches, sermons, public announcements and so on. This vast collection of registers and subregisters is more than any one person could know, and one aim of teaching is to give the child access to some of the more important parts of it.

Children who are brought up speaking the standard dialect at home clearly have an advantage over other children in areas where standard and non-standard are in competition. However these differences seem quite small compared with the vast amount to be learned by all children, regardless of dialect background, about the written, formal and technical registers. To take an optimistic view, then, the advantages of being a native speaker of Standard English will dwindle as children advance into these registers.

In the first part of this chapter I recommended that the standard dialect should be taught to non-standard speakers only after they have studied the relevant parts of their own non-standard dialect. I argued that this would be a good way to teach standard dialect features. However I also believe that this treatment of the dialect conflict will prove its value in relation to the other registers of Standard English. If standard dialect is presented to children as a substitute for their non-standard dialect, and is rejected as such, then this rejection is also likely to apply, irrelevantly, to the registers where standard and non-standard are not in competition. If, on the other hand, it is presented as an addition to the children's repertoire of varieties, for use in certain 'schoolroom' contexts, then there is no conflict with non-standard dialect and consequently no resistance to the other registers.

Conclusion

What, then, *is* Standard English? I have given a very long answer to this apparently simple question, so let me try to summarise the discussion. Standard English, as this term is generally used, covers (a) a dialect, namely the ordinary speech of a small social elite and (b) a collection of registers, including those which I have labelled 'written', 'formal' and 'technical'.

The standard dialect is in structural competition with non-standard ones, in the sense that it provides alternative ways of saying things that can be expressed just as well in non-standard dialects. It must therefore be clear to all concerned that standard dialect is in no sense better than non-standard dialects, and is reserved strictly for use in certain contexts where it is required for purely conventional, social reasons.

The situation is quite different with the standard register-collection. This does not compete structurally with non-standard dialects, so all children can be introduced to it as a vast resource to help them to communicate more easily and efficiently.

In short, there is a sense in which Standard English is better than non-standard varieties, as so many people have insisted in spite of the inflated claims that we linguists have sometimes made. But there is another sense in which we were right all along: Standard English is just one dialect among many.

Part II

Some grammar lessons

The following are some rather specific teaching suggestions. Each might take up just a lesson or two, but I hope they are suggestive of a much longer list of topics in grammar that could be applied. The suggestions consist of goals or areas of knowledge that children could explore, rather than methods; in some cases I shall suggest some ways of running the lesson, such as turning it into a game or dividing into little research teams, but these suggestions are very tentative, as I have no expertise whatsoever in classroom management at school level.

In choosing my topics for teaching I have made use of the National Curriculum list of attainment targets at different levels, given in appendix A. (Five-year-olds start at level 1, and high-achieving 16-year-olds are at level 10; average 16-year-olds are at level 6 or 7.) I offer one topic for each level, to counter any idea that grammar is relevant only to older and more academic children. I have also tried to vary the topics so that they span as many areas of grammar as possible.

For each lesson I shall explain just enough about grammar to enable you to teach that lesson, or at least to understand how the lesson might be taught if everything went to plan – as recognised earlier, you need to know much more grammar than this in order to deal with unforeseen interventions from the class. These small doses of grammar don't add up to a satisfactory course in the subject, but I hope they will be enough to get you started. You will be able to find some more information in the part IV 'encyclopedia of grammar', which is strictly for reference only. But ultimately you will probably want to read some of the other books listed in chapter 6.

I argued a strong case for discovery-learning in the last chapter, and my lessons are all based on this method. If this is good for your pupils it ought also to be good for you, so I use it in presenting my fragments of grammar. There are obvious limitations on using discovery-learning in a book, since the method ideally requires face-to-face interaction and free flow of information in both directions; so I shall supplement it with a more didactic style for which I apologise. In each lesson, therefore, I pose two questions, one for you to answer, and the second for your pupils.

Level 1

Inflections and dictionary-words

The National Curriculum lists the following items in its Programme of Study for infants, though it makes no specific recommendations for teaching about language at level 1.

Activities should ensure that pupils . . .
– notice how words are constructed and spelled;
– refer to . . . dictionaries . . . as a matter of course.

The aim of my first lesson will be to show the children ways in which words are constructed and spelled, and in the process to help them to refer to dictionaries.

A lesson for the teacher

The key to success in discovery-learning, in my experience, is to start with a clear question whose answer is to be discovered. My question for you is this: how many words are there in sentence (1)?

(1)   Mary swims superbly and Bob swims quite well and even the twins swim after a fashion.

You may think this a silly question but as soon as you try to answer it I think you will see the point. For the children, your question is a different one. How do you say the s that can be added to a word? Needless to say, the answers to both these questions are less important than the facts and ideas that lead up to them.

We start with your question. As you have surely recognised, the problem in counting the words in (1) is in the meaning of the word *word*. First, does it mean 'word-length units' into which this sentence can be divided, or does it mean 'distinct word-length units'? In the technical terminology of linguistics, does it mean 'tokens' or 'types'? If we are asking for the number of word-tokens, the answer is 16 (*Mary, swims, superbly, and, Bob, swims, quite, well, and, even, the, twins, swim, after, a, fashion*). But if we are asking for word-types, we count the words *and* and *swims* only once each, giving a total of 14. If you were measuring the length of an essay you would count the number of word-tokens; but if you were measuring the size of someone's vocabulary you would count the number of word-types.

As you probably know, one standard way of measuring the maturity of someone's written style is to take an example of their written work and calculate the ratio of word-types to word-tokens. A high type-to-token ratio (such as 0.8 types to 1 token) would indicate a wide range of vocabulary, with each token tending to be a different type, but a low ratio (such as 0.4 types to 1 token) would show a less mature style, because the same types are being used over and over again.

So far, then, you have discovered the difference between types and tokens, corresponding to the answers 16 and 14, but you have probably noticed the possibility of a third answer, 13. This would be the answer if we treated *swims* and *swim* as 'the same word', a step that you would presumably find quite reasonable. Indeed, if you were measuring vocabulary size it would surely be much more reasonable to count these tokens as only one item, on the grounds that they involve the same item of vocabulary in each case.

What shall we call these 'items of vocabulary'? We can't call them words, for the reasons we have just seen, nor can we call them simply word-types, because we want to keep this term up our sleeves in case we want to treat *swim* and *swims* as different word-types. Linguists have a number of alternative names, built on the Greek root *lex-* meaning 'word', notably 'lexical item' and 'lexeme'; but though short these sound rather forbidding. I shall opt for a rather longer but more transparent term: 'dictionary-word', showing that these are the units that are listed separately in any dictionary. We can say, then, that *swims* and *swim* are the same dictionary-word, but different forms of it.

But what can we call this particular dictionary-word? If we call it just *swim*, we shan't distinguish it from one of its forms, and it could be confusing to say that *swim* is a form of *swim*. The convention I shall use (which incidentally is quite widespread in linguistics) is to call a dictionary-word by its shortest form, and I shall write its name in capital letters; so *swims* and *swim* are different forms of the dictionary-word SWIM. You may have noticed that I occasionally used this convention in earlier chapters.

We could rewrite our sentence using this convention instead of the standard orthography:

(2) MARY SWIM SUPERBLY AND BOB SWIM QUITE WELL AND EVEN
     THE TWIN SWIM AFTER A FASHION.

You will notice that we have not only changed *swims* into SWIM, but also *twins* into TWIN, on the grounds that *twins* and *twin* are forms of the dictionary-word TWIN. The sentence in (2) is the same as the one in (1), but it is analysed differently, in terms of dictionary-words instead of orthographic words.

A third analysis would represent the pronunciation more directly, using what is called a 'phonological' transcription whose units are 'phonemes':

(3) /mɛːri swɪmz supɜːbli n̩ . . ./

(By convention, phonological transcriptions are always enclosed between diagonals.) Several other analyses are possible, as we shall see, but the main point is that, as with any other kind of object you can think of, a sentence can be analysed, studied and represented from a number of distinct points of view.

The relevance of all this to the National Curriculum is that when children look words up in a dictionary, the units that they find in the dictionary are dictionary-words, but what they see when they are reading is orthographic words, representing particular forms of dictionary-words. For example, they see *swims*, but need to look up SWIM. They need to learn that they won't find *swims*, as such, in any dictionary; so they have to remove the final *-s*. This is a fairly trivial problem, but in some cases they have to do far more; for example, to look up *swam* they have to convert the vowel into *-i-*.

However there is more to finding dictionary-words than ignoring differences between forms like *swim, swims* and *swam*. For one thing, you have to distinguish 'homonyms' – dictionary-words whose shape happens to be the same, but which in other respects are entirely different. For example, I can now ask a more sophisticated question than my original one: how many dictionary-words are there in sentence (4)?

(4)   A cross bear can't bear to cross rivers.

A silly sentence, but it makes the point clearly because it contains two examples of the spelling *cross* and two of *bear*, each of which conceals important differences – that is, the first *cross* is an adjective meaning 'angry', whereas the second is a verb meaning 'go across'. These would certainly count as different items in any dictionary, so children have to learn to recognise such differences as well.

If they are different dictionary-words, then they need different names. My (personal) system uses a mnemonic word added to the basic spelling: CROSS/angry and CROSS/go; but there is no standard system, so if you prefer some other system, by all means use it. An analysis of (4) in terms of dictionary-words now looks like this:

(5)   A   CROSS/angry   BEAR/animal   CAN   BEAR/tolerate   TO
      CROSS/go   RIVER.

(You will notice that I have written *can't* as CAN, on the assumption that *can't* is a form of CAN.)

Just to complete the explanation of dictionary-words, your

children will also have to learn to cope with some dictionary-words that are more than one word long – what are sometimes called 'fixed phrases'. Some obvious examples are *in spite of* and *get on like a house on fire*, where the meaning of the whole cannot be distributed among the individual words (as is normally possible). The first example is most likely to be listed in a dictionary under SPITE rather than IN, and the second under HOUSE, but it is really best to consider them each as a separate many-word dictionary-word. Such examples pose real problems, and the child has to learn to explore a dictionary in order to find them. For our own purposes we might label such dictionary-words in various ways, but the most obvious is to hyphenate the parts: IN-SPITE-OF, GET-ON-LIKE-A-HOUSE-ON-fIRE.

I can now summarise what I have helped you to discover in this lesson. You have found that the word *word* can mean a variety of things which need to be kept clearly distinct: in particular, 'orthographic word' (that is, the ordinary spelling) and 'dictionary-word'. The same orthographic word may be a form of a variety of dictionary-words (which are homonyms), and different orthographic words may be forms of the same dictionary-word; or even a dictionary-word may consist of more than one orthographic word. (Everything said here about orthographic words could, of course, be paralleled by similar things said about phonological words.) A word can also be counted either as a 'token' or as a 'type', but if we are counting types we can now see that we have a choice between counting orthographic words (that is, counting *cross* as the some type whatever it means) and counting dictionary-words (distinguishing CROSS/angry from CROSS/go).

A lesson for the pupils

The question for the children to answer is: How do you say the *s* that can be added at the end of a word? Their first task is to find some words that can take a suffix -*s*. The following is one sequence of activities that would produce the right results, but an experienced infants teacher can no doubt improve on my suggestion.

1   With the whole class, write *cat* and *cats* across the board (on the same line), and ask them what they mean. Draw a picture of a single cat over the first, and a pair of cats over the second. Now ask them whether they can break the words into smaller parts which have a meaning – for instance, does the *c* mean anything? Now what about the *s*?

2   To help them think this through, write *book* and *books* (beware of writing *dog*, *dogs*, because the *s* is pronounced differently!) below *cat* and *cats*. What do the words mean? Draw one book over the first, and two over the second. So what does the *s* mean? Does it mean 'two'? Or just 'more than one'?

3   Having found that *cats* and *books* can be divided into two parts, you can call the *s* an 'ending'. This is a technical term for a bit of grammatical structure, but not too frightening, I hope! The next question is, what other words can take *s* as an ending, with this meaning? This part of the discussion can be a free-for-all, with the children offering examples, because the aim is to collect a wide range of word-types. The children needn't know how to spell the words; as they suggest them, you can write them on the board (or on paper if by this time you have organised them in groups). I suggest you write both the singular and the plural, to bring out the visual similarities.

4   Now we come to the question I have set: how are all these *s*'s pronounced? In the first examples, *cats* and *books*, they are 'voiceless', as at the end of *bus*, but in *dogs* and *shoes* the *s* is 'voiced', like a *z*. ('Voice' is the buzzing sound made when your vocal chords are vibrating; you can feel the vibration in an extended *z* if you put your finger on your throat just over where men have their adam's apple.) The next activity, then, is to let the children sort the words collected so far into two groups, according to whether the *s* buzzes or not. (Of course, this activity would be very much easier if you had written each of your word pairs on a separate card.) The answer, then,

is that the ending *s* is pronounced sometimes like an ordinary *s*, and sometimes like a *z*.

5 You may feel that it is a pity to draw their attention to a letter which has two different pronunciations at a stage when they are still struggling with the idea that letters correspond to pronunciations at all. One reason for doing this is because plural nouns like *dogs* are so common, and it is important to acknowledge that a word like *dogs* is in fact an exception to the general principle that *s* is pronounced as in *bus*.

But an even better one is that you can lead them into the analysis of their own speech at the phonetic level by discovering a very useful and simple generalisation: the ending which means 'more than one' and which is written as *s* is voiced or voiceless according to whether the preceding sound is voiced or voiceless.

To reach this discovery you go through the words that they have given you and which are now in two lists, which we can now call the voiced and voiceless lists (because *s* is voiced and voiceless respectively). You might call them the buzzing and whispering lists, because whisper is all voiceless. (Try distinguishing *Sue* and *zoo* in a whisper!). Assuming the children understand the difference between buzzing and whispering sounds, ask them to tell you whether the s-less words end in a buzzing or whispering sound.

Be sure to concentrate on how the words are pronounced and not on how they are spelt, because the generalisation applies to pronunciation – whether or not there is a buzzing sound. However, it may be helpful to you to know that the pronunciations that are most typical of our consonant letters in most accents can be classified as follows:

voiced: z, v; b, d, g; m, n, l, r
voiceless: s, f; p, t, k

This list does not include the tricky letters *c, h, j, q, w* and *x*, nor letter combinations like *th, sh* and *ch*.

One great virtue of this generalisation about pronunciation is that it is absolutely regular: the 'voicing' (that is, the choice between 'voiced' and 'voiceless') of an ending *s* is always the same as that of the sound before it. You will find this generalisation even extends to vowels; when used after a vowel sound (as in *shoes, potatoes, zoos*) the ending *s* is voiced, because all vowels are voiced. It also makes no difference whether the vowel is part of the word's basic form, as in the examples just given, or is the short vowel which is introduced to separate the *s* from a similar consonant like *s, z, sh,*or *ch* as in *buses, wishes, churches*. (I am about to say something about the 'magic *e*' in words like *faces*, which has a different status from the one in *churches*.) And to make the rule even more useful, it doesn't only apply to the ending *s* that we find in nouns, but it also extends to the *s* which is added to verbs, as in *swims* and *chats*.

6   There are many directions in which this little project could be extended, but a particularly useful one would involve the magic *e*. If your list includes words like *cake* and *line* you will find that the pronunciation of the ending *s* follows the pronunciation and not the spelling – voiceless after *cake*, but voiced after *line*. In other words, what counts is the preceding sound, and not the preceding letter. This is an important point because it shows that ordinary speech is rule governed, and governed by rules some of which are absolutely general and regular – a useful antidote to the widely held view that rules are the prerogative of writing. Moreover, the pronunciations they have been considering have been those that they themselves use, so these rules must *already* be in their minds. (You could prove this to them, if they are doubtful, by trying some nonsense words on them. If they produce a voiced plural for the nonsense word *glay*, and a voiceless one for *glat*, the point is made: they must have applied rules in producing these forms.)

Returning to the magic *e*, you could now start a fresh project in which they explored the effect of adding magic *e*, leading to the discovery that it lengthens the preceding vowel; which in turn would show them how sounds can be classified. Voiced sounds (as defined in this unit) can be further subdivided into consonants and vowels, and vowels into long and short.

Once again this classification is a matter of pronunciation and not of spelling, because there are various ways in which a long vowel may be spelt (including the use of a magic *e*, doubling and so on).

What you have achieved so far is to explore their own grammar – the rules for pronouncing the regular plural suffix. In order to do so you have had to introduce various important grammatical ideas: that words can be divided into a basic part and an ending, each of which makes its own contribution to the word's meaning; that speech sounds can be classified; and that ordinary pronunciation is controlled by rules. Let us now link these ideas to the use of dictionaries.

By now the children should be good at stripping suffixes off words. You can reinforce this skill by a group activity in which you offer them a mixture of real and nonsense words, including some inflected words and some obscure real ones, and they have to use a dictionary to decide which are genuine English words – that is, forms of listed dictionary-words. For example, the stars in the following list mark the word-forms which are not English words.

floods, bus, *glids, *pags, puss, *dasks, peers, cactus

(If they are ready for Scrabble they will appreciate the great importance of this distinction!) They cannot make the distinction unless they can distinguish dictionary-words from forms, and successfully strip suffixes. By the end of the activity they should be able to use the terms 'dictionary-word', 'form' and 'ending' with confidence. And incidentally they will have had a lot of practice in sorting words alphabetically.

Theoretical synopsis

The distinction between dictionary-words and their forms is fundamental to grammar, and is one part of the discovery made by the Greek and Roman grammarians which I mentioned earlier. The basic idea is that the analysis of a word like *swims* relates it to two different sets of other words. On the one hand, it is related to the other forms of the same dictionary-word, SWIM (for instance, to *swim, swam, swimming* and *swum*). On the other hand, it is related to the same form of other dictionary-words, such as *sings, comes, goes, eats,* etc., etc.   Just as we needed a name for the dictionary-word, we also need a name for the form, so that we can express general rules about how forms are used. The obvious name is simply 's-form', which allows us to express rules about how the 's-form of a verb' is used. Some linguists use a simple notation for distinguishing the forms of a verb, in which the suffix is added to 'V' for verb: 'V-s'. We can combine this system with our system for naming dictionary-words by adding the suffix to the name of the dictionary-word: SWIM-s. This allows a further advance on our dictionary-words-only transcription of sentence (1):

(6)   MARY SWIM-S SUPERBLY AND BOB SWIM-S QUITE WELL AND
      EVEN THE TWIN-S SWIM AFTER A FASHION.

You will notice that I am calling *twins* the s-form of TWIN. This is fine so long as we remember that TWIN is a noun whereas SWIM is a verb – in other words as long as the distinction between nouns and verbs is applied to the dictionary-words it doesn't need to be applied to the forms as well.

You may be wondering why we need to recognise both the suffix -*s* and the notion 's-form'. If the s-form of a word always contains the suffix -*s*, why can't we refer directly to this suffix in whatever rules need to refer to it? I have to recognise that some linguists believe that this is precisely what we should do. The main reason for my controversial answer is that there are irregularities: when we refer to the s-form of a word, what we mean is 'the form which normally – but not necessarily – contains -*s*'.

For example, alongside *twins*, the s-form of TWIN, we find *children* as the corresponding form of CHILD. Everything points to *children* being the s-form of CHILD in all but appearance. A typical noun dictionary-word has an s-form; CHILD has none but *children*. The s-form of a typical noun refers to a group of two or more; so does *children*. The s-form of a typical noun is used after *these* but not after *this*; this is true of *children* (*these children* but **this children*). And so on. If we say that *children* is the s-form of CHILD, then everything works smoothly except that the s-form of this dictionary-word is irregular. But if we deny it, then CHILD is irregular in not having an s-form, and we have no other way of explaining the similarities between *children* and s-forms of other nouns. In conclusion then, *children* = CHILD-s, just as *twins* = TWIN-s.

You may find it helpful to explore what you know, as a native speaker, of these rules and regularities by completing the following table for some common dictionary-words, in which I have only filled some of the boxes. You may find some of them more interesting than you expect – even surprising. I indicate the form of the noun without any suffix simply as 'N-' (to be pronounced 'en-zero').

	TWIN	CHILD	GOOSE	SHEEP	PERSON
N-	*twin*	*child*			
N-s	*twins*	*children*			*cattle*

You will have noticed that my 'N-s' and 'N-' are equivalent to the traditional categories 'plural noun' and 'singular noun'. For present purposes the two sets of distinctions – form-based and traditional – are equivalent and interchangeable, but I should mention two reasons for maintaining both sets. One is that in the case of verbs there is no established and satisfactory traditional name for 'V-s' and 'V-' (for example, *swims* and *swim*), so our names are useful. (The term 'third-person singular' is misleading because it implies that the verb is singular, whereas in fact it is the verb's subject that is singular, and third-person; it is also irrelevant to those dialects in which V-s is the only present-tense form, as in *I/you/she/we/they swims*.)

The other reason is that in some areas of grammar we need to supplement names like 'V-s' and 'V-' with other names which are based even less directly on the presence or absence of suffixes. For example, if V- includes all verbs which (even by the most normal rules) have no ending, then it includes both the *swim* in (7) and the one in (8).

(7)   I swim every morning.
(8)   Now swim to the bank and get out!

But these are different from each other in many important ways, so we shall want to distinguish them as 'present tense' and 'imperative' respectively (in a later lesson). The conclusion is that we may well need both our system of names based on suffixes, and also the traditional more abstract one.

You may be interested to know that the area of grammar that we have just been exploring is the interface between 'morphology' and 'syntax'. Morphology is the study of word-shapes, such as the presence or absence of particular suffixes; and syntax is the study of word-combinations, for instance, how singular and plural nouns combine with other words like *this* and *these*. The general conclusion that we have reached (nearly two thousand years after the Greek and Roman grammarians did the same) is that the links between strictly morphological patterns and strictly syntactic ones are mediated by abstract categories like 's-form' and/or 'plural'.

Level 2

Ambiguity

The National Curriculum gives general recommendations for teaching junior pupils which are relevant to level 2:

Pupils should consider the way word meanings can be played with, e.g. in riddles, puns, jokes, spoonerisms, word games, graffiti, advertisements, poems; the use of nonsense words and deliberate misspellings, e.g. in poems and advertisements. (16.29)

British children have a reputation for being particularly keen on verbal humour based on double meanings so it will be easy to find suitable material for this lesson. The sources for my examples are *The Ha Ha Bonk Joke Book*, by Janet and Allan Ahlberg (1982) and the *Crack-a-Joke Book* (collected by children for Oxfam, 1978).

For the class the question is this: do jokes (1) and (2) both work in the same way, and if not, what's the difference?

(1) – How can you keep cool at a football match?
     – Stand next to a fan.
(2) GIRL: Last night I had to get up and open the door in my nightie.
     BOY: That's a funny place to have a door.

But your question is (apparently) much easier: how many meanings does (3) have, and why?

(3) You saw the logs there.

A lesson for you

Let me help you with your question by breaking it down into two simpler questions. How many meanings does each of (4) and (5) have, and why?

(4)   You saw the logs.
(5)   He saws the logs there.

We start with (4).

As you have probably noticed, it is possible to take *saw* in two quite different ways – in fact, as an example of two different dictionary-words, which are distinguished in (6) and (7).

(7)   He saws the logs.
(8)   He sees the logs.

The dictionary-words are the verbs SAW and SEE, and the ambiguity arises from the fact that, by pure chance, one form of each of these dictionary-words has the same spelling and pronunciation, *saw*. Whenever this spelling or pronunciation occurs, we can therefore link it either to SAW or to SEE, and write it in either of these ways:

(4a)   YOU SAW THE LOG.
(4b)   YOU SEE THE LOG.

We could make the analysis more sophisticated by showing the forms as well as the dictionary-words. In relation to SAW, *saw* is the bare form, but in relation to SEE, *saw* is like the forms containing -*ed* that belong to regular dictionary-words like WALK (for instance, *walked, looked*). Let's assume then that *saw* is the ed-form of SEE, and improve the analyses:

(4a′)   YOU SAW- THE LOG-S.
(4b′)   YOU SEE-ed THE LOG-S.

We now have an answer to my question about (4). This sentence has two meanings because the word *saw* is either the bare form of SAW or the ed-form of SEE. We can follow standard practice in calling this kind of ambiguity 'lexical' – two analyses are possible, but the only difference is in one dictionary-word. This particular example also involved a difference in the form – V-ed or V- – but this isn't important, and many commonplace examples are more straightforward:

(8)   The ears are too small.
(8a)   *ears* = EAR/bodypart
(8b)   *ears* = EAR/corn

(9)   She lifted her trunk.
(9a)   *trunk* = TRUNK/luggage
(9b)   *trunk* = TRUNK/elephant

(10)   We passed the box.
(10a) *passed* = PASS/go
(10b) *passed* = PASS/hand

These are all clear cases of lexical ambiguity.

You may have noticed some other ambiguities in *You saw the logs* in addition to the one just discussed: *You* could refer to the person spoken to or it could mean people in general, like ONE; and the logs could have been a set of records. Ambiguity is all-pervasive in any language, and inescapable; but most of the time it is also harmless because we eliminate most of the possible meanings without even noticing them. Precisely how we do this is a long, fascinating and still incomplete story.

Let's now move on to your next problem, example (5).

(5)   He saws the logs there.

This too has two different meanings, but they have a very different explanation. You may see the ambiguity straight away, but in case you don't I shall need to 'disambiguate' this sentence – that is, to force one or other of its interpretations, by excluding the other. Try the following:

(5a)   He saws them there.
(5b)   It's the logs there that he saws.

As you can now see, *there* can relate either to *saws*, as in (5a), or to *logs*, in (5b). In (5a) it tells us where he does the sawing (he saws them there), and in (5b) it tells us which logs he saws (the logs there).

Unlike the first problem, this one has nothing to do with dictionary-words because the dictionary-words are just the same in either interpretation of (5). What varies is the relations among the words, and specifically the relation between *there* and the rest of the sentence. In one meaning *there* links to *saws*, in the other it links to *logs*; in traditional terminology, it 'modifies' either *saws* or *logs*. The modern description is much the same: it is a 'modifier' of either *saws* or *logs*. Roughly speaking, if we say that *there* is a modifier of *logs* we mean two things: that the word *there* takes its position from the word *logs* (*there* has to be just after *logs*), and that its meaning refines ('modifies') the meaning of *logs* (*there* tells us which logs).

These different relations can most conveniently be shown by means of a diagram; modern linguists have a number of different diagramming systems, but I think you will probably find the following more helpful than any of the standard ones:

(5a′)

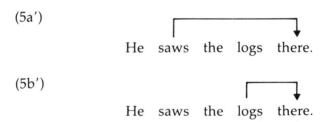

He   saws   the   logs   there.

(5b′)

He   saws   the   logs   there.

The arrows in these diagrams point from the modified word to the word that modifies it.

This kind of ambiguity is normally called 'structural', because it involves the structure of the whole sentence – how the words in it are related to one another. More specifically, it is a 'syntactic' ambiguity, because it concerns the relations among the words themselves, and not just the relations among their meanings. We can see this from the fact that the ambiguity arises only when *there* is immediately after *logs*; it disappears if we reverse this order, as we can if we move *there* to the front of the sentence:

(11)   There he saws the logs.

In this case we can't take *there* as a modifier of *logs* because the rule mentioned above says that the modifier has to come straight after the noun.

Why, then, does an ambiguity arise in sentence (5), *He saws the logs there*? This is because the rules for positioning modifiers happen to allow the same word to be taken either as a modifier of the verb or as a modifier of the immediately preceding noun. Precisely what those rules are, and why this coincidence arises, is a matter of detail which you might like to ponder. I will return to it in the next section but one.

We are now ready to tackle your main problem: how many meanings does sentence (3) have, and why?

(3)   You saw the logs there.

As you can no doubt see, this sentence is made up out of the bits of the other two sentences (4–5), and contains the ambiguities of both of them. Consequently the answer is that it has $2 \times 2 = 4$ meanings. (I mentioned two further lexical ambiguities, involving *you* and *logs*, so it actually has $2 \times 2 \times 2 \times 2 = 16$ meanings! For simplicity I shall ignore these extra possibilities.) The first pair are as in sentence (4):

(4)   You saw the logs.

Here the ambiguity is lexical: SAW versus SEE. The other pair comes from the ambiguity in sentence (5):

(5)   He saws the logs there.

This ambiguity is the syntactic one: does *there* modify *saws* or *logs*? Here they all are, using a mixture of the analytical systems that I have given you so far.

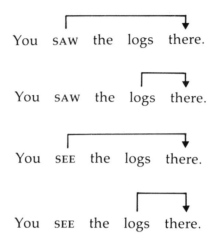

You SAW the logs there.

You SAW the logs there.

You SEE the logs there.

You SEE the logs there.

To summarise this lesson, you have discovered that sentences have a structure in which words are related to each other. The words in the sentence are each related to some dictionary-word, as we saw in the first lesson, so one source of ambiguity is that one word may be taken as an example of either of two different dictionary-words (as with *see* = SAW or SEE). Another source, however, is the fact that alternative sets of relations may be possible among the same string of words (such as *there* modifying either *logs* or *saws*). We call these two kinds of ambiguity 'lexical' and 'structural' respectively.

A lesson for the children

The children's question is whether jokes (1) and (2) both work in the same way, and if not, what the difference is.

(1)   – How can you keep cool at a football match?
       – Stand next to a fan.

(2) GIRL: Last night I had to get up and open the door in my nightie.

BOY: That's a funny place to have a door.

You can no doubt see the answer I would give: that (1) is an example of lexical ambiguity but (2) involves structural ambiguity. The meanings of (1) vary according to whether *fan* = FAN/ventilator or FAN/supporter, and those of (2) vary according to whether *in my nightie* (or just *in*, if you prefer) modifies *open* or *door*. I obviously don't expect the children to be able to use this terminology in their answer, though I see no reason why you shouldn't teach it to them (if you think it would be helpful) after they've discovered the relevant distinction in their own terms.

I also leave it entirely to you to decide whether to explore the reasons why the jokes are funny. I take it that the humour comes from the fact that the first sentence pushes one hard towards one interpretation, but then the second sentence forces the other one; but it's hard to turn this into a comprehensible 'explanation' for the humour without provoking yawns all round. It may be best to leave the humour as the driving force which will motivate them to search for more examples.

The point of the lesson might be achieved in many different ways. One would be to ask the class to provide further examples of jokes which they thought were like (1) but not like (2), and then to do the reverse. This would no doubt throw up a mass of funny debris (in my sense of 'debris', meaning worthy but irrelevant examples), which would give you a chance to explain why the irrelevant ones didn't fit the pattern; but of course it would be most helpful if at least the first few examples fitted clearly into one or the other pattern. You could achieve this by starting with your own special collection, and asking them to put them into one or the other category. (You might write each joke on a separate card to make classification easier, and provide yourself with two baskets.)

Here are some more examples from my collection (that is, from the *Ha Ha Bonk Joke Book* and the *Crack-a-Joke Book*); we start with some lexical ambiguities (which, incidentally, are ten-a-penny):

(12) – What was the tortoise doing on the motorway?
      – About ten yards an hour.

Explanation: *doing* = DO/what or DO/speed. ('DO/what' is a gesture of despair; it is meant to be the DO found in expressions such as *What are you doing in my bedroom?*)

(13) – How can you stop an elephant from smelling?
      – Tie a knot in his trunk.

Explanation: *smelling* = SMELL/perceive or SMELL/stink.

(14) – What's yellow and stupid?
      – Thick custard.

Explanation: *thick* = THICK/stiff or THICK/stupid; notice that in this one the ambiguity is in the answer, not the question; but again there is a conflict between the meanings required by the question and by the other word in the answer.

And now some examples of structural ambiguity, with the minimum of lexical ambiguity. I should admit that not many of the jokes in my source books seemed to fit into this category. First a couple of near-clones of our original joke:

(15) SHOW-OFF: . . . so I just leapt out of bed, grabbed my gun and shot the tiger in my pyjamas.
      CLEVER DICK: Goodness me, what was a tiger doing in your pyjamas?

Explanation: *in my pyjamas* modifies either *shot* (how was I when I shot it?) or *tiger* (which tiger?).

(16) CUSTOMER: I would like to try on that suit in the window, please.
      ASSISTANT: I'm sorry, sir, you'll have to try it on in the changing-rooms like everybody else.

Explanation: *in the window* modifies either *try* (where shall I try it on?) or *suit* (which suit?).

(17)   BILL: The police are looking for a man with one eye called Murphy.
   WILL: What's his other eye called?

Explanation: again, *called Murphy* could be a modifier of *man* (a man called Murphy) or of *eye* (an eye called Murphy). Diagrams may be helpful:

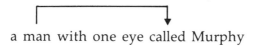

a man with one eye called Murphy

a man with one eye called Murphy

only the first meaning survives if we change the order of words, bringing *called* next to *man*: 'a man called Murphy with one eye.'

(18)   – Doctor, doctor, my hair's coming out. Can you give me something to keep it in?
   – Certainly – how about a paper bag?

Explanation: either (a) *something* is related to *keep* (something keeps the hair in) or (b) it is related to *in* (I keep the hair in something). The diagrams are:

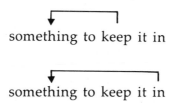

something to keep it in

something to keep it in

Unfortunately neither of these relations is the relation referred to in your lesson, 'modification', but you can probably see how the ambiguity arises. If not, compare *something to keep it in* with (a) *something to make me happy* and then with (b) *something to sit on*.

(19) A lady went into a pet shop.
'I want a parrot for my little girl,' she said.
'Sorry, madam,' said the shop-keeper. 'We don't do swops.'

Explanation: *for my little girl* is related either to *want* ('I want it in exchange for her') or to *parrot* ('It's a parrot for my little girl that I want').

I want a parrot for my little girl.

I want a parrot for my little girl.

In relation to *parrot* it is a modifier, but its relation to *want* is, again, something else.

(20) – Who invented the five-day week?
– Robinson Crusoe. He had all his work done by Friday.

Explanation: *by Friday* modifies either *had* (when did he have it done by?) or *done* (who was it done by?).

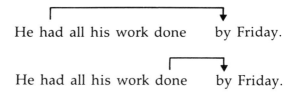

He had all his work done   by Friday.

He had all his work done   by Friday.

Compare the meanings of 'By Friday he had all his work done' and 'He had all this work done by Friday by Thursday.'

(21) – How do you make a Maltese cross?
– Stand on his toe.

Explanation: either *Maltese* is an adjective and modifies *cross*, or it is a noun, meaning 'citizen of Malta', and *a Maltese* is related directly to *make*:

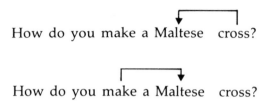

How do you make a Maltese cross?

How do you make a Maltese cross?

If you can encourage the children to look very carefully and in detail at the words in the jokes, in search of ambiguities, you will have achieved as much in this lesson as you can reasonably expect. I don't see any point at this stage in trying to provide any analytical tools more sophisticated than the notions 'dictionary-word' and 'syntactic link' (as illustrated in particular by the 'modifier' relation).

You should be prepared for a wide range of joke types that don't fit either of these neat categories. Here is just a small selection of the other types, intended to illustrate the wide and baffling range of possibilities. A complete and exhaustive analysis would involve a very large-scale (and challenging) research project.

(22) – Knock, knock!
      – Who's there?
      – Cook.
      – Cook who?
      – That's the first one I've heard this year.

(23) – Why is getting up at three o'clock in the morning like a pig's tail?
      – Because it's twirly.

(24) – Where do you find giant snails?
      – On the end of giants' fingers.

(25) – Where did Humpty Dumpty put his hat?
      – Humpty dumped 'is 'at on the wall.

(26) – Shall I tell you the joke about the empty house?
  – There's nothing in it.

(27) – Why is an elephant big, grey and wrinkly?
  – Because if he was small, white and round he'd be an aspirin.

(28) – What did the first mind-reader say to the second mind-reader?
  – 'You're all right, how am I?'

(29) – What did Tarzan say when he saw the elephants come over the hill?
  – 'Here come the elephants.'

The fact that primary-school children find jokes like these funny tells us a lot about the complexity of their minds, and also about the complexity of language. In many of them the humour revolves around an ambiguity in the analysis, but the ambiguity may be at different levels, and may involve different kinds of uncertainty – for instance, uncertainty about where the word boundaries are, about which of two homonymous dictionary-words is involved, about the relations among the words. You may feel that some of the later examples derive their humour from uncertainties that are too complex or too abstract for young children, but again they are worth storing up for use with older classes.

Many of these jokes make sense only when spoken, which allows you to make the point that there are some situations where writing is a poor substitute for speech; which in turn could lead into a discussion of appropriateness of registers. You could also discuss the very abstract nature of word boundaries, of which the jokes in (22)–(25) are evidence. Many adults firmly believe that they separate words in speech by silent pauses, so some children may believe this too and may be puzzled by the difficulties they sometimes face in writing. A speculative discussion of precisely how a listener processes one of these jokes could teach the pupils a lot about the basic principles of communication: above all, that listening is a highly active problem-solving activity, rather than a passive 'decoding' operation.

Theoretical synopsis

We have seen that a single string of words can correspond to two different syntactic structures, which in turn indicate different semantic structures – that is, different meanings for the same sentence. For example, *I opened the door in my nightie* allows two different syntactic structures according to whether *in my nightie* modifies *opened* or *door*, and corresponding to these two syntactic analyses we have two different meanings: 'Wearing my nightie I opened the door' and 'I opened the door which is in my nightie'. Examples like these might suggest that the notions 'syntactic structure' and 'semantic structure' were pretty much the same, but this is not so. I shall now explain why.

First, there is the very elementary fact that words and their meanings are quite different kinds of things. For example, my name is Richard, so I am presumably the meaning – or at least one of the possible meanings – of the dictionary-word RICHARD; but the dictionary-word contains seven letters, while I don't; and I have a beard, but the dictionary-word RICHARD doesn't; and so on. This is very obvious, but it is surprising how often even undergraduates confuse words and their meanings, saying things like 'The first word in *I like beer* is the speaker.'

Second, the semantic relations among words need not be shown directly by their syntactic relations; in other words there are sentences which have just one syntactic structure, but several different semantic structures. An example of this is (30).

(30)   We only invited Mary to the reception.

This can mean various things, according to which words are the 'focus' of *only*. It could, for example, mean 'we invited Mary, and no one else, to the reception', where *Mary* is the focus of *only*. If we call the meaning of the focus word F, then ONLY means something like 'F and nothing but F'. But (30) could also mean 'we invited Mary to the reception, and did no more than that to get her there', where the focus is *invited*; and of course the focus could be *to the reception*: 'we invited Mary to the reception and to nothing else.'

But alongside these three meaning structures there is no reason to think that there is any variation in the syntactic structure of the sentence, where *only* seems to have the same relation to all the other words throughout. The rule that allows this proliferation of meanings all sprouting out of one syntactic structure is very simple: if ONLY immediately precedes a verb (here, *invited*) then any word which follows it (in the same sentence) can be its focus.

It is true that the pronunciation varies according to which word is in focus, because we can use the loudness (technically, the intonation-focus or sentence-accent) to pick out the focus word for us: as in *We only invited* MARY *to the reception*. But this shows only that the 'phonological structure' (which is quite separate from the syntactic structure) shows focus; it does not prove that the syntactic structure varies. You will notice, incidentally, that this explains why the sentence pattern in (30) is so much more successful in speech than in writing, where the pronunciation cannot remove the ambiguities; hence the need to encourage children when writing to use the other rule, which places ONLY next to its focus (*We invited only Mary to the reception*).

There are a great many other reasons for distinguishing between the grammatical structure of a sentence, in which we are dealing with words and their syntactic relations, and its semantic structure, in which the units are word-meanings and their interrelations. Some of these other matters will come up in later lessons, but let me finish with one final point. If we say that one word is the modifier of another word, this tells us a great deal about the relations between the words – for example, that the two words need to be as near to each other as possible, and that the modifier must stand either before or after the modified word, according to the types of word involved, with adjectives that modify nouns standing before them (*big book*), but most words that modify verbs standing after them (*run quickly*).

On the other hand, when we know that one word modifies another this tells us very little about the semantic relations between their meanings. For example, the syntactic relation is the same in both *grammar book* and *exercise book*: the first word modifies the word *book*; but the semantic relations must be quite different, because *grammar book* means 'a book about grammar' but *exercise book* means 'a book full of exercises'. Even more dramatically, *big books* means 'a set of big books' whereas *numerous books* means 'a big set of books'; but the syntactic relation between the adjective and the noun seems to be precisely the same in both examples.

We can now assume a distinction between syntactic facts and semantic facts. Let's now see how this distinction applies to the notion 'dictionary-word' which we explored in the lesson at level 1. What we saw there was that a dictionary-word is a 'family of words' which are related to the dictionary-word as its different 'forms'. (You may have noticed that we have allowed dictionary-words to have just a single form, which allows us to take a word like *in* as the one form of a dictionary-word: IN.) What then unites the various forms of a dictionary-word? The answer is: a collection of syntactic and semantic facts, and of facts about their shape (such as their pronunciation and spelling). For example the dictionary-word SWIM brings together all words which combine the following characteristics:

- they are verbs (a syntactic fact);
- they can occur with nothing after them (e.g. *He is swimming*.), that is (technically) they have no obligatory complements (another syntactic fact);
- they mean 'swim' (a semantic fact);
- their pronunciation contains the sounds represented by the spelling ⟨swim⟩, or a closely related sequence ⟨swam⟩.

Any word that has all these characteristics is an example of SWIM, so we can see why dictionary-words are so important, as a major source of the interconnections between the syntactic, semantic and form-based structures.

Level 3

Tense

The study programme for writing at level 3 includes the following two recommendations:

(i) Pupils working towards level 3 . . . should be taught to look for instances where . . . tenses or pronouns have been used incorrectly or inconsistently.
(ii) They should be taught, in the context of discussion about their own writing, grammatical terms such as sentence, verb, tense, noun, pronoun.

The incorrect use of tenses referred to in the first recommendation is presumably illustrated in the following examples:

(1a) There **was** a swimming pool which you **can** go in. (age 9)
(1b) It **was** hopeless to escape because the window **is** about 4½ yards off the ground. (age 10)

(These examples are taken from Perera 1984.) The highlighted words are all verbs, and the relevant problem is that the choice of tense wobbles uncertainly between present and past. This problem is not restricted to writing, as can be seen from the following:

(2) and she and and at the end/ she's um . . . these er two men/ and um they **were** angels/ **stop** you know/ and he**'s** going to run out/ and she **came** through the door/. . .and then they **played** rugby/ (age 10; from Fawcett and Perkins 1980)

(The slashes mark the end of intonation units; I have omitted a number of other phonetic symbols.)

Our aim in this unit will be to clarify the notion 'tense', and explore some ways of tackling this problem. Your question is simply, 'How many tenses does English have?', and the question for the children is about the difference between past and present verbs in a narrative.

A lesson for you

How many tenses does English have? As you are no doubt aware, there is a long and powerful tradition which answers 'three: past, present and future'. These three tenses are illustrated in (3).

(3a)   I am a teacher.
(3b)   I was a teacher.
(3c)   I will be a teacher.

But you probably also know that we can make a lot more distinctions that have something to do with time, which presumably has something to do with tense. The sentences in (4) illustrate just a few of the possibilities.

(4a)   I am teaching.
(4b)   I have taught.
(4c)   I have been teaching.
(4d)   I used to teach.
(4e)   I am about to teach.
(4f)   I will teach.
(4g)   I will have taught.
(4h)   I will have been teaching.
(4i)   I will have been about to have been teaching. (!)

Most of the words in these sentences other than *I* and TEACH are called 'auxiliary verbs' (a very traditional name), and as you can see these can combine quite freely with one another to form monsters like the last one.

So, how many tenses does English have? Three? Or as many as can be expressed by piling up auxiliary verbs? If the second answer is correct we may have to reconcile ourselves to a large number; I make it 24, if we include all the possible combinations of the words in (4). If the children's problems involve all of these possibilities, your problem is pretty serious!

It all depends, of course, on what you mean by 'tense'; and when you do grammar by discovery-learning, the terminology is up to you. Let's rephrase the question. What rules in English grammar are relevant to the children's wrong choice of verb-forms, and what categories do these rules mention? Whatever these categories turn out to be, we may as well call them 'tense'; this will at least be in line with the National Curriculum, since this links 'tense' with the notion of 'tenses being used inconsistently', as in the examples quoted above. This apparently cavalier approach to matters of terminology is typical of modern linguistics, where the focus is on the rules in the grammar rather than on the terminology for naming things.

Let's call the various word-forms and word-combinations that I illustrated in (3) and (4) 'time-wordings'. (This isn't a standard name, but it will do for the time being, and it illustrates the need to invent new terminology at times.) Our new task is to find some rules which have something to do with time-wordings, and which in particular have something to do with time-wordings at different places in a sentence or story being 'consistent' with one another. Any rule of this kind must (by definition) divide the time-wordings into at least two groups, so that it can impose some kind of restriction on the ways in which members of the different groups combine with one another. The groups are what we are really interested in, because the groups are what we are going to call 'tenses'. Before we start you may like to lay a bet on the number of tenses that will emerge from this exercise.

1   For our first rule we start with the following examples.

(5a)   It is 10.45.
(5b)   He told me it was 10.45.

Assuming that (5b) reports the words in (5a) we see that *is* has been changed into *was*. It is easy to explain this change in the light of the meanings of these two words, on the assumption that the time of the reporting was no longer 10.45: we can't use *is* to refer to a state of affairs which is no longer true. But now look at the next pair.

(6a)   The square root of 9 is 3.
(6b)   He told me the square root of 9 was 3.

In this example our explanation fails, because the fact expressed in (6a) is just as true at the time of the reporting as it was when reported. Why, then, do we find *was* referring to an eternal truth?

   The traditional explanation is that this is a peculiarity of 'reported speech' – speech produced at one time and reported at another. This can't be true, however, because *was* is not possible if the reporting is done by a present-tense verb – a standard device as in (7a), used even when the original 'utterance' was in the past:

(7a)   Homer says that the sea is/?was like wine.
(7b)   He tells me the square root of 9 is/*was 3.

This example shows that the presence of a reporting verb is not sufficient to allow this use of *was*. Nor is it necessary, because we find just the same pattern in examples where there is no speech to report:

(8a)   He discovered that the square root of 9 was 3.
(8b)   He believed that the square root of 9 was 2.
(8c)   He wondered whether the square root of 9 was 2.
(8d)   He worked out the number that was the square root of 9.

   The generalisation we need in order to explain these examples is a very simple one:

RULE: If a past-tense verb (e.g. *was*) is used after a past-tense verb (e.g. *discovered, told*), then the former may be understood as though it were a present-tense verb.

(This is not quite accurate as it stands, but it will do for the time being and it works for the examples given. Notice that I am not saying that the verb in these cases *has* to be past tense, just that it can be, contrary to the normal rules for interpreting past-tense verbs.) In other words, a preceding past-tense verb lets a following verb 'agree' with it, regardless of its meaning. We can call the two verbs involved in this agreement V1 and V2.

Now we come to the main question: how does this rule divide up the world of time-wordings? So far the examples we have considered have been very simple, with just a single verb in each position:

V1 = told, discovered, . . .   V2 = was

What happens if we add auxiliary verbs? For example, we might think that since *has taught* and *taught* both refer to events in the past that they would receive the same treatment. Let's see what happens when we replace the simple past-tenses with HAVE + V-ed (for instance, *has taught*).

(9a)   He has told me that the square root of 9 is/*was 3.
(9b)   He discovered that the square root of 9 was/*has been 3.
(9c)   *He has told me that the square root of 9 has been 3.

Assuming you accept my judgements, it appears that *has been* and *was* are not interchangeable. They are distinguished by this rule, and more generally HAVE + V-ed does not count as a past-tense verb. If V1 is *has told*, the options for V2 are just the same as when V1 is *tells*, and if V1 is *told*, then *has been* can't refer as V2 to an eternal truth, though *was* can.

I should issue a brief warning about my terminology, which is downright sloppy by professional standards. I am using 'past-tense verb' and 'V-ed' as though they were interchangeable, and I am also calling the verb-form found after HAVE 'V-ed'. You have probably noticed that in some cases these forms are in fact different – such as *was* versus *(has) been* – so we ought to give them different names ('past tense' versus 'perfect participle') although in most verbs they have the same shape, V-ed. I don't want to get sidetracked into this question here, but you will find a discussion in the encyclopedia in part IV below, under 'tense' and 'perfect participle'.

If we carry out this kind of test on all our various auxiliary combinations, we find the following kinds of time-wordings can satisfy both V1 and V2 in the rule – that is, if both V1 and V2 are drawn from the following list, then V2 can be interpreted as though it were present tense. ('Present tense' isn't quite right here, as I shall explain below.)

V-ed	e.g. told, was
BE-ed + V-ing	was telling
HAVE-ed + V-ed	had told
HAVE-ed + BE-ed + V-ing	had been telling
USE-ed TO + V-	used to tell
BE-ed ABOUT TO V-	was about to tell
WILL-ed V-	would tell
WILL-ed HAVE- V-ed	would have told
WILL-ed HAVE- BE-ed V-ing	would have been telling

What generalisation leaps out from this list? If you look at the first word in each formula, you will notice that it is the ed-form – that is, the past-tense form – of the verb concerned. The rule makes a simple two-way division, then, into time-wordings whose first verb is past tense, and those where it isn't – in other words, where it is present tense.

You may think I have cheated in order to arrive at this neat generalisation. First, notice that I have treated *told* and *was* as the ed-forms of their respective dictionary-words, in spite of their lack of an -*ed* suffix. I doubt if this worries you, given that I am using V-ed as another name for 'past tense', and we all know that verbs can have irregular past tenses. Second, you'll see that I treat *used* as USE-ed, although this is in fact the *only* form that this verb has (you can't say *I use to do it*, meaning 'I habitually do it'). Again I don't see why this should worry you.

The third assumption is where you may stick: *would* = WILL-ed; that is, that *would* is the past-tense form corresponding to *will*. The form isn't too worrying; after all we find much the same difference between *can* and *could*, which are obviously present- and past-tense forms of the same dictionary-word (compare *I can swim now, and I could already swim when I was three*). The problem is the meaning: in most of its uses, *would* doesn't refer to something true in the past, as most past tense verbs do. Where is the past-time meaning in an example like the following?

(10)   If you asked him nicely he would tell you the answer.

The meaning of *would tell* is a hypothetical state of affairs rather than one that existed in the past.

Nevertheless, *would tell* does have precisely the same effect on a following verb that one expects of a past-tense verb according to our rule on p. 92. You can see this in the following example.

(11)   If you asked him nicely he would tell you the square root of 9 was 3.

Notice that here again we find *was* referring to an eternal truth – something which is not possible after *will tell*:

(12)   If you ask him nicely he will tell you the square root of 9 is/*was 3.

We have two alternatives. One is to rephrase our rule, so that it allows past-tense verbs to have meanings like those of present-tense verbs either if they follow a past-tense verb or if they follow *would*. The other is to classify *would* as the past-tense form of WILL, and leave the rule as it is. We shall see that there are quite good reasons for preferring the second choice.

One of these reasons is that *would* behaves like an ordinary past-tense verb when it is in the second position as well. The next examples make the point:

(13a) I calculate that he will be 90 next week.
(13b) I calculated that he will/would be 90 next week.

You can see that *would be* refers to a state of affairs which is still in the future at the time of speaking, just as for *will be*. Once again we have the same choice: either we change our rule or we classify *would* as a past-tense verb. But this time we can see that if we opt for changing the rule, we shall have to change it into the following:

> If a past-tense verb (or *would*) is used after a past-tense verb (or *would*) then the former may be understood as though it were a present-tense verb.

How much better to kill two (or more) birds with one stone and classify *would* as a past-tense verb.

One conclusion to which we have been driven, rather unexpectedly, is that *would* is the past-tense form of WILL – that is, it can be analysed as WILL-ed. The same kind of evidence leads us to take *should* as SHALL-ed, *could* as CAN-ed and *might* as MAY-ed. But more importantly, we have found that as far as this rule is concerned, there are only two kinds of time-wording: those introduced by a past-tense verb, and those introduced by a present-tense one. If you backed a number bigger than two, your money is in danger!

2 The next rule is rather similar to the one we have just discovered, as it involves special meanings that time-wordings may have when combined with other words. In this case, though, it is the present-tense verbs that have the extra meanings. We start with the examples in (14).

(14a) I ate when I was/*am hungry.

(14b)   I eat when I am hungry.
(14c)   I'll eat when I am hungry.

If *I am hungry* occurs on its own it has to refer to a state of affairs which is true at the time of speaking. This is the case in both the first two examples, but in (14c) the state of being hungry is still in the future. Suppose I plan to eat in about three hours time; I can't say **I'm hungry in three hours*, though I can say *I'll eat when I am hungry, in three hours*. In short, *I am* has the meaning you would expect of *I will be*, and takes its time reference from the verb in front of it, *I'll eat*. (In French, a future tense is obligatory in such sentences: *Je mangerai quand j'aurai/*j'ai faim.*)

The same pattern, is found across a wide variety of words other than WHEN: BEFORE, AFTER, WHILE, AS, IF, BECAUSE, ALTHOUGH. It is also found in examples like (15), which involve relative clauses (explained in the encyclopedia).

(15)   I'll eat the food that I buy.

But in none of these constructions can a present-tense verb take its time reference from a past-tense verb; that is, we can't say *I ate when I am hungry*, with the times linked as in *I will eat when I am hungry*. Once again there is a simple two-way distinction between time-wordings introduced by present-tense verbs and those introduced by past-tense ones.

3   Our last rule is about 'tag questions', the little questions that we often add to statements to turn them into semi-questions.

(16a)   You like grammar, do you?
(16b)   You liked grammar, did you?

The point of these examples is to show that the tag question agrees in tense with the statement: after *like* (i.e. LIKE-) we have *do* (DO-), and after *liked* we have *did* – i.e. LIKE-ed ... DO-ed. (It is somewhat more usual for a tag question to be negative after a positive statement, that is, *don't you* in the case of (16a), but I have chosen the simpler structure to avoid having to talk about negation, which isn't relevant here.)

Once again we must ask what happens if we use the more complex kind of time-wording, containing auxiliary verbs. For example, after *will like* do we find *will do*? The answer is obvious: the only bit of the time-wording that is at all relevant to the tag question is its first word, which is either a present-tense verb or a past-tense verb. You can see this in the following examples.

(17a) You will like grammar, will you?
(17b) You would like grammar, would you?
(18a) You have understood, have you?
(18b) You had understood, had you?
(19a) You are enjoying it, are you?
(19b) You were enjoying it, were you?
(20)   You used to like grammar, did/?used you?
(21a) You may have been dozing, may you?
(21b) You might have been dozing, might you?

In all these examples, the verb in the tag question has to have the same tense as the first verb of the statement, but the rest of the statement is irrelevant.

We have seen three rules which mention past-tense and present-tense verbs, but none at all which refer to traditional tenses like future (*will teach*), perfect (*has taught*), pluperfect (*had taught*), imperfect (*was teaching*) and so on. You will just have to take my word for it that there are (to the best of my knowledge) *no* rules at all that do refer to these notions. You will have noticed, of course, that past and present are the only tenses in English which are distinguished by the endings on the verb itself; all the others are marked by adding some kind of auxiliary verb. The other traditional tenses were excellent for Latin, where they were also marked by endings on the verb; but for English they are quite irrelevant. So the answer to my question is: there are just two tenses in English, past and present.

A lesson for the pupils

Your lesson aimed to combat some assumptions you may have had about the English tense system. These questions are important for you, but irrelevant to children who have no assumptions at all about tense systems. For them the most important question seems to be exactly what the meanings of past and present are. (I am assuming that I can now use 'past' and 'present' as the names for types of word, without necessarily implying anything about their meaning; remember the points I made about *would* being the past-tense form of WILL in spite of not referring to anything true in the past.)

Their problem only seems to arise when there is a sequence of sentences referring to closely related events, such as you find in a narrative or description of a scene. In these cases the first verb always seems to be appropriately tensed, and chaos arises only in later verbs. What this indicates is the need to help them to sort out how tenses are chosen in non-initial verbs. I suggest confronting the problem head-on by asking them to discuss the difference between various past–present pairs of examples. If you can locate relevant examples in their own writing, so much the better.

We start with a very simple example, to give the idea of the contrast between past and present verb-forms.

(22a)   I am little.
(22b)   I was little.

What is the difference in meaning between these? You could ask them which they might say now; which they could combine with *a few years ago*; and which they can combine with *now*. Then you can repeat the operation with sentences containing some regular verbs, such as the following:

(23a)   I look like a baby.
(23b)   I looked like a baby.

The verb-forms can be listed (by you or by them, working in

groups) in two columns, according to whether they allow *now* or *some time ago;* the columns can be headed 'present' and 'past'. (I recommend that at this stage you avoid all verb-combinations, especially those involving auxiliary verbs like *would!*) I think it would also be helpful at this stage to tell them that the choice between past and present is called tense; the term will be useful later, and they already know the concept that it names.

This listing will not only teach them how to recognise past- and present-tense verb-forms, but will also allow them to see that for most verbs the past-tense form ends in *-ed* in the spelling. If you wanted to continue the work of the first unit, you could let them find that, just like the *-s* ending, this can be either voiced or voiceless when pronounced, following just the same rules as *-s*.

Assuming that they can now recognise the tense of a verb, we move on to the next stage of the unit: tense choice in narrative. I suggest that you ask each of them to write a little story containing just three verbs, and that you ask them to leave a blank where each verb should be, but to make a note of the dictionary-word needed in each blank. An example might look like this.

(24)   One day I _____ home from school, and my mum _____ me to do some shopping. She _____ a bag of sugar.

   COME, ASK, WANT

The class can now discuss the choice of tense in each of these blanks; as usual, this can be done in groups if you prefer. Your instructions should be to try each tense of each verb, and to pick the one that sounds best.

You may find that their choices are as expected for every verb. If so, you have discovered that their grammars are like adult grammars in this respect, so if they make mistakes in their normal writing it is a matter of application rather than of knowledge: they know what to do, but find it hard to apply this knowledge. This would be like the problems that even experienced writers have in maintaining consistency in a hypothetical discussion. I think I am typical in often switching between *will* and *would*, *can* and *could* and so on in such situations. Indeed, these chapters have raised the problem in an acute form: when I am describing a lesson, do I say 'You can do such and such' or 'You could do such and such'? And having embarked on one particular course, I then have to remember which one I have chosen – not an easy task, as the choice itself is near to being arbitrary.

My guess is that you will find something different: a firm adult choice for the first verb, but not for the later ones. My reason for making this prediction is an impression that by the age of a level-3 class (aged about 9 or 10 as a median) the choice of tenses in isolated verbs is already like that of an adult. In that case I think you can assume that the problem comes from their knowledge of grammar rather than from how they apply this knowledge. Specifically, they must believe that the rules for choosing tenses in non-initial verbs are different from those for isolated verbs, whereas in adult grammars the same rules apply, but with the twists that we explored in your lesson. They need to learn that if an event took place in the past, any verb that refers to it must be in the past tense (unless the whole narrative is shifted into the 'narrative present' for vividness).

The methods you need for solving this problem are quite different from those that would be appropriate if the problem was just a matter of applying their existing knowledge better. Getting the class to discuss their own examples won't in itself improve matters. One possibility would be to prepare a short and straightforward narrative extract from a book they are reading in class: replace all the past- or present-tense verb–forms by their dictionary-word names, and ask the class to try to guess which forms the writer chose. When you compare their choices with those made by the writer you can explain the reasons for any differences, and hope thereby to improve their understanding of this area of grammar.

Theoretical synopsis

The meaning of tense in English is primarily utterance-based, meaning that the basis for our choice of tense is the moment of uttering – 'now'. The choice hinges on whether or not the state of affairs being described existed before now. For example, if I say *I feel hungry*, the state of hunger must exist now, at the moment of speaking, whereas in *I felt hungry* it existed at some time before now. If we want to refer to a state of affairs which will exist at some time after now, we generally use an auxiliary verb such as SHALL or WILL: *I shall/will feel hungry*; but we have decided not to analyse these combinations as tenses, and in any case we have seen that in some cases it is possible to use an ordinary present-tense verb to refer to a state of affairs in the future (such as *I'll eat when I* **am** *hungry*).

In this respect the meaning of tense is like the meanings of words like ME and HERE. If you hear the sentence *Mary met me here*, you don't know who Mary met, or where the meeting happened, unless you know the details of the utterance – who was speaking, where, when and so on. (Such meanings are graced with the technical name 'deixis', from the Greek word that means 'to point'.) One of the problems facing a child is learning how to translate utterance-based meanings in terms that are relevant to writing. Presumably speaker = writer, but in many written sentences it is not at all clear who the writer is; and if the child hears the teacher reading a book in which a character is reported as saying *The horse picked me up*, who on earth does *me* refer to? This character, or the writer of the book, or the teacher?

Similar problems arise with tense, but in both cases the child basically follows the rules which apply primarily to speech, with some kind of adaptation for writing. The main adult rule for choosing tenses in speech is simple:

RULE: If the state of affairs being described existed before the moment of speaking, use the past-tense form of the verb concerned.

(Slightly more accurately, this rule is in competition with one for using the sequence HAVE + V-ed, as in *I have seen him*; but this pattern doesn't seem to raise any problems for children so I shall ignore it.) This rule applies in narrative and complex descriptions just as it does in choosing isolated verbs. If a series of events all took place before now, every verb is in the past tense. This is the system which we want children to learn.

Why don't all children use this system? The problem, I suspect, lies in the time structures that children are aware of. In a narrative, each of the verbs after the first one refers to an event which is located in time in two directions at the same time: in relation to the moment of speaking, but also in relation to the time of the previous event.

Imagine a simple scenario in which Mary knocks on a door and John opens it; and assume that it took place in the past. Here is the adult version:

(25)   Mary knocked on the door and John opened it.

We know that the time of the knocking is before now, but nothing else; but when we come to the time of the opening we know two things about it: like the knocking, it is before now, but it is also after the knocking. The question the child has to answer is: which of these two time relations is signalled by the tense of *opened*? As the child sees it, the really important relation is the one between the two events. The fact that the whole sequence is located in the past has already been signalled by the past tense of the first verb, so this doesn't need to be signalled yet again (as it does according to the adult rule). Instead, why not use the present tense for OPEN, to show that it happened at about the same time as the knocking? This makes good sense given that the present tense on isolated verbs shows that their state of affairs is at the same time as the speaking; by extension, the use of the present tense could well show an identity of time between the verb's event and some other event just mentioned.

This may or may not be what goes through the mind of some children; and I certainly can't claim that it is supported by research. What is certain, however, is that this is how some languages organise their tense choices, so it is a perfectly viable system, though not the English one. And even more relevantly, this is precisely what English does in sentences like *I will eat if I am hungry*: the present tense of *am* relates its time to that of *will eat*, rather than to the moment of utterance. As you can see, the adult system is much less obvious to the child than it is to us, and adults provide enough distractors to leave children in great uncertainty. The aim of this unit is to give guidance to those who are still wavering between the two systems.

Level 4

Phrases and the apostrophe

The requirements for level 4 include the following.

[Pupils should] (d) begin to use the structures of written Standard English and begin to use some sentence structures different from those of speech; e.g. begin to use subordinate clauses and expanded noun phrases.

And the study programme includes this suggestion:

[Pupils should] be introduced to some of the uses of the comma and the apostrophe.

The aim of my lesson at this level is to bring together two of the patterns mentioned here: expanded noun-phrases and the apostrophe. I hope to be able to throw some light on this very problematic punctuation mark, which tends to be used enthusiastically rather than correctly; but at the same time I shall explain what 'expanded noun-phrases' are, and how children might be encouraged to use them.

Your question is: What is the rule for using an apostrophe? The children's question is about the separability of -s and 's from the preceding noun.

A lesson for you

You may find my question surprising: what do I mean, *the* rule for using an apostrophe? Surely there are a number of rules? Here is a list of examples, each containing an apostrophe, and each apparently illustrating a different use:

(1a) Mary's bike was stolen.
(1b) The girls' bikes were stolen.
(1c) Mary's gone home.
(1d) Mary's going home.
(1e) Mary isn't going home.
(1f) Let's go home.
(1g) You have to go home, 'cos your mother says so.
(1h) Mary left at one o'clock.
(1i) There are three i's in that word.

(Most of these examples are taken from Quirk et al. (1985: 1636).) Surely there must be a list of rules something like the following:

1 To show possession, add 's to a singular noun, s' to a plural one. (1a,b)
2 To show that an auxiliary verb is in its short form, replace the parts which are not pronounced by an apostrophe. (1c,d)
3 To show that NOT is in its short form, replace o by an apostrophe. (1e)
4 To distinguish *let's* from *let us*, write *let's*. (1f)
5 To show that BECAUSE is pronounced /koz/, write 'cos or 'cause. (1g)
6 O'CLOCK is always spelt like that. (1h)
7 Add an apostrophe to any item that has no conventional spelling before adding plural -s. (1i)

I admit total defeat over rules 6 and 7, but I doubt if such examples are very important in school teaching. Look at the rules 2, 3, 4, 5. What do they have in common? In each case, the apostrophe stands for a part of a word which could have been pronounced, but wasn't – in traditional terminology, it shows where letters have been omitted. More specifically, it shows the gap left by at least a vowel and possibly some consonants.

The following is a complete list of the auxiliary verbs that can be abbreviated in this way. I have bracketed the parts that can be replaced by the apostrophe.

(2)   (a)m, (i)s, (a)re, (ha)s, (ha)ve, (ha)d, (wi)ll, (sha)ll, (wou)ld, (shou)ld.

In addition to the auxiliary verbs we have *n(o)t, let(u)s* and *(be)cause*, which show the same property. I shall now forget about *'cause*, which doesn't fit the general pattern in other respects.

We are left with two apparently different groups of uses for the apostrophe: one indicating 'possession', and added to a noun (*John's hat*); the other indicating the omission of a vowel (plus consonants) in an auxiliary verb, NOT or US (*John's working, John isn't working, Let's go!*). We shall come back to the possessive use shortly, but first we must deal with a couple of other matters to do with the omission use.

You will certainly have noticed that the apostrophe does more than mark the omission of a sound or two: it also marks a downgrading of the word containing it. This is shown very clearly in our spelling, because we write the contracted word and the word before it as a single word, without a word-space. This indicates an important fact about the contracted word: after the contraction, it is no longer a complete word as far as its pronunciation is concerned. It cannot be pronounced (naturally) on its own. For example, if you were dictating *John's working* at slow speed, would you pause after *John* and after *'s*? Surely not. The problem is that a typical word contains at least one vowel, so by losing their vowel these words have ceased to be typical words, and have become parasitic on the word before them. (The technical term for words which are reduced in this way is 'clitics'.)

How about the syntactic status of the reduced word? Is it less than a complete word in the syntax as well as in the pronunciation? Try omitting it from one of these sentences:

(3a)   Mary's asleep.
(3b)   *Mary asleep.

(4a)   I'm going home.
(4b)   *I going home.
(5a)   We'll be good.
(5b)   *We be good.

As you can see, the reduced verb is still an essential part of the syntactic structure. Why is this?

What kinds of verbs are reduced? Admittedly they are all auxiliary verbs, but the reducible forms are all either past- or present-tense forms; for example, there is no reduced form for *be, being* or *been*, which are also forms of BE. A standard term which covers past- and present-tense forms is 'tensed': a verb-form is tensed if it has a tense. *Am* is tensed, but *be* isn't (at least, not in Standard English).

What is the connection between reduced verbs being tensed and being essential for sentence structure? Look at the following examples:

(6a)   He has gone away.
(6b)   *He gone away.
(7a)   I like analysing sentences.
(7b)   *I analysing sentences.

To cut a long story short, a sentence normally needs a 'main verb'. (This was one of the main edicts of traditional grammar, but traditional or not, it was right – provided that we remember not to apply it to perfectly good sentences which for special reasons need no main verb such as *How about a cup of tea?*.) What is a main verb? It is either a tensed verb or an imperative verb (that is, one used to make a command, an invitation, a request, etc.):

(8a)   Be good!
(8b)   Come in!

This is the reason why the reduced verbs can't be omitted in sentences like *Mary's asleep*: *'s* is syntactically essential because it is the sentence's main verb. And this in turn tells us what the syntactic status of a reduced word is: if it is the main verb, it must still be a separate part of the sentence structure, identifiable as the main verb (just as though it had been unreduced). This is rather an unexpected and odd conclusion: we reduce (to almost nothing) the word that is most essential to the sentence's structure! You may like to ponder this paradox.

We can now start the return journey towards the *'s* of possession. Let's summarise what we have discovered.

1 What we can call the 'apostrophe of omission' shows that the word containing it has been reduced phonologically to the status of a mere word-part, which is why we write it as part of the preceding word.

2 But the apostrophe of omission has no effect whatsoever on the syntactic status of a reduced auxiliary verb: this verb is still a distinct and essential part of the sentence structure. (We didn't discuss NOT and US; the conclusion there would have been very different, but not directly relevant.)

So how many words are there in a sequence like *I'm*? The answer has to be complex: one word in terms of pronunciation, but two in terms of syntax.

This brings us back to the apostrophe of possession. Let's start by comparing *'s* with the plural suffix *-s*. They look rather similar in the following examples:

(9a) The boys went home.
(9b) The boy's friend went home.

But now try this pair:

(10a) The boys from next door have gone home.
(10b) The boy from next door's friends have gone home.

Here a big difference emerges, as the *s*'s occur in completely different places. To see how rigid and clear the rules are, contrast the pair above with the following, where I have reversed the positions of the two forms:

(11a) *The boy from next doors have gone home.

(11b) *The boy's from next door friends have gone home.

Our next subproblem is clearly to find an explanation for this difference.

What is the rule for positioning 's? Once again I hope I can cut a corner by assuming that you can recognise a 'phrase' – a sequence of words that hangs together syntactically and that has a single meaning. For example, take sentence (12).

(12) The girls saw their friends yesterday.

The phrases include *the girls* and *their friends,* but they do not include *girls saw* or *friends yesterday* or *their friends yesterday.* What phrases can we find in example (10b)? One of them must surely be *the boy from next door,* but if that's so then we have answered our question about 's: this is positioned directly after the phrase to which it belongs. That is, it is actually *outside* the phrase, just like a preposition (or more accurately, like a 'postposition', a preposition that stands after its object rather than before it; English has just a handful, including NOTWITHSTANDING). We find, then, that *the boy from next door's* is actually like *the boy from next door notwithstanding;* and 's cannot stand next to *boy* for just the same reason that *notwithstanding* can't stand there.

In short, 's is syntactically a 'word', not a suffix. In contrast, the plural -s is very clearly a suffix, as witness its inability to be separated from the noun that it belongs to.

Let's look at another difference between 's and -s. The latter is the regular marker of plurality, but there are a great number of exceptional plural forms:

(13) children, oxen, geese, mice, fish, cacti, phenomena, people

This is typical of suffixes; you find the same kind and quantity of irregularity in past-tense verb-forms. But what about possessive 's? Here there are no irregular nouns at all – that is, there are no nouns which have an irregular 'possessive' form.

(It is true that there are special 'possessive pronouns', traditionally called 'possessive adjectives', whose forms are mostly highly irregular, such as *my*, *her*, etc., but these aren't comparable with irregular forms like *children*, which is a common noun and not a pronoun.) This is a strange fact if *'s* is a suffix, but entirely to be expected if it is a separate word.

Our conclusion, which is widely accepted among linguists, is that *'s* is in fact a separate word as far as the syntactic structure is concerned, though not of course in its pronunciation. This conclusion makes it just like the reduced auxiliary verbs in every respect except one: the possessive *'s* has no 'unreduced' form. Whereas *I'm* could be expanded to *I am*, there is no way to expand *the boy's friends*. (You may be tempted to treat *'s* as the reduced form of *his*, giving *the boy his friends* as the expansion of *the boy's friends*. This won't work unless you are willing to accept *'s* as the reduced form of *her* and *their* as well, as in *the girl's friends* and *the children's friends*.)

What then is the relation between *'s* and *-s*? We have decided that the former is a word which is pronounced as a word-part, but the latter is a word-part, a suffix, in every respect. (This very different status results from a thousand years of linguistic change, because in Old English they were both ordinary suffixes; the possessive *-s* was a genitive ending like the one still found in modern German.) Their statuses are very different, and the more you can emphasise these differences in your teaching, the easier it should be for children to learn to keep the apostrophe out of the suffix.

There is an important connection which I haven't mentioned but which is relevant to spelling. This emerges from examples like the following:

(14a)   That boy's shouting is unbearable.
(14b)   Those boys' shouting is unbearable.

What is the rule for choosing between *'s* and *s'* (if that is indeed the right way to express the choice)? These examples suggest that *s'* may be used after plural nouns, but the next ones overturn this idea:

(15a)   That child's shouting is unbearable.
(15b)   Those children's shouting is unbearable.

Children is of course a plural noun, but we follow it with *'s*, not *s'*. Nor is it merely a question of whether the noun marks its plural by *-s*:

(16a)   The boy next door's shouting is unbearable.
(16b)   The boys next door's shouting is unbearable.

As you have no doubt seen, the rule is very simple: *'s* is replaced by just an apostrophe if it immediately follows the plural *-s*. (Alternatively, and preferably, we can say that in a sequence *-s* + *'s*, the two *s*'s merge into one, leaving the apostrophe at the end.) No doubt this interaction between *-s* and *'s* results from their shared history; even after a thousand years the change is still a messy compromise between two clearly distinct sets of rules.

Finally we are back at the beginning, ready to answer my question about 'the rule' for the apostrophe. The apostrophe, we can say, is used to mark the absence of a vowel (and possibly some consonants) from a word which is thereby made unpronounceable and parasitic on the preceding word. The same rule now covers *all* the uses of *'s*, including the possessive use as well as the reduced auxiliary one.

A lesson for the pupils

The easiest way to clarify the difference between *-s* and *'s* is to focus on the first difference between them that I pointed out to you: the fact that *-s* can't be separated from its noun, but *'s* can, being added to the whole phrase and not just to the noun in it.

This suggests a group activity in which each group invents a list of examples. You provide a simple example which they try to elaborate by inserting extra material at a specified point. I suggest starting with an example like this:

(17)   We know every star's name.

The challenge to them is to insert as many words as possible between *star* and *'s* without changing the meaning of the rest of the sentence. For example, they could insert *of tv*, or *in the list*, or *with long hair*, but not *knows his mother*, even though the latter makes a fine sentence! Any discussion of the pros and cons of particular examples will deepen their understanding of sentence structure, and the exercise will also involve expansion of noun-phrases (*every star* is a noun-phrase, as is *every star of tv*) and, our main concern, the discovery that *'s* is added at the end of the whole noun-phrase.

Having done this you can then repeat the operation with a different example, containing *-s* instead of *'s*:

(18)   We know all the stars.

The challenge once again is to insert as many words as possible between *star* and *s*, without changing the meaning of the rest of the sentence. Sooner or later they will realise that the task is impossible, at which point you will of course ask them why, and guide them through the relevant facts. In order to emphasise the point, you can ask them to duplicate the expansions in their first list, but this time with the *'s* glued to the noun; this will fail. And they can try expanding (18) by adding extra material, this time after the *-s*, which will of course succeed.

A supplementary activity would emphasise the similarities between the possessive *'s* and the reduced auxiliary verbs, by showing that they are both added to phrases. This may reveal an interesting difference between the two: because of its history, possessive *'s* is still relatively closely tied to the noun before it, so although it does allow intervening material the possibilities are limited compared with what is possible before a reduced auxiliary verb. The difference is apparent in examples like the following:

(19a)   The man who wrote this book's a linguist.
(19b)   ?The man who wrote this book's name is Dick Hudson.

(19c)   Everyone I know who works in London's going home for Christmas.

(19d)   *Everyone I know who works in London's plan is to go home for Christmas.

Therefore if you want to encourage them to expand noun-phrases you can repeat the exercise I outlined above, but using the reduced auxiliary verb instead.

Theoretical synopsis

Although the pedagogical focus in this unit was on the apostrophe, the most important theoretical concept underlying the discussion was the notion 'phrase'. I defined it earlier as a sequence of words that hangs together syntactically and has a single meaning – a rough and ready definition, but one that contains the main points. When linguists study sentence structure they generally call it 'phrase structure', in recognition of the importance of phrases; and in my opinion sensitivity to phrases is well worth developing in any language-user.

In this section I should like to give a few tips on how to recognise phrases, which you may choose to pass on to your pupils. In English word order is rather inflexible (at least when compared with many other languages); in particular, phrases are generally required to be continuous strings of words, uninterrupted by words which belong to other phrases. This makes phrases relatively easy to recognise. For example, it is easy to recognise that *big books* is a phrase in *He buys big books*, because you can't split it into two, with *buys* between the two parts: **He big buys books*. On the other hand you probably didn't need that evidence, because it is obvious that *big books* is a phrase: it has a meaning (it is the name of a class of objects which are both big and books), and it obviously hangs together syntactically, with *big* as a modifier of *books*, following the usual word-order rule for adjectives that modify nouns.

There are other cases which are somewhat less obvious. Let us take the following two sentences as our test case:

(20a)   She finds interesting children.
(20b)   She finds children interesting.

No doubt you feel these have very different structures, but where, precisely, does the difference lie? I shall show that part of the difference is in the division into phrases. It is useful to show phrases by enclosing them in square brackets:

(21a)   She finds [interesting children].
(21b)   She finds children interesting.

In other words, *interesting children* is a phrase, but *children interesting* is not. How can I prove this? By three tests.
    (a)   Mobility. *Interesting children* can occur freely in many other positions and with many other words outside it.

(22a)   I met [interesting children].
(22b)   [Interesting children] attend that club.
(22c)   They are thinking about [interesting children].

In contrast, the non-phrase *children interesting* can't survive this kind of transplantation:

(23a)   *I met [children] [interesting].
(23b)   *[Children] [interesting] attend that club.
(23c)   *They are thinking about [children] [interesting].

This immobility shows that *children interesting* is really two phrases, whose co-occurrence depends very heavily on one particular syntactic environment, the preceding *She finds*.
    (b)   Internal rigidity. A phrase is relatively rigid in its internal structure, so we generally can't change the order of words within a phrase; if two strings of words can swap positions, they can't constitute a phrase. This is true of our phrase as can be seen from (23a), but the internal order of the non-phrase *children interesting* can be reversed if we expand

children into a longer phrase worth delaying till later; so the two sentences in (24) are stylistic variants with precisely the same meaning:

(24a) She finds [children with strong feelings] [interesting].
(24b) She finds [interesting] [children with strong feelings].

(c) Ability to be treated as 'focus'. One particularly useful way of focusing the reader/hearer's attention on a particular phrase is to embed it in what is called a 'cleft sentence' – a sentence consisting of IT + BE + focus + rest, where 'rest' means the rest of the original (unclefted) sentence. For example, we can focus on *sweets* in *We gave the children sweets* by converting it into *It was sweets (that) we gave the children*. The relevance of this construction is that the focus has to be a complete phrase. Let's see how it applies to our sentences:

(25a) It is [interesting children] that she finds.
(25b) *It is [children] [interesting] that she finds.

As expected, we can focus on *interesting children* but not on *children interesting*, because the latter is not a phrase.

Let me end by showing that *the boy from next door* is a phrase, as I claimed in the discussion of the apostrophe (where I showed that *'s* has to be added to the whole noun-phrase). First it is highly mobile.

(26a) [The boy from next door] is coming round to play.
(26b) She's going out with [the boy from next door].

Second it is internally rigid.

(27) *I know [from next door the boy].

And third, it can be focussed.

(28) It is [the boy from next door] that she's going out with.

Level 5

Vocabulary and style

Among the requirements of the National Curriculum at level 5 is that pupils should be able to:

show through discussion an awareness of a writer's choice of particular words and phrases and the effect on the reader; e.g. recognise puns, word-play, unconventional spellings
. . .
show in discussion the ability to recognise variations in vocabulary according to purpose, topic and audience and whether language is spoken or written ...; e.g. discuss the use of slang in dialogue and narrative in a published text and in their own writing and comment on its appropriateness.

This kind of sensitivity to what I shall call 'style' is of course one of the main goals of English teaching, and no doubt the National Curriculum is reflecting not only best practice, but normal practice. Nevertheless I think I may be able to offer you a new perspective on this extraordinarily complex phenomenon.

The National Curriculum focuses on vocabulary as a marker of style ('variations in vocabulary according to purpose, topic and audience and whether language is spoken or written'). As I explained in chapter 2, linguists generally see vocabulary as part of grammar, and to many of us the boundary between vocabulary and general rules is anything but clear. In principle, then, a book on grammar ought to have something coherent to say about vocabulary. The trouble with vocabulary, though, is that it is messy by nature: rich in detail and complexity but poor in generalities. The best one can do is to select one little corner of the jungle and hope that by showing its structure one can throw light on other parts as well.

I shan't even try to define 'style', since there are already quite enough competing definitions. Instead I propose to focus on just two phenomena which might reasonably be covered by this term. One is the way in which the choice of words shows what kind of person is speaking, and the other is the way in which it shows the source of authority for the content of the words. As we shall see, these phenomena are closely connected.

For the pupils I have a question about a longish text, so I shall leave this question till I introduce the text. But for you I have a straightforward question: what is the meaning of the word APPARENTLY?

A lesson for you

Here are some sentences containing APPARENTLY:

(1a) He apparently missed his train.
(1b) It's snowing in Scotland, apparently.
(1c) Apparently you have to apply through the local post-office.

In asking for the meaning of APPARENTLY I am asking what contribution this word makes to the meaning of a sentence containing it; that is, what difference does the presence of APPARENTLY make? Well, let's compare the sentences in which it is present with their equivalents where it is absent:

(2a) Fred missed his train.
(2b) It's snowing in Scotland.
(2c) You have to apply through the local post-office.

Let us first make another comparison, between (2a) and the same sentence with JUST added:

(3)   Fred just missed his train.

The addition of *just* modifies the description of the event described; as we all know, there is a difference between simply missing one's train, and just missing it. It is easy to imagine an event which could accurately be described by (2a) but not by (3) – if he missed it by three hours, for instance. Similarly, if we add ONCE or DELIBERATELY we change the definition of the event by making it more precise.

Returning to APPARENTLY, you will notice that its effect on the sentence's meaning is quite different. Instead of changing the definition of the event being described, it changes the speaker's role in speaking. Suppose we hear (2a), without APPARENTLY; what conclusion do we draw? Under normal circumstances (excluding jokes, novels, etc.) we assume that the speaker vouches for the truth of what is said; that is, that Fred missed his train. But (1a), containing APPARENTLY, tells us that the speaker believes that Fred missed his train, but is quoting someone else's authority for it. So if it turned out that Fred didn't in fact miss his train, (2a) would count as a lie, but (1a) wouldn't.

On the other hand, APPARENTLY doesn't simply mean that the speaker has heard someone reporting what follows. Suppose little Ann tells her mother that the Tooth Fairy left some money where she had left the tooth that had fallen out, the mother wouldn't report this to the father as *Apparently the Tooth Fairy left Ann some money for her tooth*. This choice of words would imply that she herself believed the report. So if I say (1a), I am telling you that I believe Fred missed his train, but that I only have someone else's word for it. Because of this I can't then deny the report by adding *but I don't believe it*.

The 'meaning' of APPARENTLY, then, can be defined along the following lines: the speaker of a sentence containing APPARENTLY does not vouch personally for the truth of the sentence, but does accept it as true on the basis of information supplied by others.

What other means does English provide for expressing this kind of meaning? The list is surprisingly long and varied, and includes: ACCORDING TO, SAY, SEEM, PRESUMABLY and tag questions (which you will remember from the lesson at level 3). Here are some example sentences:

(4a) According to Bill, Fred missed his train.
(4b) Bill says Fred missed his train.
(4c) Fred seems to have missed his train.
(4d) Presumably Fred missed his train.
(4e) Fred missed his train, did he?
(4f) Fred missed his train, didn't he?

I am not suggesting that these sentences all express the same meaning; far from it. But they are similar in that they all contain the words *Fred . . . missed his train*, and that in every case these words express the notion 'that Fred missed his train', but without actually telling us, on the speaker's authority, that this is so, in the way that the bald statement *Fred missed his train* does.

This little study highlights one of the important contributions of recent work in linguistics, which has been to distinguish various radically different kinds of 'meaning' – the meaning of APPARENTLY being radically different from that of a word like RECENTLY. But it also shows us something important (though obvious) about the meaning of an ordinary statement: in the absence of a word such as APPARENTLY (or some contextual clues such as the opening *Have you heard the one about . . . ?*), the speaker does vouch for the truth of what is said. In other words, the speaker is also 'the authority' (for the message).

A lesson for the pupils

I have chosen a text that might be read by a pupil at level 5, *The Finding* by Nina Bawden (1987: 48):

'Six years old is too young for a key,' Laura grumbled out loud. *She* hadn't been given a key until she was ten. 'Bob is such a sensible boy,' her mother had said when Laura had pointed this out, as if

Laura had not been sensible at that age, and Laura felt the unfairness burn hotly inside her. Mum was always on about things being fair, but she wasn't fair herself, was she? It wasn't fair to make her keep a secret from Alex, particularly when it was something so interesting. It was making her tell a lie in a way, Laura thought indignantly, turning her into a cheat and a liar!

My question for your class is: does the narrator think that Laura's mother behaved unfairly?

What is particulary interesting about this passage is the way in which the authority for what is said varies between the narrator and Laura, and how these changes are marked. At some points the narrator herself is the authority, but at others the authority is Laura. This is clearly so where Laura's own words are quoted directly, but it is sometimes the case even where the narrator is the speaker. Even though the narrator's words include *Mum ... wasn't fair*, it is vitally important that the reader should realise that this isn't part of the story, but just what Laura thinks. This is of course the answer to my question, but what matters is the evidence for the answer.

Here is the passage presented as a sort of dramatic dialogue, with the speaker and authority indicated:

SPEAKER	AUTHORITY	TEXT
1 Laura	Laura	'Six years old is too young for a key,'
2 Narrator	Narrator	Laura grumbled out loud.
3 Narrator	Laura	*She* hadn't been given a key until she was ten.
4 Mother	Mother	'Bob is such a sensible boy,'
5 Narrator	Narrator	her mother had said when Laura had pointed this out,
6 Narrator	Laura	as if Laura had not been sensible at that age,
7 Narrator	Narrator	and Laura felt the unfairness burn hotly inside her.
8 Narrator	Laura	*Mum* was *always on about* things being fair, but she *wasn't* fair her-

			self, *was she*? It *wasn't* fair to make her keep a secret from Alex, particularly when it was something so interesting. It was making her tell a lie *in a way*,
9	Narrator	Narrator	Laura thought indignantly,
10	Narrator	Laura	turning her into a cheat and a liar!

Every one of the changes in authority or speaker is marked in some way by the choice of language, but some of the clues are very subtle. In order to answer my question the class have to pick up the clues in part 8, so let's concentrate on them. I have highlighted the clues that I noticed.

The general strategy is to present what is said as Laura's words, not the narrator's, without actually claiming that Laura said or even thought literally these words. The narrator is still the speaker (unlike the passages between speech marks), as we can see from the choice of tenses: past tense throughout part 8. But she is speaking, as it were, on behalf of Laura. The clues to this are as follows:

(a)   the word *Mum*, which is stylistically wrong for the narrator (compare *her mother* in 5). It is also used here as a proper noun (like *Laura*), as you can see from the absence of any word like *her* before it; when used in this way it generally means 'my mother', which makes sense in the mouth of Laura but not of the narrator.

(b)   the expression *was always on about*, which suggests a teenage speaker rather than a mature writer. This expression can be broken down into two parts: the complex dictionary-word BE ON ABOUT (as in *My dad's on about my homework again*) and the exaggerated use of ALWAYS (as in *My dad is always telling me off*).

(c)   the tag question *was she?*, which indicates an interactive dialogue (in which the speaker is actually talking to herself), rather than part of the narrative. As you can probably see, this kind of tag question is used to share the authority for the statement with the hearer.

(d)   the expression *in a way*, a marker of tentativeness

which is common in speech but not in writing, and therefore suggests Laura talking (to herself) rather than Nina Bawden writing as a narrator.

It is tempting to include *wasn't*, which occurs twice, as a clue, on the grounds that a shortened form like this (containing an apostrophe to show the absence of a vowel!) is more appropriate to spontaneous speech than to the narrative part of a novel. However 6, which also comes on Laura's authority, contains *had not* rather than the expected *hadn't*; and the next sentence after my extract is *She couldn't see Alex at first*, which is clearly part of the narrative rather than Laura's thoughts. We therefore have to resist the temptation.

As I said earlier, I know that close reading of texts is already part of many English lessons, so this activity as such may already be familiar to you. What is new is the analytical apparatus that an explicit study of grammar provides – notions like 'tag question' and 'dictionary-word', plus the ability to break down complex expressions into simpler parts (as I did with *was always on about*). Another change is that the descriptive approach of modern grammar allows colloquial expressions (such as BE ON ABOUT, IN A WAY, tag questions, shortened auxiliary verbs) to be accepted and discussed objectively, as objects of interest on the same footing as parts of the written standard language.

It would be easy to apply this kind of analysis to other material, though the passage I chose is probably unusually rich in its structure. Advertisements often pretend to put words into the mouths of people other than the advertiser, and would provide ample opportunity for analysing the clues to the purported speaker's identity.

Another useful activity would be the production of material by the class. You could imagine some event such as an accident in the canteen, and get the class to provide a number of different reports of it, each suited to a different speaker: the school secretary, the cleaner who had to deal with the mess, a junior child, a senior child, a teacher, the school newspaper, the local newspaper, a radio reporter, etc. Some of the reports will naturally be spoken, others written, and the class should consider the different kinds of clues available in the two mediums. Having done enough of this, you could increase the difficulty of the task by separating speaker from authority: how would a child report a report from the secretary? This may be beyond the ability of most of the class, but any members of the class with a feel for acting could have a field day.

Theoretical synopsis

From a grammarian's point of view the discussion in this chapter has been all over the place, jumping from simple dictionary-words to tag questions to shortened forms, and from purely stylistic matters (such as the choice between MUM and MOTHER) to questions about meaning (such as the meaning of APPARENTLY). And yet there has been a consistent theme running through the chapter: our choice of words is not determined entirely by the events and situations we want to describe.

For example, consider all the variations on the simple sentence *Fred missed his train* that we reviewed. These all described the same event, and indeed they all described it in precisely the same way, giving just the same amount of detail about it; and yet they varied enormously in their meaning. At the most general level the meaning differences involved the triangular relation between the speaker, this event and the authority for the truth or otherwise of the event. This kind of meaning does not fit at all comfortably with the popular view that meaning is simply a matter of providing names for people, things and events in the world. Instead, we see that many sentences tell us something about the speaker at the same time that they tell us something about the rest of the world.

It is hard to justify a line between this kind of meaning and what is generally seen as matters of dialect or register, most of which also serve the purpose of giving information about the speaker over and above the 'basic content' of the sentence. For example, the choice between MUM and MOTHER tells us something about how the speaker wants us to see them, or about how the speaker views the situation of which the speaking is a part; and similarly for the choice between BE ON ABOUT and GRUMBLE ABOUT. These choices are not made by looking at the person or event being described – is she a mum or a mother? is that an example of going on or of grumbling? – but rather by deciding what the total information package conveyed by the sentence should contain. In other words, what do we want to say about ourselves as well as about the things being described?

To a grammarian, then, there seems to be little point in dividing the contents of the grammar into neat compartments bearing labels like 'grammatical information', 'meaning', 'dialect', 'register', 'style'. What really matters is that when we learn a language we have to learn how to use all the words and other patterns (syntactic constructions, intonation patterns and so on). And learning how to use a pattern involves learning not only how to combine it with other patterns but what information we convey to hearers by using it. Although the territory of grammar has traditionally been restricted largely to matters of how to combine patterns, the modern emphasis on 'mentalism' (which I described in chapter 2) means that grammar, as the study of linguistic knowledge, includes far more than you might expect.

Level 6

Subjects, verbs and dialects

My text for the next lesson is the following collection of extracts from the National Curriculum:

[Pupils should be able to] show in discussion an awareness of grammatical differences between spoken Standard English and a non-standard variety; e.g. take note of different ways in which tense and person are marked in the verb 'to be' after listening to recordings or participating in classroom improvisations.

Pupils should be given the opportunity to consider:
– any grammatical differences between the speech of the area and spoken Standard English, e.g. in verb forms, pronoun use, prepositions.

[Pupils should] demonstrate, through discussion and in their writing, grammatical differences between spoken and written English; e.g. in a group, identify some of the differences between the language used in a tape recording of someone talking and a piece of writing by the same person.

All these extracts have something to do with the difference between non-standard and standard English, and since verb-forms receive special attention in the National Curriculum we shall follow suit.

This unit can be seen as a continuation of chapter 3, 'What is Standard English?', where I distinguished between Standard English as a dialect similar to all other dialects, and Standard English as a large collection of registers. All the differences with which we shall be concerned now are matters of dialect, simply different ways of saying the same thing. The main aim of the chapter will therefore be two-fold. First, we must counteract the widely held view that Standard English is inherently better than non-standard dialects, by showing how arbitrary the differences are. But second, we must help the children to understand the rules of Standard English better in order to improve their use of it.

Your question is: What use is subject–verb agreement? The pupils' question is: When does a verb end in -*s*?

A lesson for you

Let me explain first what 'subject–verb agreement' is with an example:

(1a)   I snore.
(1b)   You snore.
(1c)   She snores.
(1d)   We snore.
(1e)   They snore.

As you are no doubt aware, a present-tense verb has two different forms, according to whether or not its subject is 'third-person singular', like *she*. You may wonder why this is called 'agreement', given the lack of distinctions in the other combinations of 'person' and 'number'. I share this doubt, and would prefer to talk about the 'so-called agreement' between subjects and verbs.

My question to you is: What use is this so-called agreement? This is a sensible question, because one would imagine that grammatical rules exist in order to make communication more efficient. If a language contained vocabulary but no rules for combining words (that is, no syntax) we should never know what anyone meant; for example, if English were like this we could express the idea that John saw Mary by saying any of the following:

(2a)   John saw Mary.

(2b)   John Mary saw.
(2c)   Saw John Mary.
(2d)   Saw Mary John.
(2e)   Mary saw John.
(2f)   Mary John saw.

Unfortunately precisely the same list of sentences would also express the idea that Mary saw John, so if we heard any of them we would not know whether John saw Mary or Mary saw John. To cope with this problem, we have rules which position subjects before the verb and objects after it, and other rules which tell us that the subject of SEE names the 'see-er' and the object names the thing seen.

Some other languages, such as Russian and Latin, adopt a very different strategy. They allow completely free word order, but distinguish the subject and object by their word-forms; these differences are called 'case', and subjects typically have a 'nominative case' while objects have 'accusative case'. Our distinctions between forms like *me* and *I* for some pronouns are the dying embers of just such a system.

Other languages again adopt a third strategy for distinguishing subjects from objects, which is called 'cross-referencing'. In this system the verb carries a marker which shows what kind of subject it has – for example, that it has a first-person singular subject – and if it has an object it also carries another marker linked to the object. Here is an example of this system in operation in an Australian language called Warlpiri (Andrews 1985). (This language happens to use case-markers as well; we can ignore them, and also their strange names.)

(3a)   Nya-nyi ka-rna-palangu wawirri-jarra ngajulu-rlu. 'I see two kangaroos.'
(3b)   Nya-nyi   see – 'non-past'
         ka-rna-palangu   'present' – 'first singular subject' – 'third dual object'
         wawirri-jarra   kangaroo – dual, absolute case
         ngajulu-rlu   I – ergative case

The main point of this example is the second word, a kind of auxiliary verb, whose endings show that the subject is 'I' and the object is a noun referring to two things. Regardless of word order and cases, this system removes any ambiguity in sentences like the one considered here; and in particular it prevents us from understanding it as 'Two kangaroos see me'.

We can see our so-called subject–verb agreement as a feeble attempt at this system, because the form of the verb tells us something about the subject: if the verb ends in -*s*, the subject must be some singular noun other than *I* or *you*, and without the -*s* this kind of subject is excluded. But do we really need this information? Let me parade some facts before you.

(a) We make no such distinction in past-tense verbs (except for the distinction between *was* and *were* which is unique), but this doesn't seem to matter. *Snored* is compatible with any kind of subject, but we don't seem to have any difficulty in finding its subject.

(b) Some dialects of English make no such distinction even in the present tense. In East Anglia *no* present-tense verbs have an -*s*, while in many western and northern dialects they *all* do – giving *I like* and *she like* in the first case, and *I likes* and *she likes* in the second. The people who speak these dialects presumably communicate perfectly satisfactorily without the distinction.

(c) There is a small list of very common auxiliary verbs, called 'modal verbs', which never carry -*s*. (We discussed most of these verbs in the chapter on tense.) The main ones which can occur in the present tense are WILL, SHALL, MAY, CAN, and MUST, whose invariance is illustrated in the following:

(4a) I/he/they will come late.
(4b) I/he/they must work hard.

(d) The positions of the subject and object are fixed by rather rigid rules, as I have already mentioned, so it is almost always easy to tell which is which just by listening to the order. The subject is generally the one just before the verb, so even if the object is shifted to the front of the sentence, as it may be, it is still clearly different from the subject:

(5a) Children like sweets.

(5b)   Sweets, children like.

There is no danger of (5b) being misunderstood as meaning that sweets like children!

(e)   One particular word-order rule that overrides the general one applies (among other uses) in questions like (6).

(6a)   Do children like sweets?
(6b)   What do children like?

In these sentences it is clear that *children* is the subject of *do*, although the normal order is reversed. (In case you aren't convinced that *children* is the subject of *do*, see how the latter changes, by so-called agreement, if you replace *children* by *he*.) The subject of a question stands just after a tensed (that is, past-or present-tense) auxiliary verb, such as DO, but since these verbs don't allow an object there is virtually never any ambiguity.

(f)   Every tensed verb in English has to have an expressed, audible, subject, so there is no need for the verb to tell us about this subject. In some languages the subject can be omitted, in which case it is useful for the verb to carry some information about the missing subject. For example, in Italian the single word *amo* means 'I love', so the hearer misses nothing if the pronoun *io*, meaning 'I', is omitted. In English we have to provide every tensed verb with an expressed subject; this rule is so strict that even a verb like RAIN, whose meaning doesn't call for a subject, has to have one, so we supply a meaningless *it*.

(g)   In most dialects, including the standard dialect, a handful of important words have distinct forms according to whether or not they are the subject of a tensed verb. These are the 'personal pronouns' which I mentioned above: *I/me, he/him, she/her, we/us* and *they/them*. (In some dialects in the south-west of England, and in some creole-based dialects, even these contrasts don't exist.) When you hear or read *he*, you can be sure that it is the subject; and in contrast, *him* can't be the subject. On the other hand it is important to recognise that these contrasts tell hearers very little that they don't know already from all the other clues listed above. This is why they can safely be dispensed with in some dialects. It also explains why they can be linked to the presence of *and* as well as to the subject/non-subject distinction, giving sentences like (7), which are widely used though (presumably) not part of Standard English.

(7a)   Mary and him are good friends.
(7b)   I saw Mary and he together.

These very widespread alternatives to the system of Standard English are worth exploring in their own right.

This list of facts shows clearly that so-called subject–verb agreement is very little use to anyone, and can best be explained as the residue of an earlier system in which word-order was much freer and the cross-referencing between subject and verb may have played an important part in preventing misunderstandings. In general, when non-standard dialects differ from Standard English in this area of grammar, it is the latter which is more conservative, with a greater role for this useless contrast. No wonder most non-standard dialects have no contrast to match the Standard English *was/were* (using either *was* or *were* for all subjects); and no wonder others have abandoned the distinctions in the present tense. In view of this conclusion, it is hard indeed to argue that Standard English is inherently superior to the non-standard alternatives.

A lesson for the pupils

When does a verb end in -*s*? Before starting this lesson you need to know something about the local dialect, because we are going to take that as the object of study. In order to study it, you need expert speakers, a role which can of course be filled admirably by your pupils. The aim will be to get them to supply information about the dialect.

How can you make sure that they tell you about the local dialect, rather than about Standard English? One question is what to call it, and as I suggested earlier, I think the best policy here is to give it the name of the local town or area. I shall call it 'Town'. But how can you be sure that they don't confuse Town with Standard English? Part of the answer comes from your own knowledge of the local dialect, even if this is only partial. Another possibility would be to ask some of them to make a tape recording of free speech in a non-school situation – for instance, in the school canteen or in a youth club. This is a valuable exercise for them and can produce a great deal of interesting information, but it raises serious organisational problems, and may not in fact produce a great deal more or better information than you can get through a discussion in class. If the whole class agrees on some claim, then it is probably right. Some more sophisticated techniques may be appropriate where disagreements arise.

With these preliminaries behind us, let's start the lesson. You select any verb – say SNORE – and ask them what the present-tense form is in Town. In some dialects, as we have seen, there is only one present-tense form, which is either *snore* or *snores*; if this is true of Town you should still go through a range of possible subjects to make it clear to them that this has no effect on the verb's form. You may know that some verbs in Town do still have different present-tense forms for different subjects; this is especially likely for the three non-modal auxiliary verbs BE, HAVE and DO. If any verbs do make a distinction between forms with and without -s, explore the rules with the class, as they may be useful as a basis for learning Standard English. You also need to know whether THOU survives in Town, and if so whether it takes a special form of the verb; but THOU is unlikely except in very rural areas.

If Town has two distinct present-tense forms for SNORE, you should push the class to give you both. You write the two forms on the board and ask them to explain the difference between them. From this point on, the course of the lesson follows their suggestions. For example, if they say the forms have different meanings, you have to challenge them to define the difference in meaning; and in the absence of such a definition, they have to accept that the meanings are in fact the same. The aim is of course to arrive at a set of rules which can be compared with those of Standard English, so you should make sure that the discussion covers those irregular verbs, especially BE, in which Standard English differs most from other dialects.

One case which is of particular interest, because it involves meaning, is the possibility of using a singular subject with a verb that has no -*s*, provided the subject names a collection of individuals (that is, is a 'collective noun'). The class might like to compare examples like these:

(8a)   My family consists of four people.
(8b)   My family argue with each other all the time.

The rules allow a singular collective noun to take the verb-form appropriate to a plural subject provided this applies to the members of the group individually. This is the kind of rule they can easily work out for themselves from examples like these. (If they are studying French or some other foreign language you could explain to them that this is an English curiosity; most languages, including French, are much more strict.)

Whatever the outcome of this research project on Town, it provides a point of comparison for Standard English. You announce the change of dialect, and start again with *snore* and *snores* on the board. What are the rules for Standard English? You will of course know in advance what the important differences are, and will be able to guide the class to discover them if they don't already know them, or to bring them into the open if they do.

Theoretical synopsis

The most important assumption underlying this discussion is that sentence structure is organised in terms of 'grammatical functions' – notions like 'subject' and 'object'. A word's grammatical function – which I shall call its 'function' from now on – is its relation to the rest of the sentence, and the functions 'subject' and 'object' define the relation that a noun has to the verb. (Many linguists prefer to see these functions in terms of the relation between a phrase and its parts – seeing, for instance, the subject as the subject of a 'clause', a verb-centred phrase, rather than in terms of the relation between one word and another. For present purposes the two views are interchangeable, so I shall stick to the more traditional word–word view.)

What we have been discussing is the way in which these functions are distinguished from one another – by case-marking on the noun, by word-order, or by cross-referencing alias agreement. These questions are important, but there is a danger of getting lost in the details of the clues and forgetting what they are clues to.

The main points about functions are that they are by and large similar across languages, and that they provide the crucial link between sentence structure and sentence meaning. Every language allows you to express the idea that John saw Mary, and in every language the words for John and for Mary have different functions, different syntactic relations to the verb. A language must provide some audible means of distinguishing one from the other, which is where the main differences between languages arise; but once the functions of the words concerned have been recognised, the semantic structure follows automatically – we know whether John saw Mary or the other way round.

You should notice that I am distinguishing carefully between a word's grammatical function and the semantic relations found in the sentence's meaning. For example, in *John saw Mary* I say that the word *John* is the subject of *saw*, but this relation is different from that between the person John and the act of seeing that is described in this sentence. The subject function of *John* is a clue to the semantic function of the person John. I suppose this point is obvious because the word *John* and the person John are totally different, as I pointed out in an earlier chapter.

It is convenient to be able to show these relations in a diagram, and the system of arrows that I introduced in the lesson at level 2, the unit about ambiguity, is as good as any. The following diagram shows two separate but linked structures, a syntactic one which involves the words and a semantic one which involves their meanings (called 'm1' for 'meaning 1', etc.). The words are linked to their meanings by the dotted lines. Let's assume that the person who sees something is the 'experiencer' of the vision, and the person or thing which is seen is its 'cause'.

(9)

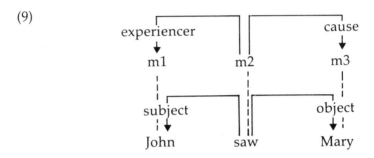

Diagrams like this can be used to show the links that hold phrases together, as a supplement to the bracketing system that I introduced earlier.

This is a very simple sentence, of course, but it makes the main point clearly: that grammatical functions can be seen as a means to an end, as a link between the audible shapes and positions of the words we hear and the meanings that we build for entire sentences. The rules of grammar are restrictions, but in principle these restrictions are not pointless infringements of our liberty; they are essential for communication. It is only because both you and I recognise the same restrictions that you can identify the grammatical functions of the words I use in this book; and if you don't know a word's grammatical function, you can't work out its semantic function either, so you don't know how it fits into the sentence's meaning.

The trouble is that languages are not ideal communication systems. One consequence of this is that they allow a good deal of redundancy, the same bit of information being conveyed by more clues than are needed. An example of this is the subject function of *he* in *He likes sweets*, which as we have seen is signalled by word-order, by the choice of *he* rather than *him*, and by the -*s* on *likes*. Word-order on its own would be quite adequate, and this has allowed our ancestors to reduce the other clues to the messy handful that we now have. Non-standard dialects have taken this process further than Standard English but the mess is still around, and as long as we want to be accepted as native speakers of Standard English we have to toe the line.

Level 7

Purposes and indirectness

The requirements for level 7 include the following:

Pupils should be able to ... show in discussion that they can recognise features of presentation which are used to inform, to regulate, to reassure or to persuade, in non-literary and media texts. e.g. ... verbal emphasis through repetition, exclamation, or vocabulary.

The purpose of this lesson is to explore some of the more standard 'features of presentation which are used to inform, to regulate, to reassure or to persuade'.

When we speak we normally have a reason for doing so. After all, speaking is a form of action which involves a certain amount of energy and thought, so it is easier not to speak than to speak. The hearer's main task is to work out what purpose the speaker had. On most occasions, of course, this is so easy that the hearer doesn't even notice the question, but sometimes we fail completely and are aware of the problem. A hearer might react by saying something like *Why on earth did you say that?*, or *What do you mean?*, or (to another hearer) *What do you think she meant by that?* Occasionally speech is more like a reflex than a purposeful activity; for instance a friend of mine admits that he once found himself apologising to a fly for swatting it! In the vast majority of cases, however, speech is a highly purposeful activity; perhaps the purposeful activity *par excellence*.

The reason for focusing on purposes in this lesson is to dispel any impression that the only reason for speaking is to convey factual information – what the National Curriculum means by 'informing'. We all know, of course, that we can also use speech for other purposes, including persuasion and control, but it is worth exploring the ways in which we apply our linguistic resources to these purposes.

My question for you is about the different ways in which we use language in order to control other people's behaviour; and for the children it is about the persuasive use of language found in teenage magazines.

A lesson for you

Suppose you are sitting in a room and a colleague called John comes in, leaving the door open. This causes a draught, so you want the door closed; and specifically, you want your colleague to close it because he is nearer to it than you are. What do you do? More precisely, what do you say? (In this unit it is essential to remember that speaking is a form of 'doing'.) Here are a number of obvious options.

(1a) Close the door!
(1b) Close the door, please.
(1c) Will you close the door, please?
(1d) Will you close the door?
(1e) Would you close the door?
(1f) Can you close the door, please?
(1g) Can you close the door?
(1h) Could you close the door?
(1i) Would you mind closing the door?
(1j) I wonder if you'ld mind closing the door.
(1k) It's cold with that door open.
(1l) You've left the door open.
(1m) Door!
(1n) I'm trying hard to keep warm in here.
(1o) Brrr!

No doubt you could extend the list; we might mention in

particular the possibility of not using language at all, but making some kind of gesture, such as pretending to push the door closed.

How do these various solutions work, and how would you choose among them? You may have noticed that my list moves from relatively direct solutions to very indirect ones. The first one is direct because it uses a grammatical device – the imperative sentence structure, with V- and no overt subject – which is provided by the grammar precisely for this kind of purpose: for getting the listener to do whatever is described in the sentence. This is very direct, in the sense that anyone who knows English can go straight to the speaker's purpose.

At the other extreme we have *Brrr!*, which is (presumably) part of English, meaning 'I'm cold', but certainly doesn't mean 'Close the door!' In order to arrive at that message, the listener has to do a lot of thinking, so we can say that the link between the expression and the speaker's intention is indirect. (It would be very easy to find examples with an even more indirect link between the expression and the intention; for example, you could say just *John!*, the colleague's name, in order to remind him of a long-running battle about doors.)

Between these two extremes we have a large number of grades and types of indirectness. First you can add *please*, in recognition of the fact that it's up to John to decide whether or not to do it. Then you can add *Will you*, to ask whether or not he is willing to do it. This is recognised conventionally as a way to make a request, but it can also be taken at its face value, as a request for information rather than action; so he could (just about) say *Yes*, and do nothing. At the direct end of the scale, he can certainly say *No*, and do nothing. But you will find that this becomes harder when the request is expressed less directly; for example, John could hardly say *No* when all you say is *Brrr!*.

You can decrease the directness further by making the question into a hypothetical one (*would* instead of *will*), and then by questioning John's ability (which is surely hardly in question) instead of his willingness. The verb MIND comes in next, to raise the question of John's feelings in the hypothetical situation where he closed the door; and less directly still, you state that you are curious about this question, using WONDER.

At this point you drop the verb CLOSE altogether, but point out that the door is open. In (1k) you link this to the cold, but leave him to work out that you want him to do something about it. In (1l) you miss out the link to the cold, but point out John's responsibility for the door being open; so this time he has to work out what the problem is. And in (1m) you say nothing but *Door!*, leaving him to find a problem, his responsibility, and your plan of action. In general we can assume that none of these sentences have any conventional link to the meaning 'Please close the door', such as one could reasonably include in a grammar of English; but we can easily imagine a recurrent situation in which your saying *Door!* to John becomes directly linked in both your minds with him closing the door after him.

Finally you can drop all reference to the door and concentrate on yourself and your problems, with sentence (1n) and *Brrr!*, (1o). The link between either of these sentences and John closing the door is extremely indirect, since the idea of his closing the door isn't mentioned explicitly by a single word in either sentence.

The situation and the examples that we have been considering are extremely commonplace and unremarkable, but they show how indirect the link can be between the words we utter and the effects we achieve. They show that as listeners we are good at 'reading between the lines', by which we mean applying our intelligence and our knowledge to things we hear, in order to make sense of them. The general principle that we follow as hearers is to assume that the speaker has some rational and sensible purpose for speaking; so if we can't find a rational explanation for a direct interpretation of an utterance, we look for an indirect one. When John hears you say *Brrr!*, he could take this at face value, but in some situations it wouldn't make sense to him, so he looks for a hidden meaning.

This raises an obvious question. If reconstructing hidden meanings gives the hearer so much mental work, why do speakers inflict it on them? Why don't we always say directly what we mean? We shall return to this question in the third section.

A lesson for the pupils

My question for your class is based on an extract from a feature in *Smash Hits* (25 January 1989) about a pop singer. The title is just 'Roachford'.

(2) His top-rate tune 'Cuddly Toy' is romping up the charts! He'll be a jolly famous pop star before you know it! And Alex Kadis is itching to spill the beans on his 'fascinating' past!

(Alex Kadis is the feature writer.) The question is: Could the meaning of this passage have been expressed more briefly and straightforwardly, and if so, why wasn't it?

The first task for the class, then, is to construct a paraphrase which gives all the information that (2) gives, but without the frills. Here is my suggestion, which is only one of many possibilities.

(3) His excellent tune 'Cuddly Toy' is rising up the charts, and he'll soon be a very famous pop star. Alex Kadis wants to talk about his 'fascinating' past.

So far as I can see this carries the same objective information as the original. So what have I changed in the paraphrase, and what have we lost?

1 I have removed all the exclamation marks.
2 I have merged the first two sentences into one, and removed *and* from the start of the last sentence.
3 I have substituted some 'ordinary' words for less straightforward ones: EXCELLENT for TOP-RATE, RISING for ROMPING, VERY for JOLLY.

4 I have substituted single words for some idiomatic phrases: SOON for BEFORE YOU KNOW IT, WANT for BE ITCHING, TALK for SPILL THE BEANS.

What have we lost? This is for your class to decide, but I feel sure that they will pronounce the new version thoroughly boring. They may feel obliged to declare the original boring too (I wonder if JOLLY was really part of 1989 teenage vocabulary?), but the revision is even worse. Why? Why should VERY be more boring than JOLLY, or SOON more boring than BEFORE YOU KNOW IT? The class will surely have some views on these questions, and may well produce interesting new insights.

Let's consider the four groups of changes that I distinguished.

1 The exclamation marks are a conventional signal of intense feeling. They are like the balloons on the door of a house with a birthday party; whatever the quality of the party, at least the conventional symbols are there, saying (optimistically) 'We're having fun,'

2 The short sentences increase the number of places where an exclamation mark is possible, and also reduce the difficulties of processing the sentence. A long and complicated sentence may be fascinating to those with quiet and academic tastes, but not for teenagers in search of kicks.

3 The vocabulary like TOP-RATE, ROMPING and JOLLY achieves its effect just by not being ordinary adult usage. Excitement is the opposite of the humdrum routine adults seem to follow, so if you want excitement you do something out of the ordinary, like using TOP-RATE. If you overdo it, then what used to be out of the ordinary becomes humdrum; hence the need for teenage slang to be forever changing.

4 The idioms BEFORE YOU KNOW IT, BE ITCHING TO and SPILL THE BEANS are conventionalised to different degrees, but they all reveal their origins more or less clearly, and they all allow a literal interpretation. This

presents a double challenge for the hearer: did the speaker intend the literal or the idiomatic meaning? But even if they are intended idiomatically, the literal meaning still lurks in the background, contributing something to the meaning. (If I am itching to have a go, I don't just want to have a go but I have an almost physical need to do so, a need which is as pressing as the need to scratch an itch.)

The last category is particularly interesting because it seems to be related to the notion of indirectness which we explored in your lesson. Instead of presenting a message 'straight', we wrap it up in an information package which the hearer then has to unwrap. What is interesting is that we all seem to enjoy this challenge (just as we prefer our birthday presents to be wrapped up), and at least on occasion we prefer it to a straight presentation, for reasons which may be similar to our reasons for enjoying jokes: simply for the intellectual challenge. A lot of entertainment on the media is of this kind – jokes, innuendos, repartee and so on.

Why, then, are teenage magazines written like this? I think it is important not to be too condescending, and to consider the following hypothesis. The publishers face a major problem: how to persuade teenagers to read anything at all. They recognise that the major problem is boredom; as soon as this sets in, reading stops. So the task is to make the reading experience itself interesting, and if possible exciting. To do this they use some conventional means (like the exclamation mark), but they also recognise the value of indirectness – of making the reader work on the meaning, instead of presenting it on a plate. The intellectual excitement and pleasure of this kind of reading may be shortlived, but at least it achieves its immediate effects. You will notice that this explanation brings us back to the National Curriculum's interest in the uses of language for persuasion – in this case, persuading the reader to read on.

This lesson suggests a great number of possible activities for the class – collection and analysis of further examples, comparison of different kinds of magazine for teenagers, comparison of the teenage press with publications for younger and older age-groups, production of a page of a class magazine in different styles, and so on. No doubt such activities are already commonplace in many classrooms.

Theoretical synopsis

The main theme of this unit has been the notion of degrees of directness in the link between the words we say and what we mean. Some links are conventional and part of the grammar; thus in order to know what I want when I say *Close the door!*, all you need to do is to look up the meaning of 'imperative verb' in your mental grammar. (I speak metaphorically, of course!) In contrast, if you want to know what I want when I say *Brrr!* you have to do a great deal of intelligent thinking, so the link is indirect.

You might think that the only purposes that are directly signalled by language are very mundane ones: informing and perhaps regulating, but not reassuring and persuading. (These are the four purposes mentioned in the National Curriculum.) After all, we have declarative sentences (alias 'statements') to inform, imperatives (alias 'commands') to regulate the hearer's behaviour, and interrogatives (alias 'questions') to regulate the hearer's sharing of information:

(4a) You will be back by 10.   (= I hereby inform you that . . .)

(4b) Be back by 10!   (= I hereby instruct you to . . .)

(4c) Will you be back by 10?   (= I hereby ask you whether . . .)

You might think that meanings that fall outside these types must be expressed indirectly.

This is not in fact so. We have a wide range of useful devices for making other purposes explicit. Here is a list of examples which you may find helpful. In my explanations, H stands for the hearer and X stands for the idea expressed (hence 'X') in the sentence. You will see that I am not at all certain about the purposes of some of these expressions.

AFTER ALL

We've got plenty of time. After all, the train doesn't leave till 8.00.   Purpose: to persuade H that X is relevant.

HOW ABOUT

How about a cup of tea?
How about the next example?
Purpose: to get H to pay attention to X, and to draw conclusions.

LOOK

Look, I can't take much more of this arguing.
Purpose: to get H to accept X as the last word (?).

NOW

Now where did I put my glasses?
Purpose: to introduce a new topic (?).

OH

Oh, alright, I suppose so.
Purpose: to acknowledge a message received from H (?).

PLEASE

Where's the post-office, please?
Purpose: to show that H has the right to refuse.

PROMISE

I promise to help you.
Purpose: to make a promise.

SURELY

Surely that must be wrong.
Purpose: to persuade H that X.

Tag questions
  This is your coat, isn't it.
  Purpose: to get H to confirm X.

WELL
  Well, I'm not going to, so there!
  You know that man we met yesterday? Well, he's died.
  Purpose: to prepare H for important information linked to
  what has preceded (?).

WHY + V-
  Why work so hard?
  Purpose: to persuade H not to X.

WHY DON'T YOU
  Why don't you have a break?
  Purpose: to persuade H to X.

YOU KNOW
  You know, you really ought to work harder.
  Purpose: to prepare H for X as new and important infor-
  mation.

It should be easy to add to this list. In class you could use the
list as the basis for drama work, say, choosing one word at a
time, and asking the class to produce a scene in which it is
used appropriately.

One final point that is worth making explicit is that it can
be difficult to distinguish between grammar and personality,
and that this difficulty can lead to social friction. This would
also provide very suitable material for a drama lesson. Suppose
someone irritates you by always sounding dogmatic and condescending. If you were to analyse their speech you might
find that this impression comes from their over-use (by your
standards) of words like NOW and YOU KNOW, which (for you)
mean that the speaker wants to tell you something you don't
already know. These words are fine when used appropriately,
as in (5).

(5)   You know, I never did like the way she dresses.

But when you already know the facts being communicated they sound condescending (because they suggest that the speaker doesn't expect you to know them):

(6)   You know, people live much better now than when I was a boy.

The crucial question is, why do these people say things like (6)? Does the problem lie in their grammar or in their personality? If their rules for using YOU KNOW are the same as yours then they must arrogantly assume that they know more than you do, which is a personality problem. But what if they have different rules for YOU KNOW? Then the problem turns into a trivial matter of grammar, which is no reason for feeling badly towards the speaker. But how do we know which is which? Unless we can take the speaker aside and do some careful linguistic fieldwork the only evidence for the grammar comes from what we can observe, which is their problematic behaviour. I have no solution to this problem, but time spent in alerting pupils to the dangers may be time very well spent.

Level 8:

Presuppositions

One of the study-programme suggestions for this level is as follows:

Pupils should be able to . . . recognise authorial viewpoint and . . . persuasive or rhetorical techniques in a range of texts.

One contribution that grammar can make to this effort is in the area that is called 'presupposition'.

The trigger for your exploration of this area is the question: What is the difference in meaning between KNOW and THINK? For the class the question is somewhat different: What does YET mean?

A lesson for you

What's the difference between (1a) and (1b)?

(1a)   Ann thinks Father Christmas exists.
(1b)   Ann knows Father Christmas exists.

In case the answer isn't immediately obvious, try adding the sentence *but in fact she's wrong.*

(2a)   Ann thinks Father Christmas exists, but in fact she's wrong.
(2b)   Ann knows Father Christmas exists, but in fact she's wrong.

As you can see, sentence (1a), with THINK, tells us what Ann thinks, but nothing at all about whether the speaker agrees with her. Sentence (1b) containing KNOW is also about her beliefs, but this time the sentence presents the beliefs as factually correct (in the speaker's opinion, of course). In technical terminology, it 'presupposes' that her beliefs are correct.

In a sense, then, (1b) tells us two things about Father Christmas's existence: that Ann believes it, and that it's true. However the meaning of this sentence isn't simply a combination of these two bits of information, because their statuses are quite different. The first is on the surface and available for argument, criticism or denial, but the second isn't – it lurks in the background, so to speak, but won't come out and fight properly.

You can see this difference by simply negating our first two sentences, which is a straightforward way of denying them.

(3a) Ann doesn't think Father Christmas exists.
(3b) Ann doesn't know Father Christmas exists.

Negating (1a) produces (3a), which as you can see denies the only thing that (1a) tells us, namely that Ann believes in Father Christmas. But negating (1b), to give (3b), leaves Father Christmas's existence untouched; all it denies is that Ann believes in him. The truth of his existence is taken for granted (presupposed) in (3b) just as firmly as it is in its opposite, (1b).

This surreptitious character of presuppositions makes them an enormously effective weapon in the armoury of a persuader – an advertiser, a politician, a school-teacher or a grammarian writing for school-teachers. Advertisers and politicians continually tell us what they claim we 'know' already, when all they are telling us is just their own beliefs or opinions. (Imagine a poster saying 'Vote ____, you believe it's right!') School-teachers remind pupils that they 'know' (not believe) that smoking is bad for them, that they'll have to find a job or grow up one day, and so on. And grammarians write sentences like the following (from the previous chapter):

(4) We all know, of course, that we can also use speech for

other purposes, including persuasion and control . . ..

By using *know* I avoided the need for persuasion, as our shared belief now counts as a fact; had I used *believe* I should have needed to explain and justify the claim.

Presuppositions are much harder to react to in a critical way, precisely because they are presented as background information which needs to be taken for granted in order to allow communication to take place. As soon as you question a presupposition you can be accused not merely of being wrong, but of rejecting the very fabric of assumptions shared by all decent members of the society.

A very simple example of this kind of effect is the use of BUT in examples like (5).

(5) Jones is a Tory but he's a very good MP.

If you say (5), then you tell your hearer that you don't expect Tories to be virtuous, whereas no such information would have been conveyed if you replaced *but* by *and*. But of course (5) doesn't allow me to accuse you of saying that Tories are generally bad MPs, because you didn't say it – you just implied it. Similarly suppose you said (6).

(6) This is a new one, but I'll sell it to you for £10.

This implies strongly that a new one normally costs more than £10, but doesn't actually say so; consequently, if I later discovered that they normally cost less than £10 I can't accuse you of having lied, as I could have if you had said (7).

(7) This is a new one, which would normally cost more than £10, but I'll sell it to you for £10.

Presuppositions are not always reprehensible even when they slip new information past in the guise of old. They are a standard device for making language less routine, blunt and wordy. For example, a letter from my insurance company starts with the following:

(8)   I am delighted to be able to tell you about our latest range of services designed to help minimise your inconvenience in the event of an accident.

Taken at its face value this sentence tells me about the chairman's state of mind, but we all know (!!) that this isn't really the point, which is simply to tell me what could have been conveyed much more briefly by (9).

(9)   We have just introduced a new range of services to minimise your inconvenience in the event of an accident.

I don't object to the personal touch (whose sincerity is no business of mine), and in general I feel the world would be a worse place if presuppositions were reserved strictly for straightforward cases where the presupposed beliefs really are shared between speaker and listener.

Grammarians have uncovered a wide range of grammatical patterns that carry presuppositions. Here is a selection of examples, in which I have highlighted the words that carry the presupposition:

(10)   Fred **accused** Bill of writing the letter.
      (presupposed: someone wrote the letter; writing the letter was bad)
      (stated: Fred said it was Bill)
(11)   Fred **criticised** Bill for writing the letter.
      (presupposed: Bill wrote the letter)
      (stated: Fred said it was bad)
(12)   Fred ate **the** cake.
      (presupposed: there was a cake)
      (stated: Fred ate it)
(13)   **Who** ate the cake?
      (presupposed: there was a cake; someone ate it)
      (questioned: who was that someone?)
(14)   **If** Fred **had** been clever he **would have** come.
      (presupposed: (a) Fred is not clever; (b) Fred did not

come)
(stated: (a) alone explains (b))

(15) **Why don't** you read a book?
(presupposed: you should read a book)
(questioned: your reasons for not doing so)

(16) You've been at the biscuits **again**.
(presupposed: you've been at the biscuits before)
(stated: you've been at the biscuits recently)

(17) Will you have **another** cup of tea and some **more** cakes?
(presupposed: you've already had a cup of tea and some cakes)
(questioned: will you have a cup of tea and some cakes)

(18) He's gone **back** to Glasgow.
(presupposed: he was in Glasgow before)
(stated: he's gone to Glasgow.)

(19) He **even** likes pop.
(presupposed: you wouldn't expect him to like pop)
(stated: he likes pop.)

It is hard to see any pattern running through all these examples, other than the semantic structure which distinguishes presupposed information from information which is stated, questioned or whatever. What the list does show, however, is how all-pervasive and important the phenomenon is.

A lesson for your class

Here is the question for your class: What is the meaning of YET in the following sentence?

(20) Have you got a car yet?

In order to work out the answer they will need to see the effect of removing *yet*:

(21) Have you got a car?

The discussion will hopefully show that YET carries a presupposition, though this term clearly won't be used (unless you introduce it, as you may). The presupposition is that the state of affairs described will come true though it is still untrue at present.

Since this is a presupposition it can't be driven away by negation:

(22a) No, I haven't got a car yet.
(22b) No, I haven't got a car.

Yet still has precisely the same effect in (22a) as it did in (20), so (22a) still carries the presupposition that I will have a car in the future. And (22b) is free of presupposition, just like (21).

How do you answer question (20) if you have in fact got a car? In the case of (21) you can simply reverse the subject and auxiliary verb, and add *Yes*; so you might expect to be able to do the same with (20).

(23a) Yes, I have got a car.
(23b) *Yes, I have got a car yet.

How strange! And yet (a different YET!) this is really precisely what we should expect if *yet* carries the presupposition 'I will have one in the future though I haven't got one now.' Either I have got one, in which case the presupposition is false; or I haven't, and the expressed statement is false.

The class could easily develop this theme by looking for examples of YET in advertisements. A standard example found in posters advertising school magazines is *Have you got your copy yet?* As they become more aware of presuppositions they could expand the range of linguistic forms to be collected; for instance, *your copy* in the last example carries the presupposition that everyone has a copy (cf. *You can buy your copy from your class rep*).

What might be more interesting for them, however, would

be to conduct their own campaign. You can divide them arbitrarily into two groups, and then assign to each group some person or thing to be promoted. If you give a pop star to one group and a food to the other they won't be in competition, but each group can try to persuade the other group by means of posters, speeches or any other linguistic means they can think of. The one rule of the game is that they score a mark (from you) for each presupposition they use; and each group can challenge your decisions about the other's presuppositions. The group with the most points wins. The class can then decide whether this was also the group with the best arguments.

Theoretical synopsis

The discussion of presupposition has shown that the ideas that make up a sentence's meaning have a variety of statuses. We can distinguish three kinds:
   (a)   Those which are claimed to be true.

(24)   Someone is snoring.

The entire meaning of this sentence is claimed to be true.
(b)   those whose truth is uncertain.

(25)   They think someone is snoring.

If we embed sentence (24) into a larger one containing a verb like THINK or BELIEVE, its meaning turns into a type (b) idea, about which the hearer is uncertain. Sentence (25) states that the speaker thinks this idea is true; but we can't tell whether someone really is snoring.

   (c)   Those which are presupposed to be true.

(26)   They know someone is snoring.

Here the idea that someone is snoring is assumed true, and the only idea that is open to possible doubt or denial is the idea that they know it. And this, as I said earlier, is why a sentence like this is so hard to argue against.

Level 9:

Passives

According to the National Curriculum, by level 9 pupils should be able, among other things, to:

(c) make an assured and selective use of a wide range of grammatical constructions which are appropriate for topic, purpose and audience, demonstrating awareness of the means whereby a writer may choose to achieve a desired emphasis ...; e.g. vary sentence beginnings; alter word order; use lexical or structural repetition, passive constructions, adverbial connectives, elliptical constructions, non-finite subordinate clauses and choose varied and appropriate vocabulary such as colloquial, formal, technical, poetic or figurative.

... pupils should be taught:
– about the nature and purpose of impersonal styles of writing, and the vocabulary and grammar characteristic of those styles, e.g. the use of the passive voice and of other ways of depersonalising text, such as not using pronouns.

One of the grammatical themes that recurs in this list is the use of passives, which is my topic for this lesson. However I should make it clear that children use these structures from quite an early age in their own speech, and meet them in their earliest reading, so you may well have found it appropriate to discuss passives long before the pupils reach this level.

For your pupils I have a rather general and open-ended question: Why do writers use passive verbs? Your question is this: What is the subject of *was eaten* in *My homework was eaten by our dog*?

A lesson for you

Your question, then, is about (1), a typical passive.

(1)   My homework was eaten by our dog.

What is the subject of *was eaten*? Let's start by comparing it with the active equivalent, (2).

(2)   Our dog ate my homework.

In this sentence there is no doubt about the subject: it must be *our dog*. The two sentences appear to have the same meaning, so you might expect *our dog* to be the subject of *was eaten* as well. This would be quite wrong, though, as I shall explain.

One of the rules, or facts, that applies to subjects is that they normally precede the verb. This is not true of *our dog* in (1). Another rule is that in a question the subject follows an auxiliary verb (such as *was*); so what is the question form of (1)?

(3)   Was my homework eaten by our dog?

Once again, *our dog* is entirely out of the picture. A third rule says that a tensed verb (such as *was*) has to have a subject, so if *our dog* is the subject, it ought to be obligatory. But provided we also miss out *by*, we can drop *our dog* without any problems:

(4)   My homework was eaten.

And finally, we know that *was* is used with a singular subject and *were* with a plural one; so changing *our dog* into *our dogs* should trigger a change from *was* to *were*. But it doesn't:

(5)   My homework was/*were eaten by our dogs.

The outcome is conclusive: *our dog* is definitely not the subject of *was eaten*. The only alternative to this conclusion is to abandon all these otherwise excellent rules.

The point of this little exercise was to prepare for a discussion of passive verbs. I have treated *was eaten* as a single unit, but it really consists of two words, only one of which is a passive verb: *eaten*. In English (unlike Latin, on which so many of our grammatical ideas are based) 'passive' is the name for just one form of a verb. In contrast, the word *was* is not a passive verb, but the past-tense form of BE. We can vary this form a great deal, without changing the passivity of *eaten*: so *is eaten, are eaten, were eaten*, even *am eaten*, are all passive in precisely the same sense as *was eaten*.

Indeed, the passivity survives if we replace BE by GET: *get eaten, gets eaten* and *got eaten* are all still passive. To show that BE and GET in these examples are just the ordinary verbs BE and GET, we can even add further auxiliary verbs before them:

(6a)   This plant **is being eaten** by slugs.
(6b)   This plant **has got eaten** by slugs.
(6c)   This plant **will be being eaten** by slugs (if we don't do something).
(6d)   This plant **has been being eaten** by slugs for weeks.

What makes all these examples passive is that they contain *eaten*, and you can think of the other verbs – BE, GET and the various auxiliary verbs – as mere syntactic props for the passive verb.

One last piece of evidence that the passive verb is just *eaten*, and doesn't include BE or GET, is that *eaten* can occur without any verb before it, but modifying a noun:

(7)   The plant **eaten** by the slugs is over there.

As I hope you can see, *eaten* is still passive in this example.

But what, precisely, does it mean to say that *eaten* is passive? Let's survey the differences between *eaten* and *ate*:
   (a)   *Ate* is a tensed verb (specifically, past-tense verb), so

it can be the only verb in the sentence; *eaten* isn't, and there-fore can't. *Eaten* has to occur after BE, GET or a noun (or in a few other contexts that we can ignore for the present). In this respect, *eaten* is just like *eating*. These are both called 'participles': 'passive participle' and 'present participle', respectively.

(b) What would have been the subject of *ate* is 'demoted' to being a mere optional modifier of *eaten*, introduced by the preposition BY. This is why *our dog* is not the subject of *(was) eaten* although it is the subject of *ate*.

(c) Having 'lost' the normal subject, *(was) eaten* takes a different noun as its subject; this is often the one that would have been the object of *ate*, as with *my homework* in *My homework was eaten by our dog*.

(d) A peculiarity of English is that another possibility is allowed for the subject of a passive verb: the object of a preposition. Compare the following.

(8a)   Somebody ate from this plate.
(8b)   This plate was eaten from.

The removal of its object leaves this preposition 'dangling', a pattern that traditional grammarians inveighed against simply because it was not allowed in Latin. English speakers have been doing it for centuries.

To summarise these four points, passivising a verb replaces the ordinary subject by some other noun that would otherwise have followed the verb – such as *my homework* or *this plate*; and at the same time it allows us to leave the subject unex-pressed (as in *My homework was eaten*, or *This plate was eaten from*) if we wish. Passivising is a very useful source of flexi-bility because it allows us, in effect, to pick almost any noun we want as the subject, and then choose between an active and a passive verb-form as necessary. The price we pay for this flexibility is that the passive verb is a mere passive verb, not a tensed verb, so we need extra words to support it.

Some more examples of passive verbs in sentences may be helpful. The following is part of a feature in the *Guardian*

(April 1991) in which I have highlighted the passive verbs. I have omitted sentences that don't contain any.

(9)   In the south [of Iraq], the plight of the Shia population is not much better – some 4,000 are **reported** to have been **executed** in two towns alone, Najaf and Talme. Many of the Kurds, their rebellion **crushed** by tanks and helicopter gunships, have been **trapped** as the Turks and Iranians periodically close the border to try to stem the influx. . . . Mr Major now began to take the initiative and won enthusiastic endorsement from other European Community leaders meeting in Luxemburg for a proposal to set up an enclave in northern Iraq as a safe haven for Kurdish refugees, to be **policed** by United Nations forces. . . . Sanctions would remain in force until the safety of the Kurds was **guaranteed** – whether by Saddam Hussein or by his successor. The plan was due to be **put** before the UN security Council, but it was not **expected** to get an easy ride. While the Security Council voted last week in favour of final ceasefire terms for the Gulf war, grudgingly **accepted** by Iraq, there was more opposition to a further resolution, **sponsored** by Belgium, France, the USA and Britain, condemning the repression of civilians in Iraq, especially Kurds, and demanding that Baghdad allow humanitarian access to those in need – to Cuba, Yemen, India, Zimbabwe and China this looked like intervention in the internal affairs of a state, **forbidden** by the UN charter.

I hope that you can now recognise passive verbs reliably. We shall be considering their value in the next section but we can't finish this general outline of how passive verbs work without saying something about their morphological form. As you can see from the passage just quoted, most of them end in -*ed*, just like a past-tense verb. This is the regular pattern, which applies to the vast majority of verbs, but there are a fair number of irregular verbs in which it is not true. The passage contains two: *put* and *forbidden*. The former is again just the same as the past-tense form of the same verb, but the latter isn't (the past tense being *forbad(e)*). Very many irregular verbs have *-en* on their passive forms, but not on their past-tense forms: EAT (*ate/eaten*), HIDE (*hid/hidden*), BREAK (*broke/broken*), FORGET (*forgot/forgotten*), and so on. In recognition of this fact, linguists often call the passive form of a verb 'V-en', even though in most verbs the ending is actually *-ed*. This is a useful convention, because passive verbs are very different from past-tense verbs in many ways other than their shape (as we saw in the comparison of *ate* and *eaten*).

One final little twist to the story is that the passive form of a verb is always, without exception, the same as the form that occurs after HAVE, as in *have eaten*. V-en, then, can be used in two different ways: either as a passive, or after HAVE. In the latter case it is called 'perfect' (or a 'perfect, or past, participle'). The classification of these verb-forms that we have now achieved is summarised below:

V-ed past-tense form   We **baked/ate** a cake.

V-en perfect (participle)   We have **baked/eaten** a cake.

V-en passive participle   A cake was **baked/eaten** by us.

A lesson for your pupils

Why do writers use passive verbs? The point of this lesson is to try to guide the pupils themselves in their own use of passives by making them sensitive to the benefits of this structure, but a prerequisite for this must be at least a rough understanding of how passivisation works. I suggest an in-depth discussion of one sentence along the lines of my lesson for you, leading up to the generalisations with which we ended.

Assuming that they can recognise passive verbs reasonably efficiently, the next step is to collect some examples. I suggest a comparison between a scientific text, where passives are generally rather common, and some very different kind of text, such as a sports report in a newspaper or a passage from a novel. Each pupil, or group of pupils, could collect, say, 20 examples from each text, and count the total number of words from the start of the passage to the twentieth passive verb. This will give some idea of how frequent such verbs are in the two texts. One would expect them to be more frequent in the scientific text than in the other, so they should have to read fewer words in the scientific text in order to gather 20 examples.

You should draw their attention to passive participles that modify nouns, such as *the examples discussed above*, where *discussed* is the passive participle of DISCUSS and modifies *examples*. I leave it to you to decide what to do with apparent examples of passive participles that stand, as a modifier, before a noun, as in *the broken bottle*. (Opinion is divided among linguists as to whether these are adjectives or verbs.)

Here are the first five examples that I find in a randomly chosen passage from Charlotte Brontë's *Jane Eyre* (1975 edition: 78). The passive verbs are emphasised.

(10) household matters were not *scrutinised* into
(11) the cross housekeeper was gone, *driven* away by the fear of infection
(12) our breakfast basins were better *filled*
(13) she was *qualified* to give those who enjoyed the privilege of her converse, a taste of far higher things
(14) for some weeks she had been *removed* from my sight to I knew not what room up-stairs

Between the point where I started reading and the fifth example there were about 600 words, which means about one passive per 120 words.

A similarly random choice in an A-level Physics textbook *Physics: Concepts and Models* by E. J. Wenham, G. W. Dorling, J. A. N. Snell and B. Taylor (1972: 377) yielded the following five examples in a mere 120 words (that is, 24 words per passive), a frequency five times that of *Jane Eyre*.

(15) no further energy has to be *provided* to free it from the gravitational pull of the Earth

(16) how much energy has to be *supplied* to get the spacecraft into such a position?

(17) at this distance the field intensity *g* is *given* by . . .

(18) In order to move the craft a further distance . . . along the radius, additional energy has to be *transformed* to gravitational potential energy.

(19) The energy *gained* per unit mass, . . . = ...

The figure for the *Guardian* feature that I quoted earlier lies between these two: 290 words, or 58 words per passive.

A recent trend in science textbooks suggests an interesting exercise for pupils who are studying science: to compare a modern textbook with an older one, such as the one I have just quoted (published in 1972). The principle behind the trend has been to make textbooks more readable, so one might expect a reduction in the number of passives. If they find this to be true, the students can also evaluate the books as consumers, to see if the change is linked to an improvement in readability.

Returning to our two texts, why did the authors of these works choose passive verbs in preference to active ones? One of the most obvious benefits of passivisation is that it allows the 'normal subject' to be omitted entirely. In the ten examples above, this option is taken in no fewer than eight cases, the only exceptions being (11) and (17). Ignoring these two examples for the time being, then, we can guess that in both texts one reason for passivising verbs was to allow the author to leave the normal subject out.

But why should the author have wanted to do so? If we look carefully at the examples, we can distinguish two kinds of example. First we have examples in which it would have been difficult or even impossible to choose a suitable phrase for the normal subject. For example, take (15) again.

(15) no further energy has to be *provided* to free it from the gravitational pull of the Earth

Suppose we were told to un-passivise this, what would we supply as the subject? The problem is that the passage describes a hypothetical thought-experiment in which space-ships can be moved out of the Earth's atmosphere, but where it is totally irrelevant how they move, whether by self-propulsion, or by some giant hand which pushes or pulls them, or whatever. By simply omitting the normal subject of *provided* the writer can sidestep this issue completely. This kind of explanation applies to several of the other examples: (13), (16) and (18) as well as (15). We might also include number (14) under this heading:

(14)   for some weeks she had been *removed* from my sight to I knew not what room up-stairs

One reason for not saying who removed her is presumably that this information is simply irrelevant.

A second group of examples without a *by*-phrase corresponding to the normal passive are presumably used not because the identity of the person concerned is irrelevant, but because it is obvious. Take (10), for example, which I now set in a larger context:

(10)   Mr Brocklehurst and his family never came near Lowood now: household matters were not *scrutinised* into.

The preceding context makes it clear who the potential scrutinisers were, so they can be left implicit. It would be interesting to discuss, with the class, whether this is preferable to using the active (20), given that only one word is saved.

(20)   Mr Brocklehurst and his family never came near Lowood now: they did not scrutinise into household matters.

Two other examples like this are (12) and (19).

Finally we return to our two examples in which the passive participle has an accompanying BY which introduces the normal subject. Given the extra complexity of passivisation, what motivation is there for choosing it in these cases? Each example illustrates a different reason.

Let's start with the scientific one, (17).

(17)   at this distance the field intensity g is *given* by ...

In this example the dots stand for a complex formula, so the advantage of passivisation here is that it allows the normal subject to be delayed till the end of the sentence. It is much easier to read a sentence that ends in a formula than one that starts with a formula. This is because all the processing of the sentence proper is completed before the reader pays attention to the formula. More generally, passivisation can be useful if the normal subject is long and/or complicated, because it can then be delayed until the end of the sentence.

The other example is (11).

(11)   the cross housekeeper was gone, *driven* away by the fear of infection

The advantage of passivisation here is that passives, like several other verb-forms, allow their subjects to be omitted in constructions like this – that is, where there is a sequence:

. . . noun . . . passive participle . . .

and the preceding noun can be taken as the 'understood subject' of the passive participle. A similar pattern, containing an active participle, is illustrated in (21).

(21)   He went to look for a dictionary, hoping to find the word he couldn't remember.

Here the relevant verb is *hoping*, whose missing subject is understood as being the person named by *he*. For similar reasons, the subject of *driven* in (11) is understood to be the housekeeper. But if the verb had been *driving*, the housekeeper would have to be understood as the 'drive-er' – not at all the intended meaning. Hence the need for passivisation in this case.

To summarise, we have found four reasons for passivizing:

1   In order to leave the normal subject unexpressed, because its identity is irrelevant.

2 In order to leave the normal subject unexpressed, because its identity is obvious.
3 In order to move the normal subject to the end of the sentence, where it is easier to process if it is complex.
4 In order to move a normal non-subject into the subject position, in order to apply the rules for subjects (e.g. for omitting the subjects of participles).

These categories will probably be all you need in order to classify the examples collected by the class.

Any examples which don't fit into any of the categories should probably be active rather than passive. My last example is taken from an official form:

(22) The cheque should be paid into your bank or building society account.

I can see no good reason to prefer this over the active equivalent:

(23) You should pay the cheque into your bank or building society account.

It would be useful to encourage the class to keep their eyes open for unnecessary passives like this, which seem to be used for the wrong reasons, as part of an impersonal 'officialese'.

Theoretical synopsis

The main theoretical point underlying this discussion has been the idea that a verb sits at the centre of a network of relations to other words – its subject, its object, and various other kinds of satellite or 'dependent' words. As I pointed out in the chapter on grammatical functions, each grammatical function (that is, relation) is bound to some semantic relation.

For example, the subject of EAT expresses its 'actor', the

person whose mouth and digestive system are involved in the eating; and its object expresses its 'patient', the food ingested. These bonds between syntactic and semantic relations are quite rigid, so once you have decided to use a particular verb to express a particular idea you have very little choice in allocating the other parts of the sentence to subjects, objects and so on.

In most cases this doesn't matter – and for very good reason, because our stock of vocabulary has presumably developed over the centuries to take account of our normal needs. But sometimes it does, and this is where passives come in: they help us to tailor verbs to our special needs. I outlined four types of circumstances which raise such needs. Therefore the most important pedagogical point to make is that passives are a friend, a useful tool, and not a nuisance, a sign of 'mature style' which novices have to learn to sprinkle randomly through their writings.

Level 10:

End-weight and readability

Pupils at this level should be able to:

(d) demonstrate, in discussion and in writing, knowledge of criteria by which different types of written language can be judged; e.g. . . . clarity, coherence, accuracy, appropriateness, effectiveness, vigour, and awareness of purpose and audience.

This lesson will touch on a variety of criteria by which a piece of writing can be judged, but it will approach them by looking at a single grammatical phenomenon, the length of subjects.
   Your question is about the structure of a particular sentence, *A book has just been published about how to teach grammar*. This will prepare you for your pupils' question, which is about the ways in which long phrases can be delayed.

A lesson for you

Consider sentence (1).

(1)   A book has just been published about how to teach grammar.

What is its structure? In particular, how does the last phrase, *about how to teach grammar*, fit in?
   As you have surely noticed already, this sentence means the same as (2).

(2)   A book about how to teach grammar has just been published.

The only difference between these two sentences is in the position of *about how to teach grammar*. Since this modifies the meaning of *book* (what kind of book?), its position in (2) is the one we should expect, because this is the one that puts the modifier next to the word it modifies. You will remember from our discussion of phrases in lesson 4 that modifiers, like other kinds of dependents, stick as close to their head as they can, so that the phrase as a whole will be continuous (hence the badness of an expression like *large in cities?* compared with *in large cities*, where *large* modifies *cities* but is separated from it by *in*). How is it, then, that *about how to teach grammar* can at least appear to modify *book* in (1), while being separated from it by all the other words that are not part of the same phrase (i.e. by *has just been published*)?

The explanation is that the grammar allows certain kinds of phrases, under certain circumstances, to be split. The grammar contains rules which define these types and circumstances, so if a phrase isn't covered by such a rule, it can't be split. *A book about how to teach grammar* is in fact covered by a rule which allows the final modifier, *how to teach grammar*, to be delayed until the end of the sentence. Let's look at some other examples:

(3a)   **A letter** landed on my desk this morning **from the Inland Revenue**.
(3b)   **Five girls** live across the road **who Fred would love to meet**.
(3c)   **That man** never turned up **who said he wanted to buy our car**.

As you can see, all these are grammatical but share the same split-phrase pattern, with the first part of the subject in its normal position but a modifier of the subject noun delayed to the end of the sentence. (I have highlighted the split phrase in the examples.) In each case the modifier could have occurred in its expected position, between the subject noun and the verb, so the delaying is completely optional.

This pattern is called 'extraposition', a slightly misleading term suggesting that the delayed modifier is moved right outside (Latin *extra* means 'outside') the rest of the sentence. This is not in fact true; the delayed modifier is still very much part of the sentence that contains it, as you can see from more complicated examples like (4).

(4a) Although **a letter** landed on my desk this morning *from the Inland Revenue*, I haven't yet opened it.

(4b) ∗Although **a letter** landed on my desk this morning, I haven't yet opened it *from the Inland Revenue*.

We must assume that the modifier of the subject noun acquires an extra syntactic link to this noun's head verb (for instance, to *landed* in (3a) and (4a)) which allows it to be delayed. We needn't go any further into the details of this analysis.

Extraposition of a modifier isn't restricted to subject phrases; for example, in (5b) it has been applied to a complement phrase.

(5a) I'm reading **a letter from the Inland Revenue** at the moment.

(5b) I'm reading **a letter** at the moment **from the Inland Revenue**.

This time extraposition has moved the modifier of the noun across a modifier of the verb, *at the moment*.

Why does the grammar allow us this option, and why do we exploit it? Presumably the first question rests on the answer to the second one: once we can explain why we exploit the option of extraposition, this will tell us what extraposition is good for; and once we know this, we may assume that the grammar has evolved in line with our interests. The explanation is bound to be speculative, but the following seems plausible.

It is easy to show that we have only a limited amount of whatever kind of memory we use for reading and listening; for instance, you reduce the memory available for reading if you try to listen to a conversation at the same time. Let's call this memory 'working memory'. (It's important to distinguish this memory from general memory, because this seems to be virtually limitless in its capacity.) One important kind of information that you have to hold in your working memory when processing a sentence is a list of the words processed most recently, plus their syntactic relations to one another. The more words we have to hold in this way, the more crowded our working memory becomes and therefore the more difficulty we face; therefore a considerate writer or speaker will ease the difficulty by minimising these demands.

Now let's see how this applies to extraposition. Take sentences (1) and (2) again.

(1)   A book has just been published about how to teach grammar.

(2)   A book about how to teach grammar has just been published.

Now compare them both with (6), in which I have simply omitted the modifier phrase, *about how to teach grammar*.

(6)   A book has just been published.

Both (1) and (2) are more complex than this, but in (1) the extra complexity doesn't hit the reader until the rest of the sentence has been more or less sorted out. In fact, the words up to *published* are precisely the same in (1) as they are in (6), so the processing demands of (1) up to this point must be precisely the same as those of (6). In (2), on the other hand, one's working memory has to cope with the extra complexity of the modifier phrase right in the middle of dealing with the rest of the sentence, which of course imposes much greater demands on working memory. The benefits of extraposition come at a price, of course: when the extraposed phrase is encountered, the reader has to find a suitable head for it in the preceding sentence. However it seems that this extra effort is outweighed by the benefits.

A lot of the details of this picture remain to be worked out, but one general conclusion can be drawn: long subjects are hard to process. Here is an example of a difficult sentence from an otherwise well-written book, *Archaeology in Britain since 1945*, edited by I. Longworth and J. Cherry (1986: 29):

(7)   The imbalance in the archaeological record due to the absence from most dryland sites of many of the main organic components – wood, leather, rope and basketry – *has* long been a source of concern.

I have emphasised the main verb (that is, the tensed verb which holds the whole sentence together), whose subject phrase consists of all the preceding 26 words. Throughout this phrase the reader's working memory contains the question: this phrase that I'm building must be linked to some word outside it – what is it? and what is the semantic role of the phrase? This is a lot of uncertainty to carry along, and explains the difficulty that I (for one) found in reading the sentence. It would have been much easier to read a roughly equivalent sentence such as (8).

(8)   Archaeologists have been concerned for a long time about the imbalance in the archaeological record due to the absence from most dryland sites of many of the main organic components – wood, leather, rope and basketry.

A lesson for your pupils

What resources does English offer for delaying long phrases till the end of the sentence? The aim of the lesson is to let the class build themselves a checklist of constructions that are worth considering as ways out of a grammatical tight corner caused by an over-long phrase.

My suggestion is as follows. First present the sentences in (9), all of which contain the long phrase *some cakes with pink and green icing and little bits of holly on top*.

(9a)   *Some cakes with pink and green icing and little bits of holly on top* were on it.

(9b) *Some cakes with pink and green icing and little bits of holly on top* attracted me.

(9c) I bought *some cakes with pink and green icing and little bits of holly on top* for them.

You start by asking them to pass judgement on these sentences, in the hope that they will be fairly scornful. You then work out the syntactic structures with the class, in order to identify the source of the problems. Diagrams like the following may be helpful:

(9a')

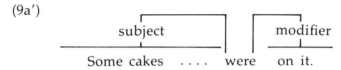

(9b')

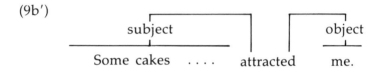

(9c')

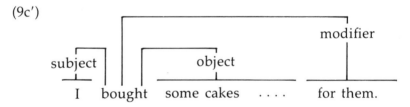

You should steer them to the conclusion that the problem comes from the fact that the long phrase is boxed in by other words.

The question then arises: how could you improve them? You can collect and classify the suggestions they make, which are likely to fall under the following headings. Some of them are constructions which, according to my syllabus, they should already know, so you should encourage them to use the technical names.

Passivisation This helps with (9b), though not with (9a) or

(9c). It allows the long phrase to be treated as a modifier introduced by BY, instead of as the subject, and this in turn allows it to be at the end of the sentence, where it is easier to process:

(10b) I was attracted by *some cakes with pink and green icing and little bits of holly on top.*

Extraposition This applies to all three sentences:

(11a) *Some cakes* were on it *with pink and green icing and little bits of holly on top.*
(11b) *Some cakes* attracted me *with pink and green icing and little bits of holly on top.*
(11c) I bought *some cakes* for them *with pink and green icing and little bits of holly on top.*

You could discuss the relative merits of these sentences in speech and in writing. I think they are more successful in speech because intonation provides a guide to their structure.

Lexically permitted structure change By this I mean a change in the structure of the sentence which leaves the sentence's meaning unchanged, and which uses the same dictionary-word for the principal verb. This applies to (9c), because BUY allows two different patterns for expressing the same semantic relations:

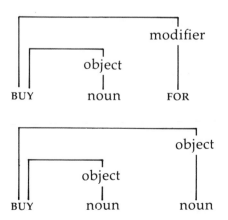

The original example, (9c), uses the first of these patterns, so we can easily improve it by changing to the second, which leaves the whole of the long phrase at the end of the sentence.

(12c)   I bought them *some cakes with pink and green icing and little bits of holly on top.*

Heavy-noun-phrase shift   This is an established name for a simple change of word-order which moves a 'heavy noun-phrase' out of its normal position and into final position. This applies only to noun-phrases which already follow the verb, such as the one in (9c).

(13c)   I bought for them *some cakes with pink and green icing and little bits of holly on top.*

Use of THERE   The spelling *there* belongs to two quite different dictionary-words. One is the 'demonstrative' THERE/dem, which means 'over there'. This is always pronounced with a long vowel, and rhymes with WHERE. The other is the one I have in mind here. It is usually pronounced like THE (with an added /r/ in some accents), and is quite meaningless. It is used as a 'dummy' subject, allowing the expected subject to be delayed to the end of the sentence. We can call it THERE/dummy.

(14)   There's a fly in my soup.

Although THERE/dummy is historically related to THERE/dem, the two are now separate to the extent of being able to occur alongside one another:

(15)   Here there's a chair and there there's a table.

This is a helpful device for delaying some kinds of long subject in some kinds of sentence. It works well in (9a), and almost works in (9b), depending on how 'high' we are willing to let the style level rise (from casual to 'highbrow').

(16a) There were *some cakes with pink and green icing and little bits of holly on top* on it.

(16b) ?There attracted me *some cakes with pink and green icing and little bits of holly on top*.

Sentence (16a) is still only a partial solution to the problem, because the long phrase is still boxed in by *on it*. To overcome this we can now apply heavy-noun-phrase shift (see above):

(17) There were on it *some cakes with pink and green icing and little bits of holly on top*.

We can even apply THERE to the result of passivizing (9c), and improve the result by applying heavy-noun-phrase shift. Here are the steps: passivise; insert THERE to delay the new subject; shift the heavy noun-phrase to the end.

(9c) I bought *some cakes with pink and green icing and little bits of holly on top* for them.

(18) *Some cakes with pink and green icing and little bits of holly on top* were bought for them.

(19) There were bought *some cakes with pink and green icing and little bits of holly on top* for them.

(20) There were bought for them *some cakes with pink and green icing and little bits of holly on top*.

Locative inversion   This means a sentence which starts with a 'locative' expression – that is, a phrase that defines a place or direction. In such sentences the subject can be delayed till the end:

(21) Here comes your Dad.

(22) In the corner of the churchyard stands an ancient yew tree.

The style level varies markedly according to the details of the sentence, as you can see from these examples, so it is a rich source of examples for discussion of style. It applies directly to only one of our examples, (9a):

(23)   On it were *some cakes with pink and green icing and little bits of holly on top.*

However it might be considered to apply to the passivised version of (9c), where *for her* somehow creeps into the category of 'locatives'.

(24)   For them were bought *some cakes with pink and green icing and little bits of holly on top.*

Topicalization   This is what happens when you put something which would normally follow the verb at the front of the sentence. A standard example is *Beans I like,* as in *I can't stand peas, but beans I like.* This allows us to move a late phrase out of the way, as in (25):

(25)   For them I bought *some cakes with pink and green icing and little bits of holly on top.*

Locative inversion is probably a special case of this.

Clefting   This is really a way of focusing the reader or hearer's attention on one particular phrase; for example, we can cleft sentence (26) in various ways:

(26)   Dogs chase cats.
(27)   It's dogs that chase cats.
(28)   It's cats that dogs chase.
(29)   What chases cats is dogs.
(30)   What dogs chase is cats.

However clefting also gives extra flexibility in positioning phrases, and could help us with all three of our problem sentences, provided the 'focusing' effects were also acceptable:

(31a)   What were on it were *some cakes with pink and green icing and little bits of holly on top.*
(31b)   What attracted me were *some cakes with pink and green icing and little bits of holly on top.*

(31c)   What I bought for them were *some cakes with pink and green icing and little bits of holly on top.*

This is a long list, but every construction is one which children use from an early age in everyday conversation, so your aim is not to teach them anything new (apart from a little terminology, which isn't really important). The point of the lesson is simply to make them more aware of the resources that are already at their disposal, in order to encourage them to use these resources more readily in their own writing, and to help them to identify the pros and cons of other people's writing.

Theoretical synopsis

We have covered too much grammatical ground in this chapter to allow a synopsis. I suppose the most general point that has emerged is that almost any message can be expressed in a wide variety of sentences, so the task of the apprentice language-user is to learn how to choose among the alternatives. What is interesting to a grammarian is how systematic a lot of the alternatives are, and how complex their interactions. For an educationalist I think the point of the chapter, as of this whole book, is that it is possible to lay all the alternatives out in a reasonably precise way, and even to get the pupils to discover them for themselves.

Part III

Aims and means

4

Why teach grammar?

Now that you know what grammar is, and some of the things that could be done with it in teaching, we can try to answer the big question: Why should we teach it? What I have said in earlier chapters may already have answered this question for you; I hope so. But it may still be helpful to see a presentation of the case for grammar, in order to round off the main part of the book. In an ideal world I would have started with this case, but that was ruled out by the need to explain first what grammar is.

Bear in mind that when I refer to grammar teaching, I am talking about the kind of teaching which I have been recommending here: purposeful teaching based on discovery-learning applied primarily to children's own non-standard language. (This warning is especially necessary if you are browsing through the book and haven't yet read the earlier chapters – be warned: what I mean by grammar and grammar teaching may well be quite different from what you expect!) Other kinds of grammar teaching are much harder to justify, and I hold no brief for them.

Here, then, is a list of reasons for teaching grammar as part of first-language English teaching. Some of them strike me as stronger than others, so I shall present the strongest and most important arguments first.

1   *To build linguistic self-respect*   One of the themes running through the reports of sociolinguistic research in Britain is the lack of linguistic self-confidence among most speakers. The subjects whose speech was investigated often told the researcher that they didn't speak very well and sometimes the self-criticism was so strong that terms like 'linguistic self-hatred' can be found in the literature.

This situation is socially disastrous. Being bad at speaking English isn't just like (say) being bad at football, or at gardening – skills that some have and others don't, but which affect only as much of your life as you allow. Speech is different, because it permeates the whole of your social life. The function of speech as a 'social badge' means that if you think your badge is second-rate, then it is only a very short step indeed to thinking that the group indicated by the badge is also second-rate. It would be naive of course to think that an improvement in the rating of badges will automatically transfer to the group as well, because so many other social and economic factors are involved in addition to the language, but at least it will be a significant step in the right direction.

Schools have a very special role to play in this process, because they have been largely responsible in the past for the downgrading of non-standard speech. Schools have been the main channels for the prescriptive ideas about the badness of non-standard dialects, and since they have been so effective in these efforts it is reasonable to hope that they can be equally effective in reversing the trends. However it is probably not enough for English teachers to express suitable general principles, such as 'All dialects are equal', and to refrain from critical comments. Much more than this is needed in order to overcome the prejudices which will still be expressed by other members of society (including teachers of other subjects).

The assumption on which this book is based is that by far the best way to raise the children's respect for their own dialect is to let them study its grammar along the lines of the lessons I suggested in part II. This is just a guess, but it seems a very reasonable one. At the very least it would dispel once and for all the myth that non-standard dialects have no grammar of their own, and are just 'slovenly' or 'lazy' failed attempts at the standard.

You may have noticed that all the lessons that I suggested required the pupils to study their *own* knowledge of language, and more specifically their knowledge of their ordinary language. In studying it, they will become aware of some of its regularities, complexities and inherent interest. As I explained in the chapter on Standard English, the differences between the standard dialect and other dialects are quite limited, so by studying their own language the class would in effect also be studying Standard English.

I focused directly on the differences between standard and non-standard in only one lesson, at level 6, but I think it would be excellent if any Standard/Town differences were pointed out whenever they cropped up in English lessons. I can think of no better way to defuse the conflict than to treat both Standard and Town as natural and legitimate objects of study in the English lesson.

The argument, then, is that teaching grammar will allow children to study their own ordinary language, regardless of whether this is a standard or non-standard dialect, and thereby to develop respect for it; and if they respect their own language more, then they should also think more highly of the social group to which that language belongs, and therefore of themselves.

However we can push the argument further. Teaching grammar in the way advocated in the National Curriculum means that the varieties taught by the school no longer threaten the child's native dialect, because all new varieties are simply additions to the existing ones, rather than alternatives in competition with them. These new varieties allow the child to operate in an increasingly wide range of social contexts, but they are not in competition with the local variety in the contexts where that is used. It seems reasonable to believe that a child is likely to be more successful in learning Standard English if this is not perceived as a threat to the child's existing dialect and social identity.

2   *To help in teaching Standard English*   These speculations about increased receptivity to Standard English may or may not be true, but there is another contribution that grammar teaching seems virtually certain to make to the teaching of Standard English: the framework of ideas and terminology will make it possible to teach Standard English directly.

This is bound to be an improvement on the present haphazard approach which exposes the children to 'good models' and hopes that they will draw their own conclusions as to the grammar of Standard English. As I explained in the section in chapter 2 on some basic principles, this approach raises a technical but very fundamental problem: in order to test a hypothesised rule derived from examples, you have to have negative examples as well as positive ones. It is not enough to see, for example, that *I did it* is part of Standard English; given the existence of alternative forms like *dreamed/dreamt*, the child also needs to know the negative fact that *I done it* is not part of Standard English; but this kind of information can never be found in a text. The whole process can be curtailed by direct instruction from a teacher.

It is hard to avoid the conclusion that a child's learning of Standard English, including the spelling system, must be helped if the teacher can bring the relevant facts into the open and express them in neat generalisations. I am not suggesting that this in itself is enough, but it will allow the teacher when correcting written work to write remarks like '*did*, not *done*, is the past tense of DO in Standard English', or even '*did* in Standard!'. And in more complex cases children are more likely to understand what they have to do if it has been explained properly.

For example, what do you say to a child who writes *We paid for the things what we bought*? It is no good saying that *what we bought* is not part of Standard English, because it is: *We paid for what we bought*. If you can refer to notions like 'relative clause', 'antecedent' and 'noun' the explanation is easy: in Standard English, *that* rather than *what* is used in a relative clause which has a noun as an antecedent. Without at least some of this conceptual apparatus, the teacher can give little help.

3 *To help in improving performance* The next argument is similar to the last: grammatical ideas and terminology are a useful tool in helping children to perform better (whether they are performing in standard or non-standard). Suppose a child writes a story containing the passage below (from material supplied by Mike Stubbs).

(1) The bells rang out louder and louder as I woke. I AM a

Polish girl I live at a Polazlogges home in Switzerland. I live at Switzerland because . . .

If notions like 'tense' are available they can be referred to not only in discussions, but also in correcting written work like this; so the teacher can count on being understood when he or she writes 'watch your tenses!', 'make sure your tenses are consistent!', or 'you switch here from past tense to present tense – why?' Without grammar teaching, the teacher can't refer to 'tense' in this way, still less explore the general principles of tense selection in narrative.

4 *To help in learning foreign languages* I have occasionally mentioned the possible links between grammar teaching in the English curriculum and applications of grammar in foreign-language teaching. This is one of the general themes of the 'language awareness' movement, a theme which I should have liked to stress more than I felt I could in a book written primarily for English teachers. The strength of the argument depends in part on the extent to which foreign-language teachers use grammatical terminology and explicit grammar-teaching, but even in these days of 'communicative' syllabuses explicit grammar plays some part in most foreign-language teaching, and is likely to play a larger part if it can be assumed that the children already know the relevant concepts.

Moreover, an increasing amount of language learning is now done by adults, for business or pleasure. This gives further point to the foundation of grammar which will be laid at school, and which will certainly be useful in adult language-learning. It will not only provide some basic terminology (which is often taken for granted), but will also make the whole enterprise more interesting because of comparisons that will be possible with the native language.

5 *To increase linguistic and cultural tolerance* The argument in this case rests in part on the assumption that the study of grammar will have included some consideration of dialects or languages other than the local non-standard and standard English. If this is so then the children should be that much

more willing to accept other varieties than their own as simply different, rather than as an object of mockery and contempt. But what if the direct consideration of other dialects and languages is minimal (as it may be, if we are realistic about what English teachers will be able to do, for some time to come)? There is some hope that the mere fact of considering their own language as an object of study may make pupils more objective about other people's language as well.

6   To teach scientific methods and analytical thinking   The mental processes involved in discovery-learning are very similar to those which scientists apply: notice a pattern or problem, guess at an explanation, make the explanation as precise as possible, then try it out on more data. More generally still, they involve three mental abilities which we should surely want to encourage in any subject: an observant awareness of structure in the world, an ability to generalise and to solve problems, and a belief that the whole world is, in principle, orderly and intelligible.

In the context of this set of aims, the study of a child's own grammar has a rather special place for the following reasons. First, the data are easily accessible at all times and absolutely free (no need for expensive laboratory equipment or school outings). Second, the data are of considerable interest and importance to the child, because they are part of its own mind. And third, the data are extremely clearly structured, so this is a good area to introduce the idea that even one's mental life can be made intelligible by objective study.

A rather fascinating line of speculation runs as follows. There is some evidence for fundamental cognitive differences between literate and illiterate communities, which are found regardless of the quality of the schooling that produced the literacy (Goody and Watt 1962; Org 1982). It seems that literates can consider hypothetical abstract states of affairs much more easily than illiterates can. The difference would emerge, for example, if the investigator asked the following question: Suppose that everyone who owned a house had to pay tax, and that some man owned a house, would he have to pay tax? Apparently illiterates find it hard to consider a situation without first filling in a lot of details such as who the man concerned was. Why should this ability be produced by learning to read and write? Is it because the acquisition of initial literacy is an example of the formal study of language structure (as it is, of course)? And if that is so, then how much more effective will a much more thorough and comprehensive study of language structure be?

7 To protect against linguistic exploitation For a long time English teachers have been trying to immunise children against the insidious effects of advertisements, propaganda and various kinds of prejudice (sexism, racism and so on). The reason why this role falls to English teachers is because of the fundamental part that language undoubtedly plays in developing our world-views. Values and beliefs are transmitted both through language and by language: through language when texts carry hidden messages, and by language when the grammar itself encourages a particular world-view. Presuppositions are an example of transmission through language (such as *Have you got your copy yet?*). Sexist bias is an example of transmission by language. One example of this is the preference for HE as a 'sex-neutral' pronoun, as in *When a pupil goes to school he makes new friends*. Another is the difference between pairs like the verbs FATHER and MOTHER, which imply very different activities (compare *He fathered the child* and *She mothered the child*), and convey correspondingly different images of the roles typically played by men and by women.

The best way to counter both kinds of transmission is to confront them head-on in the classroom, in the hope that this will make the children more aware of what is happening to them. If this happens then they may be less likely to hand on the same bundle of ideas to the next generation. But this kind of study of language is, of course, part of what I mean by the study of grammar.

8 To help understand language problems Language raises a variety of practical problems, and a formal study of language structure is likely to make some of these problems a little easier to solve. We have already considered the problems which are covered by first- and second-language teaching, but others are: what language policy to adopt within a bilingual family (for instance, should each parent speak only his/her own language to the children?), what to do about a child who seems to be developing language rather slowly, how to treat a friend or relative whose language is affected by illness (for instance, by a stroke). It is true that specialist advice is available for many of these problems, but we benefit more from expert advice the more expert we ourselves are.

9 *The deepening of general knowledge about language.* Britain is just emerging from a long period during which there seemed to be a widespread belief among highly educated people that there was no such thing as professional expertise in language. One of my main pieces of evidence for this claim is the persistence, and apparent popularity, of the series of five-minute programmes called 'Words' on BBC radio 3. These little talks are introduced as being about language, but the people who present them hardly ever have any professional expertise or training in the study of language – lawyers, clerics, philosophers, novelists, historians, but no linguists.

Publishers also seem to have very low standards indeed when it comes to matters of language. For example, a recent review in the *New Scientist* started with the startling sentence: 'English is probably the world's most lawless language.' The writer states this blandly, as though it were a well-known fact. I doubt if he would have dared to make a claim of this grandeur (and silliness) about any phenomenon other than language. Newspaper publishers also pander to the ignorance of self-appointed experts on language in their 'letters to the editors' sections, where they publish silly letters about split infinitives or recent innovations. Even the educated public seems to believe that in matters of language the amateur reigns supreme, as there is no subject-matter requiring instruction, understanding or expertise. This cannot be a healthy state of affairs.

5

Some non-standard dialect features

The following list of non-standard sentences is based on one compiled by Jenny Cheshire and Viv Edwards, who kindly allowed me to use their material. Their questionnaire was produced as part of a research project ('The survey of British dialects', project C-00-23-2264, funded by the Economic and Social Research Council), whose purpose is explained in an article containing the original questionnaire, see Edwards and Cheshire (1989). Unfortunately in revising their list I also had to omit the delightful illustrations by Dafydd Morriss.

Every sentence in the list is grammatical in some non-standard dialect. Whatever your local dialect, the list should offer some sentences which belong to it, while possibly provoking discussion on some of the other sentences. The list is certainly incomplete as an inventory of grammatical features that vary locally, to say nothing of local vocabulary, so you may well be able to add to it from your own knowledge.

There are many different ways in which this list can be used. You could use it yourself as a checklist, and never show it to the class, or they could go through it with you; and in the latter case, you could go straight through the entire list or take it in parts. It could simply introduce the idea of dialect diversity – the non-stop tourist approach. It could provide the basis for an interesting project, to find where some of the sentences that aren't accepted in your area are used – the geographer's approach. Individual local features that it reveals could be explored in some depth – the linguist's approach. Children could take it home to discuss with their parents or (better still) grandparents, to look for generation differences and changes underway – the historical approach. Each of these approaches could lead to important insights and entertaining lessons. You may photocopy it freely.

FORMS OF PRESENT-TENSE VERBS OTHER THAN BE

(1)   I **likes** toffees.
(2)   We **liken** toffees.
(3)   We **likes** toffees.
(4)   Thee **likes** toffees.
(5)   Thee **like** toffees.
(6)   She **like** toffees.
(7)   You **has** to see it to believe it.
(8)   We always **has** a big cake on our birthday.
(9)   What **have** her mother bought her?
(10) **Do** it go fast?
(11) **Does** we want to go fast?
(12) Fred **do** motor mechanics at college.
(13) I **does** it at school.
(14) You **mun** be at your music class by 9 a.m.
(15) You **maun** be at your music class by 9 a.m.
(16) He's out of tune, he **mun** be tone deaf.
(17) He's out of tune, he **maun** be tone deaf.

FORMS OF PAST-TENSE VERBS OTHER THAN BE

(18) He **done** that wrong.
(19) I **give** her a birthday present yesterday.
(20) I **gived** her a birthday present yesterday.
(21) Is that the car I **see** last night?
(22) Is that the car I **seed** last night?
(23) Is that the car I **sawed** last night?
(24) Is that the car I **seen** last night?
(25) I **writ** a letter yesterday.

PRESENT- AND PAST-TENSE FORMS OF BE

(26) Billy **be** stupid.
(27) Billy **am** stupid.

(28) Mary and John **is** getting married on Saturday.
(29) There**'s** cars outside the church.
(30) You **was** singing.
(31) You **wan** singing.
(32) We **was** singing.
(33) We **wan** singing.
(34) They **was** singing.
(35) They **wan** singing.
(36) I **were** singing, too.
(37) So **were** John.
(38) Mary **weren't** singing.
(39) There **was** some singers here a minute ago.

OTHER VERB-FORMS

(40) We've **gotten** her a present too – a car!
(41) She was **sat** over there looking at her car.
(42) He was **stood** in the corner looking at it.
(43) I've **a-found** my keys. Let's go!
(44) We'd like to **looken** at the TV you broke.
(45) We're **a-going** to start eating now.

NEGATION

(46) **Dinna** run too fast.
(47) You **shouldna** go in there!
(48) You've **no** to go in there!
(49) My friend broke that, I **never**.
(50) No, I **never** broke that.
(51) **Will you not** try to mend it – we need an expert.
(52) That **ain't** working.
(53) That **in't** working.
(54) That **ay** working.
(55) He **in arf** stupid.
(56) **Not** do that, John.
(57) Count on me, I **won't** do **nothing** silly.
(58) **Anyone** mustn't go in there!

SUBJECTS: DUMMIES, INVERSION AND TAGS

(59) He's stupid, **him**.
(60) He's stupid, **is Billy**.
(61) **It's stupid** he is.
(62) **It** was **stupid** he was.
(63) **There's stupid** he is.
(64) Would he do such a thing, **think you**?
(65) I asked him **did he** know who had taken it?
(66) The bride's walking into the church, **is it**?
(67) I'm going to see them now, **isn't it**?

VERBS IN COMBINATION

(68) One of the singers said he**'ll** not **can** stay.
(69) He **might can** do it tomorrow.
(70) The other one said he **won't can't** do it.
(71) I **done bought** them a wedding present.
(72) How the dog **do jumpy**! He'll knock it over.
(73) I **d' eat** chicken every day.
(74) I **do be eating** chicken every day.
(75) I **did eat** chicken every day when I lived there.
(76) I **did eat** chicken yesterday, too.
(77) **Let you be listening** to me, Joanna.
(78) **Do ee listen** to me.
(79) **Don't be talking** like that.
(80) We **managed mend** it ourselves.
(81) He **has** it **mended** twice already.
(82) We**'re gone** shopping.
(83) You **should of** left half an hour ago!

USES OF TENSES AND VERB-COMBINATIONS

(84) I **know** that builder all my life.
(85) She's been a walking disaster since she**'s** here.

(86) **Are** you waiting long for the plumber?
(87) **Did** you have your dinner yet?
(88) **Are** you **wanting** something to eat?
(89) Look! The kettle **boils**.
(90) I **be eating** chicken every day.
(91) Who **is** this book **belonging** to?
(92) If you **had've** been there, you would have seen her.
(93) If you **would've** been there, you would have seen her.
(94) You **haven't got to** be late, or you'll be in trouble.

VERB LINKERS

(95) I've come **for to** mend the window.
(96) I've come **for** mend the door.
(97) He's **after going** away, but he'll be back soon.
(98) I'd like to buy this house **without** you want it.
(99) Change the subject, **else** I'll go mad.

NOUN PLURALS AND NUMERALS

(100) That town is nearly twenty **mile** away.
(101) To make a big cake you need two **pound** of flour.
(102) This string is three **inch** long.
(103) This is a **scissors**.
(104) Look at these coins. I found about **a fifty** of them.

PRONOUN SUBJECT/OBJECT FORMS

(105) **Me's** got a good appetite.
(106) **Him's** got a good appetite.
(107) **Her's** got a good appetite.
(108) **Them's** got a good appetite.
(109) Give **I** a cup of tea!
(110) Give **he** a cup of tea!
(111) Give **she** a cup of tea!

(112)   Give **we** a cup of tea!
(113)   Give **they** a cup of tea!

POSSESSIVES

(114)   This is **me** cup.
(115)   This is **o'me** cup.
(116)   This is **mines** cup.
(117)   Eat up **thee** cake.
(118)   Eat up **thy** cake.
(119)   That's my car, where's **yourn**?
(120)   This is **he's** cup.
(121)   That's my car, where's **hisn**?
(122)   That's my car, where's **hern**?
(123)   **It** cover's got a mark on it.
(124)   **O'it** cover's got a mark on it.
(125)   This is **us** car.
(126)   This is **wer** car.
(127)   This is **wir** car.
(128)   This is my book. **Whosen** is that?
(129)   These are my **father** boots.
(130)   These are my **father** boots laces.
(131)   Don't break the **cup's** handle.

PRONOUNS: MISCELLANEOUS

(132)   **Himself** gets scared.
(133)   Did you see **herself** there?
(134)   We service it **usselves**.
(135)   John likes doing that **hisself**.
(136)   Lots of people do it **theirselves**.
(137)   Give **it me**. That's my book.
(138)   Give **me it**. That's my book.
(139)   **Thee's** hungry, I expect.
(140)   Are **youse** hungry, you boys over there?

DEMONSTRATIVES

(141) Look at **them** spiders.
(142) Look at **thon** spiders.
(143) Look at **they** spiders.
(144) Look at **this** spiders.
(145) Look at **yon** beetle.
(146) Look at **thon** beetle.
(147) Look at **thir** beetle.
(148) Look at **thick** beetle.
(149) Look at **thicky** beetle.
(150) Look at **thuck** beetle.
(151) Look at **theasum** worm.
(152) Look at **this here** worm.
(153) Look at **that there** worm.

DETERMINERS

(154) We've got **a old** house.
(155) Your house is **an recent** one.
(156) We've got **old** house.
(157) Look at **time**; you're late for school!
(158) I'll have **the headache** if I carry on talking.

RELATIVE CLAUSES

(159) The films **what** I like best are horror films.
(160) The films **as** I like best are horror films.
(161) The films **at** I like best are horror films.
(162) Let's go to that film that you wanted to see **it**.
(163) I've got a friend can watch films all night.
(164) The film **what** was on last night was good.
(165) The film **as** was on last night was good.
(166) The film **at** was on last night was good.
(167) That's the girl **what's** mum loves horror films.

(168) That's the girl **what her** mum loves horror films.
(169) That's the girl **that her** mum loves horror films.
(170) That's the girl **as her** mum loves horror films.
(171) That's the girl **at's her** mum loves horror films.

ADJECTIVE COMPARATIVE FORMS

(172) This is the **beautifullest** house I've seen.
(173) This is the **most beautifullest** house I've seen.
(174) I've never seen a **beautifuller** one.
(175) I've never seen a **more beautifuller** one.
(176) This is a **more better** one.
(177) This is a **more betterer** one.
(178) John's got a nice house, but yours is **more nice**.
(179) This is the **worstest** one I've seen.
(180) This is the **baddest** one I've seen.
(181) I've never seen a **worser** one.
(182) I've never seen a **badder** one.

ADVERBS, PREPOSITIONS, PARTICLES

(183) I like pasta. It cooks **real quick**.
(184) He knocks his hat **off of** his head.
(185) Goodbye, I'll **away** now.
(186) She goes to church **of a** Sunday.
(187) We live **aside** the cinema.
(188) We're going pictures.
(189) I'm going **up** my friend's house later.
(190) I'm going **down** my friend's house later.
(191) I'm going **over** my friend's house later.
(192) That's the father **on** Mary.
(193) Stop it! He's my best friend, **like**.

6

Useful books

All the books that I list here are intended for non-specialists, and should be very suitable for anyone who wants to follow up the points made in this book. I have classified them for your convenience, but of course this classification is imperfect. The full bibliographical details are contained in the list of references at the end of the book. Most of the books are paperbacks costing less than £10; I have indicated the ones which cost more than this.

Reference-work on language in general

Crystal (1987), *The Cambridge Encyclopedia of Language*, is a splendid volume, which deserves a place in every school. Beautifully presented, easily accessible and stuffed with fascinating information on everything to do with language. Cost about £27 in 1989.

Reference works on English grammar

Quirk et al. (1985), *A Comprehensive Grammar of the English Language*, is the ultimate, but at about £50 it is too dear for most – though this is in fact cheap for the 1,700 pages it contains.

Crystal (1988), *The English Language*, is billed as 'A guided tour of the language by the presenter of BBC Radio 4's *English Now*'. As readable and interesting as it sounds, but not a great deal about English grammar as such.

Greenbaum (1991), *An Introduction to English Grammar*, is a non-technical introduction with chapters on highly relevant topics like punctuation and written style.

Huddleston (1984), *An Introduction to the Grammar of English*, is a weighty and authoritative discussion of most of the main facts. Although organised as a textbook rather than as a reference work, it is probably more suitable for reference.

Huddleston (1988), *English Grammar: An Outline* is a much shorter, cheaper and readable book than the above. Good for reading straight through in order to get an overview of the grammar of English.

Leech (1989), *An A–Z of English Grammar*, is a dictionary-style reference book on all the traditional terms and some more recent ones as well. Very useful for English teachers.

Phythian (1980), *Teach Yourself English Grammar*. A very accessible and generally sensible guide to the basic concepts of traditional grammar, as applied to English.

Quirk and Stein (1990), *English in Use*, is a collection of essays on modern English, especially good on variation within Standard English.

Teaching of English as a first language

Perera (1984), *Children's Writing and Reading: Analysing Classroom Language*, is a very useful, accessible and thoughtful survey by a linguist of the 'state of the art' in research on the teaching and learning of the first language. It covers many of the topics I discuss, but in more depth.

Stubbs (1986), *Educational Linguistics*: another very interesting and useful guide to the ways in which linguistics bears on the teaching of the first language.

Hawkins (1987), *Awareness of Language: An Introduction*, is the main reference for the 'language awareness' movement.

Cheshire et al. (1989), *Dialect and Education: Some European perspectives*, is a very interesting collection of papers about how non-standard dialects are treated in various European countries – Belgium, Denmark, Germany, the Netherlands and the UK.

Walmsley (1984), 'The uselessness of "formal grammar"', is a pamphlet commissioned by the Committee for Linguistics in Education and gives an interesting review of the depths reached by grammar teaching in its death-throes, and of the way in which this was used as evidence against all grammar teaching.

Introductions to grammar

Burton-Roberts (1986), *Analysing Sentences: An Introduction to English Syntax*, takes the reader into English grammar by a discovery-learning approach.

Leech et al. (1982), *English Grammar for Today: A New Introduction*, gives a more systematic tour through English grammar, with less on background theory, while paying quite a lot of attention to matters of concern to English teachers.

Palmer (1971), *Grammar*, includes a linguistic view of traditional grammar and an introduction to the main current ideas.

Introductions to linguistics

Aitchison (1978), *Teach Yourself Linguistics*, is a simple and very accessible introduction.

Aitchison (1976), *The Articulate Mammal*, is an outstandingly interesting popular account of psycholinguistics with particular emphasis on how we learn language.

Aitchison (1987), *Words in the Mind*, shows how psychologists and linguists can throw light on the structure of our knowledge of language, with special reference to vocabulary. Very well written.

Bolinger and Sears (1981), *Aspects of Language*, is a very rich, readable and broad survey of the state of the art as of the early 1980's. Bolinger is a novelist, and his sensitivity to language shows through in this book. An attractive American textbook – like Fromkin and Rodman below – but somewhat more expensive.

Brown (1984), *Linguistics Today,* is a broad overview of the main developments in theoretical linguistics (mainly syntax), accessible to the layperson.

Fromkin and Rodman (1988), *An Introduction to Language,* is a witty, wide-ranging and best-selling American textbook, complete with cartoons. Extremely good value.

Hudson (1984), *An Invitation to Linguistics,* is aimed primarily at people who are wondering whether to study linguistics at college or university. My excuse for mentioning it here is that it surveys the kinds of activity that are included in the study of language.

Radford (1988), *Transformational Grammar: A First Course,* is an excellent introduction to transformational syntax, with every step in the argument laid out in minute detail. The fact that it takes 600 pages to give only half the story shows how much there is to know.

Smith and Wilson (1979), *Modern Linguistics: The Results of Chomsky's Revolution,* gives a very Chomskyan view of language, with interesting extensions into questions of language use.

Dialects and prescriptivism

Aitchison (1981), *Language Change: Progress or Decay?,* focuses on the inevitability, and neutrality, of language change. Very readable and relevant.

Anderson and Trudgill (1990), *Bad Language,* is about attitudes to non-standard dialects and other matters.

Coupland (1990), *English in Wales,* is a collection of articles about the accent and dialect variation found in the English spoken in various parts of Wales.

Freeborn et al. (1986), *Varieties of English: An Introduction to the Study of Language,* is the standard textbook for the NJB A-level in English Language. As its title suggests, it specialises in dialect and register differences, and contains a great deal of useful material.

Hudson (1980), *Sociolinguistics,* is an undergraduate-level textbook about this important branch of linguistics. It includes a chapter on attitudes to language variation as well as chapters on many of the other topics we have touched on in this book.

Hughes and Trudgill (1987), *English Accents and Dialects*, is shorter than Trudgill (1990), but includes a very useful checklist of the main dialect and accent features of ten cities, not all of which are within England.

Milroy and Milroy (1985a), 'Regional variation in British English syntax', was never properly published, though it may become available. It is an important quarry of facts about specifically syntactic variation among dialects, covering the whole of the British Isles, but fortunately many of the facts have been incorporated into published books like Hughes and Trudgill (1987) and Trudgill (1990).

Milroy and Milroy (1985b), *Authority in Language. Investigating Language Prescription and Standardisation*, is a scholary but very readable study of the benefits of standardisation and the accompanying danger of prescriptivism, with special reference to the UK. Highly relevant!

Trudgill (1974), *Sociolinguistics: An Introduction*, is a popular book about the whole of sociolinguistics, including chapters on how language variation reflects various kinds of social differences (in age, sex, social class, etc., as well as region of origin).

Trudgill (1975), *Accent, Dialect and the School*, is a somewhat polemical discussion of how non-standard dialects should be treated in school. Interesting and readable.

Trudgill (1990), *The Dialects of England*, is a very useful factual survey of differences among regional accents and dialects within England. Lots of material for use in the classroom!

Upton et al. (1987), *Word Maps: A Dialect Atlas of England*, is a very useful collection of 200 maps, each of which shows the geographical distribution of one set of words (e.g. words meaning 'dandruff') or pronunciations. Quite a lot of the maps show interesting grammatical variation, such as the one for the alternatives to *We are* (*We/us are/am/be/bin*). Lots of useful material for class work, but limited to England.

Grammar of other languages

Comrie (1989), *Language Universals and Linguistic Typology*, is an excellent undergraduate-level textbook on the similarities and differences that are to be expected among languages. Clearly and simply written, so the technicalities don't loom too large.

Grammars for particular languages may be available in any well-stocked library or bookshop. However a good place to start in looking for information about the languages in your school would be a series of books published by the Centre for Information on Language Teaching and Research (Regent's College, Inner Circle, Regent's Park, London NW1; 071-486 8221), which includes titles such as *Teaching Britain's Community Languages: Materials and Methods* and *Britain's South Asian Languages*. CILT also publishes a series of Resource Guides for Teachers, each of which deals with one language.

Books about language as a distorter of truth

Bolinger (1980), *Language. The Loaded Weapon: The Use and Abuse of Language Today*, is the classic in this field – very readable, stuffed with excellent material (mostly American), about a wide range of abuses of language from advertising to sexism.

Cameron (1985), *Feminism and Linguistic Theory*, is one of several recent books on sexism in language, but presents a British rather than an American perspective.

Spender (1980), *Man Made Language*, is a more popular British book on the same theme, with plenty of material.

Part IV

An encyclopedia of grammar

'Encyclopedia' is probably too grand a name for this part of the book, as it suggests a comprehensiveness which you won't find. All I have tried to do is to explain the technical terms that I have used in this book; I have not attempted complete coverage of all grammatical terms. If you read any of the more technical books about grammar and grammatical theory you will meet a lot of terms that I haven't covered; but you can also expect them to be explained as they are introduced, so there's not much point in my trying to cover them all here. If you want a more comprehensive collection I recommend Geoffrey Leech's *A–Z of English Grammar* (Leech 1989).

The reason for calling the following an encyclopedia is that it is more than a glossary or dictionary. Instead of a pithy definition for each term, you will find a little article which is intended to be self-explanatory (once you have looked up the cross-references). This policy made it necessary to introduce some additional terms which are needed as background to the concepts which I used in the text, and in principle it could have justified including just about every single term that has ever been used in grammar. I kept this proliferation to the minimum, so what you have is a compromise between a minimum list containing just the terms used here, and an 'encyclopedic', all-embracing, survey of all known grammatical terminology.

Three other points:

(a) I have assumed that you can apply ordinary English word-formation rules (as explained in the entry for 'word-formation'). For example I have used the term 'modification' in the entry for 'adjective', but there is no entry for 'modification' as such, only one for 'modifier'.

(b)   The sign '$' before a word or phrase acts as a guide to a similar headword elsewhere in this encyclopedia.

(c)   As you would expect in any academic discipline there is a certain amount of variation in terminology, with different scholars using different names for precisely the same concept. If you read other books you may find it helpful to know about these synonyms, so I have included them here by simple one-line entries containing '=' (for instance, 'ADJUNCT = $modifier' tells you that 'adjunct' means the same as 'modifier', and that the latter is the term used and explained here).

ACTIVE

Any $form of a $verb that is not $passive is active.

ADJECTIVE

'Adjective' is the name for one of the main $word-classes of English (and of many other languages, though not all). Typical examples: QUICK, ENTHUSIASTIC, FRENCH. The following $rules apply to typical adjectives:

- An adjective either takes the *-er* and *-est* $inflectional $suffixes (e.g. QUICK, with *quicker* and *quickest*) or allows $modification by a preceding MORE or MOST (*more/most enthusiastic*).
- An adjective takes the *-ly* suffix that makes it into an $adverb (standard English) or allows $conversion to an adverb (non-standard) – *He did it* QUICKLY/QUICK.
- An adjective can modify a $common noun (e.g. *quick speech*).
- An adjective can be a $predicative complement (e.g. *They are quick*).

ADJUNCT = $modifier

ADVERB

A major $word-class, whose members can $modify $verbs,

$adjectives or other $adverbs – i.e. anything other than nouns; e.g. *really* in: *I really hate it*; *a really big bottle*; *He'll come really soon*; but *a really success*. Unfortunately very few adverbs can occur in all positions open to adverbs in general, so most generalisations have to be made in relation to particular subclasses of adverb. Typical examples are QUICKLY, SOON, ACTUALLY, ONLY, VERY. Some adverbs are formed by adding the $lexical $suffix *-ly* to an adjective.

AFFIX

A part of a word which is not the $stem and which has an identifiable $morphological function, either $inflectional or $lexical; e.g. *-s* in *dogs*, *-ing* in *washing*, *-er* in FARMER, *un-* in UNTIDY. Affixes are either $prefixes or $suffixes in English, though some languages allow 'infixes'.

AGREEMENT

Words that are closely related in the $syntactic structure are sometimes required to have the same $value for some $feature (or set of features); e.g. THIS or THAT must have the same $number as its $complement (a $common noun): *this/*these book*, but *these/*this books*. This relation is called 'agreement' (or $concord). English is often said to have $subject–verb agreement, but this is debatable (for reasons stated in the entry below for that concept).

AMBIGUITY

Any word or sentence which can be analysed in more than one way is ambiguous. Ambiguity may involve only the $semantic structure (e.g. *The bank is over there*, referring either to a river bank or to a 'money shop'), or only the $syntactic structure (e.g. in *He is not coping* the word *not* can be taken as a modifier of either *is* or *coping*, without any consequences for the semantics); but most syntactic ambiguity also involves semantic ambiguity (e.g. *I can not speak*: if *not* modifies *can* it means

'I am unable to speak', but if it modifies *speak* the sentence means 'I am able not to speak').

ANTECEDENT

The word to which a $pronoun refers, and which is typically 'preceding' (Latin: *antecedent-*) it. In traditional grammar the term is mainly applied to the noun before a $relative $pronoun, e.g. to *man* in *the man who did it*, where *man* is the antecedent of *who*.

AUXILIARY VERB

A special kind of $verb whose main role is supposedly to 'help' (Latin *auxiliar-* = helping) other verbs, by providing extra information about such matters as the time of the event; e.g. WILL is an auxiliary verb, as it combines with another verb and means that the event referred to by the other verb is located in future time.

Like any other $word-class, this is justified by the rules that apply to it, and indeed a class which is traditionally called 'auxiliary verb', containing e.g. WILL but not GET, can easily be justified in English because all the following rules refer to it:

- A $tensed auxiliary verb may either be modified by a following NOT, or contain the suffix -*n't* (e.g. *will not*, or *won't*, but not *get not*, *getn't*).
- A tensed auxiliary verb may precede its subject, by $subject-auxiliary inversion (e.g. *will they?* but *get they?*).
- An auxiliary verb must not function as the $complement of DO (e.g. *They do get* but not *They do will*).

But *none* of these rules refer to the auxiliary verb's relation to the verb that it is supposed to be 'helping'. This relation is shared with plenty of other verbs which are clearly *not* auxiliary verbs according to these rules, such as GET, whose

range of possible complements is similar to those found with
BE (a clear auxiliary verb):

He was/got talking to her.

He was/got selected for interview.

He was/got to talk to the star.

He was/got fit.

The English auxiliary verbs are: BE, HAVE (e.g. *have seen*),
HAVE (e.g. *have blue eyes*, but only for the rapidly dwindling
group of speakers who allow *Has she blue eyes?* or *She hasn't
blue eyes*), DO (e.g. *I do like peaches*), WILL, SHALL, CAN, MAY,
MUST, OUGHT, USED, NEED (e.g. *Need you go now?*), DARE (e.g. *I
daren't risk it*). Most of these belong to the special subclass of
auxiliary verbs called $modal verbs.

Conclusion: the $word-class 'auxiliary verb' plays an
important part in English grammar, but its name is quite
misleading. A better one would be 'polarity verb', which
reflects the important part these verbs play in marking
$polarity: positive *will* versus negative *won't*, and $declarative
they will versus the yes–no $interrogative *will they?*.

CASE

Case is a $feature whose values tend to be given names
such as 'nominative', 'accusative', 'genitive' and 'dative' (all of
which are taken straight from traditional Latin grammar). A
noun's case typically varies with its $function: when the noun
is used as the $subject of a $tensed verb its case is nominative,
when it is used as the object of a verb its case is (typically)
accusative, and so on. Being a $morphosyntactic feature it
should be marked by $morphology, but in English only six
$dictionary-words have distinct forms for different functions:
ME (*me/I*), HIM (*him/he*), HER (*her/she*), US (*us/we*), THEM
(*them/they*), WHO (*who/whom*); and the $possessive *'s* is a
separate word (a $determiner), not a $suffix; so it is debatable
whether English has 'case' at all.

CLASSIFICATION

The 'classification' of a word is the $word-class to which it belongs, plus the $feature-values that it has; e.g. the classification of *dogs* is 'plural noun' (value 'plural' for the feature 'number'; word-class 'noun'). Classification contrasts with $function, which refers to the word's relation to other words in the same sentence or phrase. For example, in *history lecture*, the word *history* must be classified as a singular common noun, in spite of its function as $modifier of another common noun (*lecture*). A popular alternative analysis is to say that in this phrase *history* is an adjective, on the grounds that only adjectives can modify nouns in this way. If this had been correct, then *history*, as an adjective, should in turn take $adverbs, not $adjectives, as its modifiers (cf. *extremely good*, not *extreme good*); but in fact it takes adjectives, as in *recent history lecture*, 'lecture on recent history', not *recently history lecture*.

CLAUSAL OBJECT

One kind of $complement is a clausal object, which is, roughly speaking, a $clause: a $phrase $rooted in a $verb. This verb is generally a $tensed one (because otherwise its $function would be $×complement); e.g. *I know she likes me*, where *likes* is the (tensed) root of the clause *she likes me*, which is the clausal object of *know*. (Another way of saying the same thing is to say that *likes* itself is the clausal object of *know*.) In most cases, however, the clausal-object phrase is rooted in a special clause-introducing word other than this verb, such as a $complementiser (e.g. THAT) or an $interrogative $pronoun (e.g. WHO): *I know that she likes me; I wonder who she invited*. The structures for two clausal objects are given on p. 211. The clausal object is an 'object' in that it can (in some cases) be made into the $subject under $passivisation: *That the world is flat is believed only by a few people these days*.

CLAUSE

A $phrase whose $root word is a $verb; e.g. the phrase *you*

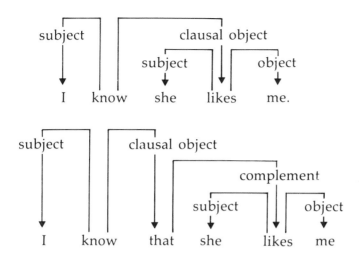

know the way and the entire sentence *Since you know the way, you can drive.* Traditionally the linking word *since* is considered part of the clause that it introduces, but nowadays it is analysed as a $preposition so *since you can drive* is a $prepositional-phrase, not a clause. Another difference between traditional and modern analyses lies in the modern assumption that one clause may be a part of another one; traditionally this sentence would have been broken into two separate clauses, *since you know the way* and *you can drive.* This kind of analysis is generally rejected now because the $function of *since you know the way* is very similar to that of a prepositional phrase like *in view of your skill,* which both traditionally and nowadays is treated as part of the clause rooted in *can.* And finally, contrary to traditional grammar *you . . . drive* is also a clause, although it is discontinuous, and more generally every verb in a sentence acts as the root of a different clause. In the diagram on p. 212 the clauses are shown by the lines beneath the words. A clause may be the whole of a sentence; e.g. *I like you.*

CLEFT SENTENCE

The following are both cleft sentences:

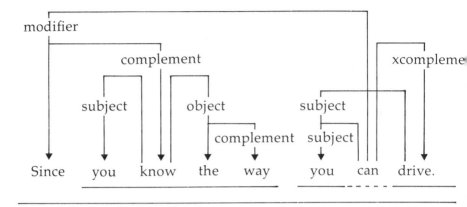

It was that pizza that I ordered. (It-cleft)

What I ordered was that pizza. (Wh-cleft)

In both cases the sentence is split ('cleft') in two: *that pizza* and the rest. The effect of this splitting is to focus attention on *that pizza* and to treat the rest as $presupposed. In both cases the presupposed part is expressed by a $relative clause, though the relative clauses are of different types. The $root verb is BE, used to identify the focused element *that pizza* as also the element missing from the relative clause.

CLITIC

In *He's tired*, *'s* must be a separate word, a $finite verb, because the sentence would be ungrammatical without one and there is no other candidate. But *'s* is like an $affix in many respects – e.g. its shortness and lack of a vowel. Words with affix-like characteristics are called 'clitics'. They play an important part in the grammar of some languages, such as French, where the rules for positioning some clitics are different from those for ordinary words; e.g. French personal $pronouns have clitic variants (e.g. *me, te, le*) which are attached to the beginning of the verb (e.g. *Jean me connait*, 'John knows me'), whereas non-clitic objects normally follow the verb (e.g. *Jean connait Marie*).

COMMON NOUN

A $noun which (a) may combine with a $determiner, and (b) if it is singular and $countable, must combine with one. For instance, DOG, DAY and DOT are countable, so when singular they must have a determiner: *a dog, every day, this dot*. In contrast, $pronouns cannot combine with a determiner (e.g. *a someone, *that him), and $proper nouns either need no determiner even when countable and singular (e.g. FRED, LONDON) or always have THE (e.g. THE THAMES, THE SUDAN).

COMPARATIVE

1. One of the values for the $degree $feature – e.g. *bigger, better, sooner, more*.
2. A range of $structures which contain comparative (in the first sense) words and a few others, and which have in common the fact that they compare one thing with another. The following are some examples:

Fred is bigger than Bill.

Fred is bigger than Bill used to be at this age.

Fred loves Mary more than her, him.

More people came to my party than to yours.

More girls than boys like languages more than science.

More girls like languages than boys like science.

Fred is more cunning than clever.

Fred is less tall than Bill.

Fred is as tall as Bill.

The sooner you come, the longer we can talk.

This government spends less on education than did its predecessor. (See %subject–auxiliary inversion.)

My name is different from/than yours.

My name is the same as yours.

Persil washes whiter.

Comparative structures are among the most complex in syntax, and have correspondingly complex $semantic structures. They are among the hardest to use and deserve serious attention in school.

COMPETENCE

Linguistic knowledge, contrasted with the behaviour that is produced on the basis of this knowledge, which is called $performance.

COMPLEMENT

$Syntactic $functions are commonly divided into two major groups, complements and $modifiers, plus a number of other individual functions, notably $subject. (Some linguists regard subjects as a type of complement, but most don't.) Roughly speaking, complements are attached more tightly than modifiers to their heads – hence the name 'complement', implying that they 'complete' the meaning introduced by the head. This difference between complements and modifiers is often (though not always) reflected in the word order; for example, in *students of linguistics with long hair*, the phrases *of linguistics* and *with long hair* are respectively the complement and the modifier of *students*, and could not occur in reversed order, with the modifier closer than the complement to their shared $head: *students with long hair of linguistics*.

The following subtypes of complement are recognised for English: $object, $particle, $prepositional object, $×complement, $clausal object and $semi-complement. In traditional grammar, the term 'complement' was used to mean the same as '×complement'.

COMPLEMENTISER

Words like THAT, WHETHER and IF are nowadays called 'complementisers'. Their syntactic characteristic is to precede a

$clause, and to mark it as subordinate to some other part of the sentence; e.g. in *I hope that it rains*, the complementiser *that* marks the following clause, *it rains*, as subordinate to *hope*. The traditional name is '$subordinating conjunction'.

The name 'complementiser' is awful, and stems from the days when the only subordinate clauses that linguists had got round to studying had the $function of $complement of a $verb; but the name has stuck and is very widely used even where the subordinate clause has a function other than complement, such as $subject or $modifier!

COMPOUND

A compound is a $dictionary-word whose $stem contains the stems of more than one other dictionary-word, e.g. BOOK–CASE, containing the stems of BOOK and of CASE. In English the second stem of a compound generally defines the general meaning of which the first stem picks out a subtype; e.g. a book-case is a type of case, not a type of book. In this respect the second stem is like the $head in a dependency relation.

CONCORD = $agreement

CONDITIONAL

A conditional $clause is a subordinate clause that expresses a condition. The simplest cases are introduced by IF, but other $structures are also relevant:

I'll go if you do.

I'll go unless you do.

Had anyone asked me I'd have gone. (See $subject–auxiliary inversion.)

I'll go whether I'm invited or not.

I'll go whatever happens.

I'll go come what may.

The $semantics of $tense in conditionals is rather complex. We can distinguish three main patterns:

(a) I'll go if you do/I (always) go if you do.

(b) I'd go if you did.

(c) I'd have gone if you had.

Terms like 'hypothetical' and 'counterfactual' are applied to some of these patterns, but the challenge is to decide precisely what these terms mean. The contrasts involve careful matching of the tenses in the conditional clause and the main clause, which children often find hard to do.

CONJUNCTION

A very small but important $word-class, whose members are AND, OR, BUT, NOR and (probably) THEN. These words signal $coordination, and are located at the start of the last $conjunct, and (optionally) at the start of each other conjunct except the first: ([*Tom*] [*and Dick*] [*and Harry*]) or ([*Tom*],[*Dick*] [*and Harry*]). The reason for considering THEN a conjunction is that it allows the $subject to be shared by two $verbs, a characteristic of coordination: *He* ([*had a bath*] [*then went to bed*]).

These conjunctions are the traditional 'coordinating conjunctions', which are traditionally contrasted with so-called '$subordinating conjunctions' like BECAUSE and AFTER. Most grammarians now treat the latter as a kind of $preposition.

CONVERSION

Conversion is the branch of $word-formation responsible for the relations between two $dictionary-words whose $shapes are the same but whose characteristics are such that one can be analysed as derived from the other; e.g. the $noun RISE (e.g. *a rise in pay*) is derived by conversion from the $verb RISE.

COORDINATION

Coordination is one kind of $syntactic relation between words in a sentence, and contrasts with $subordination. As the term suggests, the words linked by coordination have the same status, and the same relations to the rest of the sentence; for example, in *Fred and Mary snore*, the coordinated words, *Fred* and *Mary*, share the $function '$subject of *snore*'. Coordination is generally marked in English by one of the $conjunctions AND, OR, BUT, NOR. A string of words unified by coordination in the first sense is called 'a coordination'.

COUNTABLE NOUN

A $nouns is countable if it $refers to an individual entity, e.g. DOT, PIECE, STAR, TWIG, PERSON, FRED. In contrast, a '$mass' noun refers to a substance rather than to individual portions of it, e.g. STUFF, WINE, PATIENCE. Countable nouns can generally be made $plural, and when singular a countable common noun must be accompanied by a $determiner. Many English $common nouns may be used in either way, to refer either to an individual or to a substance, with syntax varying accordingly; e.g. CHOCOLATE in *He eats chocolate every evening* versus *He eats a chocolate every evening*.

DECLARATIVE

A $value for the $feature $mood, which contrasts with $interrogative, $imperative and $exclamative. A declarative $clause is an 'ordinary' one which typically expresses a statement, such as *I like you*. The same syntactic sentence- pattern could however be used to issue a command (e.g. *Hats will be worn at all times*).

DEFINITE

A $noun may be either definite or $indefinite, a distinction which relates to whether or not the hearer already knows the entity $referred to. If the noun is definite, the hearer is assumed already to know the entity, so the definiteness tells the hearer to find this particular entity in memory; but if it is indefinite the hearer introduces a new entity into the current mental 'scene'. For example, imagine the following story. 'Once upon a time, there was a king [indefinite, so new entity] who had a son [likewise]. The king [definite, so a known entity – namely the king just mentioned] said to his son [likewise] . . . .'

DEGREE

A $feature whose $values are 'positive', '$comparative' and 'superlative'; e.g. *big, bigger, biggest; much, more, most; good, better, best.* This feature applies to most short $adjectives, and a few $adverbs (e.g. WELL, SOON). Most adjectives or adverbs whose meaning allows comparison can be modified by *more, most, less, least* or *as* (e.g. *more beautiful, most successfully, less complete, least badly, as good, as quickly*).

DEPENDENT

In the $syntactic structure of a sentence, every word except the $sentence-root depends on some other word, its $head; e.g. in *Small children cry, small* depends on *children,* and *children* depends on *cry.* Dependency is a very general kind of $function, which can be broken down into more precise kinds: $complement, $modifier, $subject. It is also known as $subordination. In the diagrams that I have been using to show sentence structures, each arrow indicates a dependency, pointing from the head towards the dependent. In English most heads precede their dependents, so the following is a typical sentence structure:

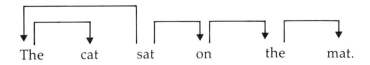

The   cat   sat   on   the   mat.

DERIVATIONAL MORPHOLOGY = $lexical morphology

DESCRIPTIVE GRAMMAR

1. When contrasted with $generative grammar, descriptive grammar concentrates on facts rather than on how to integrate them into a completely explicit, formalised, grammar.
2. When contrasted with $prescriptive grammar, descriptive grammar takes language as it is, rather than as the grammarian thinks it ought to be.

DETERMINER

The following $dictionary-words are determiners:

- $indefinite: A, SOME, ANY, EITHER, NO, NEITHER, WHICH, EVERY, EACH, ONE;

- $definite: THE, THIS, THAT;

- $possessive: MY, YOUR, HIS, HER, ITS, OUR, THEIR; whose; 'S.

What these dictionary-words have in common is that they all satisfy the following $rule: a singular $countable $common noun cannot be used without a determiner. For instance, BOOK can be used in the singular only if preceded by one of these words: *I bought book, but I bought a/the/every/your book. Another shared property is that only one determiner is allowed per common noun, though this was not always so (hence archaisms like *this my signature*).

When used with a common noun, determiners were divided in traditional grammar between 'articles' (THE, A) and 'adjectives'. This is unsatisfactory because the two groups are very similar to one another, and very different from ordinary adjectives; e.g. THE ('article') and MY ('adjective') both satisfy the need of a singular countable common noun for a determiner, but BIG doesn't (*I brought the/my/*new bike*).

Most determiners may also be used without a following common noun, in which case they are traditionally classified as $pronouns. This overlap can perhaps best be explained by saying that determiners are in fact a special kind of pronoun, which have the option of a following common noun. (The common noun is obligatory after just three determiners: THE, A and EVERY.) If determiners are in fact pronouns, they are also nouns (pronouns being a subtype of noun), so they could be analysed as the $root of a $noun-phrase – and perhaps should be so analysed, given that in *this book*, the determiner cannot be omitted but the common noun can. This is one of the reasons for my (controversial) belief that determiners are the roots of their phrases; e.g. that in *this house*, the common noun *house* $depends on the pronoun *this*, not vice versa. This assumption gives analyses like the following:

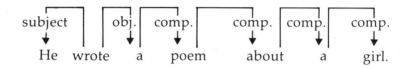

DICTIONARY-WORD

A dictionary-word is an abstraction from a collection of words which are similar in $shape, meaning, and $classification, and whose differences are due to $inflectional morphology. For instance, *boy* and *boys* are both instances of the same dictionary-word, BOY. The term 'dictionary-word' may also be applied to $idioms such as PUT UP WITH, because although they consist of several words they must be stored in the $grammar as a single unit because of their idiosyncratic meanings.

DISAMBIGUATE

Disambiguating a sentence means removing its ambiguity. This is done by changing its structure in some way so as to remove all but one of the otherwise possible meanings. For example, *Visiting relatives can be a nuisance* is ambiguous, but each of the possible meanings can be eliminated by a small change: *Visiting relatives are a nuisance* versus *Visiting relatives is a nuisance*.

DISCONTINUOUS PHRASE

A $phrase is discontinuous if it is interrupted by words which are not part of it. The most general principle is that phrases must be continuous. This explains the badness of examples like *big in cities* (instead of *in big cities*), where the phrase *big cities* is interrupted by a word which is not part of it. There are exceptional structures in which discontinuity is permitted, and which children learn to cope with very early in life – examples like *The wind stopped blowing*, where *the wind* $depends on *blowing* but *stopped* does not, so the phrase $rooted in *blowing* is discontinuous; and *What did he tell you he wanted?*, where *what* is part of the discontinuous phrase *what . . . he wanted.*

EXCLAMATIVE

The term 'exclamative' is widely applied to sentences like *What a pretty girl she is!* and *Isn't she a pretty girl!*, and contrasts with other $moods ($declarative etc.).

EXTRAPOSITION

$Clauses and $prepositional phrases can be extraposed, i.e. 'moved outside (the sentence)', by being put at the end of the clause containing them, rather than in their (otherwise expected) normal position. For instance, in the following the italicised are extraposed:

It is a pity *that he didn't make a will.*
cf. That he didn't make a will is a pity.

Any student will automatically fail *who cheats in exams.*
cf. Any student who cheats in exams will automatically fail.

FEATURE

A feature is a 'dimension' on which words may be classified (in the sense in which e.g. size, colour and shape are different dimensions on which objects may be classified), for instance, $number, $tense, $case. Each feature has a small number of contrasting $values, often but not necessarily two; e.g. the feature 'number' has 'singular' and 'plural' as its values. When a feature F is applied to some word the word is said to 'have an F' (e.g. '*dogs* has a number'), meaning that it has one of the values of F; this allows us to require the values that two related words have to '$agree' (e.g. the number of THIS must be the same as that of the $noun after it: *this boy* but not *this boys*, so the $grammar contains a $rule which requires both of them to have 'the same number').

The clearest need for features arises in connection with contrasts that are signalled by $inflectional morphology. These features may also be called '$morphosyntactic' features, because they link the $morphology of a word to its $syntactic characteristics. This is how I use features in this book.

FINITE

A $value on the 'finiteness' $feature, whose other value is (not surprisingly) 'non-finite'. A finite $verb is one which can be used without any other verb in the sentence – i.e. as the $root of the sentence. Finite verbs are either $tensed or $imperative; e.g. all the verbs in: *I like you. Are you happy? Cheer up!*

FORM

A form of a $dictionary-word is distinguished from other forms of the same dictionary-word by its $inflectional morphology; e.g. the s-form of DOG is *dogs*, which is different from its basic form, *dog*. Forms can conveniently be presented by adding the appropriate normal suffix to the end of the dictionary-word's name, e.g. *dogs* = DOG-s; and generalisations can be made by doing the same with the names of whole $word-classes, e.g. N-s meaning 'the s-form of a noun'. Forms can be made more precise by $features; e.g. the form V-en (e.g. *eaten*) may be either $perfect or $passive $participle.

FUNCTION

The 'function' of a word or phrase is its relation to the rest of the sentence, especially its $dependency relation to its $head – e.g. in *Fred tickled Sally*, the function of *Fred* is '$subject of *tickled*'.

GENDER

Gender is a $feature, whose possible values generally include 'masculine' and 'feminine', and sometimes 'neuter'. (Some languages divide the world up in other ways, e.g. as 'human' versus 'non-human', or 'animate' versus 'inanimate'.) Gender is a matter of grammar, and, being a feature, is signalled morphologically (as in French, German, etc.). It is debatable whether English has a 'gender' system in this sense, as the contrast among HE, SHE and IT relates to the sex of the thing referred to, rather than to the gender of the word used.

GENERATIVE GRAMMAR

1. A generative grammar is a grammar which is completely explicit, so that it is absolutely clear which sentences it allows ('generates', in a sense developed by mathematicians) and which it does not. No traditional grammar is generative, because it is intended for use by intelligent readers who can fill in a lot of the details, and who are probably not concerned with this kind of precision. The point of a generative grammar is not that it is more useful to ordinary grammar-users (though it is extremely useful to users in the computer world), but that we can test it against a native speaker's judgements about sentences. If the grammar and the native speaker agree about what is grammatical and what isn't, and also about how sentences are structured, then we may surmise that the native speaker's knowledge is organised along similar lines to the generative grammar. If we want to understand the native speaker's knowledge, and our surmise is correct, then we can study this knowledge via our 'model' of it, our generative grammar.

2. The term 'generative grammar' was introduced by Noam Chomsky, so it is often applied to any 'Chomskyan' grammar. Chomsky pays much less attention nowadays to explicitness, so grammars may be called generative just because they apply Chomsky's current ideas, even if they are not explicit; and generative grammars may even be contrasted with other, non-Chomskyan, grammars that are explicit. This is very confusing. On the whole it is best to avoid the term 'generative', but you should be aware of the confusion you may meet in the technical literature.

GRAMMAR

(The study of) a language, in the sense of a body of facts (i.e. $rules) that native speakers know about their language. But also more specifically 'grammar' may exclude one or more of the following parts of a language: its vocabulary, its pronunciation, its meanings, and its social and other functions. The bare minimum of grammar, on which everyone agrees, consists of (a) $morphology, (b) $syntax. The $rules that a person knows constitute that person's grammar. [Etymology: Greek *gramma*, 'letter, writing'; related, believe it or not, to GLAMOUR!]

GRAMMATICAL

'Grammatical' means 'allowed by the grammar of X', where X is the name of some language or dialect. It is meaningless to ask in the abstract whether some string of words is grammatical; for instance, *Jean a mangé une pomme* is grammatical in French, but not in English. Similarly, *I done it* is grammatical in non-standard English, but not in Standard English, and conversely for *I did it*.

HEAD

One end of a $dependency relation, the other end being the $dependent; e.g. in *tall thin boys*, *boys* is the head of *tall* (and conversely, *tall* is a dependent of *boys*, along with *thin*). If one word, H, is the head of another word, D, then you can expect the following to be true:

(a)   The combination H+D names a particular case of what H would refer to on its own; e.g. *tall boys* names a particular case of 'boys' (not of 'tallness').

(b)   H+D is part of a $phrase whose $root is H, not D; i.e. it is H that provides the link between this phrase and the rest of the sentence (e.g. the phrase *tall thin boys* is used according to the $rules for $nouns, such as *boys*, and not according to those for $adjectives).

(c)   It may be possible to omit D, without otherwise affecting the meaning or syntax of the sentence, but this is not possible for H; e.g. *tall* can be omitted from *tall boys* without changing anything else, but not so for *boys*: *Tall boys have advantages* or *Boys have advantages*, but not **Tall have advantages*.

(d)   If D can't be omitted, this is because of the grammatical characteristics of H; e.g. in *He abandoned the struggle*, we can't omit *the struggle* to give **He abandoned*. But this is because ABANDON requires an $object noun, in contrast with other verbs which don't – e.g. its synonym GIVE UP: *He gave the struggle up* or just *He gave up*. Therefore *the struggle* depends on *abandoned*, and *abandoned* is its head.

IDIOM

A sequence of words whose combined meaning does not follow regularly from the meanings of the individual words – e.g. HOT DOG ('kind of filled roll'), PUT UP WITH ('tolerate').

IMPERATIVE

An imperative $verb is a kind of $finite verb, so it can be the $root of a sentence, and contrasts with 'tensed'. (The term 'imperative' is also applied to the $clauses containing such verbs, in contrast with other $moods.) A typical imperative verb (in English) has the same form as the $infinitive, even in the verb BE (e.g. *Be quiet!*), and has no expressed $subject (unlike a tensed verb, which must have one). However, YOU may generally be supplied optionally, with unexpected (and hard to define) semantic effects: *You say that again!* Another kind of imperative verb is LET's, with the understood subject 'we' (not to be confused with the sequence *Let us ...*; compare e.g. *Let's go, shall we?* with *Let us go, will you?*).

INDEFINITE

A $noun-phrase is indefinite if its $root is either a common noun (e.g. *Peanuts (are good for you)*) or an indefinite $determiner (A, SOME, ANY, EITHER, NO, NEITHER, WHICH, EVERY, EACH, ONE; e.g. *(He ate) an apple)*. Most indefinite noun-phrases name something which the hearer does not already know (e.g. 'There was once *a king* who had *a beautiful daughter*'), but some (e.g. '*Peanuts* are good for you') refer 'generically' to all examples (e.g. to peanuts in general).

INFINITIVE

'Infinitive' is an $inflectional category (or $feature-value), i.e. a type of word defined by its morphology. Specifically, it is (in English) a type of verb which contains no inflectional affix at all (e.g. *be, come, walk*) and which can be used in various ways as a $dependent of another word (e.g. as the $complement of WILL, CAN, LET etc.: *I will/can be your friend; Let him be your friend*).

This definition conflicts with the traditional view that e.g. the infinitive of WALK is *to walk*; according to the new definition, *to walk* consists of TO followed by the infinitive of WALK, which is (just) *walk*. This conclusion means that so-called 'split infinitives' (e.g. *to boldly go*) are quite consistent with the normal rules of English grammar, which allow a verb (e.g. *go*) to be immediately preceded by a $modifying adverb (e.g. *boldly*), as in *I will boldly go*.

INFLECTIONAL MORPHOLOGY

The branch of $morphology in which a word's $shape signals its $feature-values; e.g. the presence or absence of the $suffix

-*s* in a $noun signals its value for the $feature $number. Unlike $lexical morphology, inflectional morphology makes contrasts which are normally not made in any other way; e.g. the difference between *swim* and *swam* is described in terms of the feature 'tense', which is always a matter of morphology, whereas that between SWIM and SWIMMER involves 'noun' and 'verb', two ordinary $word-classes.

INTERJECTION

A traditional $part of speech which does not appear at all in most modern grammars. It covers a rather heterogeneous collection of words like HELLO, DAMN!, HEY!, OH and HEIGH-HO, whose main shared characteristic is that they are not covered by any grammatical rules at all.

INTERROGATIVE

A $clause is $interrogative (rather than $declarative, $imperative or $exclamative) if it is like the following:

Have you finished? (yes–no)

Why have you stopped? (wh)

Was it a boy or a girl? (alternative)

(I don't know) whether/why he has finished. (subordinate)

These typically express questions, a $semantic category, but it would be confusing to call them questions because they can be used in other ways too – e.g. *Would you pass the salt, please?* expresses a request, not a question. In terms of $syntactic structure interrogative clauses have $subject–auxiliary inversion or an introductory $complementiser WHETHER or IF, and they may be introduced by an interrogative $pronoun. The main types that are generally distinguished are called 'yes–no', 'wh' and 'alternative' (see the above examples). All types of interrogative clause can be used either on their own, or $subordinate to other words.

INTRANSITIVE

An intransitive $verb is one that has no $object.

LEVEL

$Semantics, $syntax and $phonology are different 'levels' on which a linguistic form can be analysed, each involving different kinds of pattern, and described in terms of a different vocabulary of categories (e.g. 'animal', 'large', 'actor' for semantics; 'noun', 'singular', 'subject' for syntax; and 'consonant', 'voiced', 'syllable-onset' for phonology). The precise number and organisation of levels is a matter of dispute, but we all use the metaphor according to which meaning is 'high' and pronunciation (or writing) is 'low'.

The lower levels are concerned with the observable properties of uttered (or written) words, such as how they are pronounced and the sequence in which they are produced; the higher levels give priority instead to the notions expressed and the semantic relations among them. $Grammar is basically a system of rules which reconciles these two kinds of structure with one another, allowing observable low-level structures to express high-level structures.

LEXEME = $dictionary-word

LEXICAL MORPHOLOGY

A branch of $morphology, also known as 'derivational morphology'. It deals with any partial morphological similarities between different $dictionary-words which allow one dictionary-word to be considered as 'derived' from the other − e.g. FARMER from FARM. In this example the dictionary-words are both already part of the language, but some of these relations are sufficiently clear and well-established to be used for creating new dictionary-words − e.g. from the existing verb EXPECT one could derive a new noun, EXPECTER. Note that the 'source' word and the derived word may or may not belong to the same $word-class, but in either case lexical morphology (unlike $inflectional morphology) makes use of ordinary word-classes; e.g. FARMER is just an ordinary common noun, a $classification which is not affected by its relation to FARM. As well as being a branch of morphology, lexical morphology is also a branch of $word-formation, like $conversion and $compounding.

LOCATIVE INVERSION

Two examples are:

There goes our bus.
Round the corner came a long black car.

In these sentences the $subject follows the $verb, contrary to the normal rule, its normal position being occupied by a 'locative' (i.e. place) expression. This is an example of $subject–verb inversion.

MAIN CLAUSE

A $clause whose $root is not $subordinate to any other word; e.g. in *He knows that it's dangerous but he's determined to try*, there are two $coordinated main clauses (separated by *but*) and two subordinate ones: *(that) it's dangerous* and *he ... (to) try*.

MAIN VERB = $sentence root

MASS NOUN

A mass noun refers to a substance, in contrast with $countable nouns, which refer to individual entities. Clear examples are STUFF, WINE, PATIENCE, FURNITURE, EQUIPMENT. Mass nouns follow different $rules of $syntax from countable ones; e.g. they need no $determiner when singular, and can combine with determiners like SOME or with adjectives like MUCH, rather than with determiners like A or EACH: cf. *some/much equipment*, but not *an/each equipment*.

MODAL VERB

A subclass of $auxiliary verbs, whose special characteristic is that they have to be $tensed – i.e. they cannot be used in contexts which require $infinitives, $participles or $imperatives, even if the meaning would be clear. For example, *I can swim* is as grammatical as its paraphrase *I am able to swim*, but we can't say *Canning swim is important*, although we can express the same meaning as *Being able to swim is important*. Except in Scotland, this rule excludes sequences like *will can* or *may will* (many Scots use sentences like *He will can do it*). The modal verbs are: DO (e.g. *I do like peaches*), WILL, SHALL, CAN, MAY, MUST, OUGHT, USED, NEED (e.g. *Need you go now?*), DARE (e.g. *I daren't risk it*), and also BE when followed by $infinitival TO (e.g. *I am to leave soon* is similar in meaning to *I have to leave soon*, but I can't say *Being to leave soon is a nuisance*, because this BE is a modal verb, although *Having to leave soon is a nuisance* is fine).

All the modal verbs except BE are also unusual in their $morphology, because their $present-$tense forms have no -s with third-$person singular $subjects: *He can/*cans swim*.

MODIFIER

One of the two general classes of $dependent, contrasting with $complement. As explained under 'complement', a modifier is relatively loosely bound to its head, and relatively self-supporting in that it defines its own $semantic role, regardless of the word it has as $head. For instance, *big* in *big book*; *yesterday* in *I saw him yesterday*; *since (you know the way)* in *Since you know the way, you can drive.*

MOOD

A traditional $feature which embraces values such as 'indicative' and 'subjunctive', but may also be applied (especially in more modern work) to the contrasts among $declarative, $interrogative, $imperative and $exclamative. If it includes the latter, it is generally considered to apply to $clauses rather than to individual words, though some of us think otherwise.

MORPHEME

Any $radical or $affix; e.g. *farm-er-s* contains three morphemes, that is, one radical and two affixes.

MORPHOLOGY

The part of $grammar which deals with partial similarities between words which involve not only their shape but also their syntax and/or meaning – e.g. *feet* is morphologically related to *foot* (they both contain *f...t* and both belong to the $dictionary- word FOOT), and also to *geese*, which shares both its vowel and its plurality; but *feet* is not related morphologically to *fleet*, because the only similarity is in their shape, nor to *hands*, because all they share is plurality. Morphology divides into two main branches: $inflectional and $lexical.

MORPHOSYNTACTIC FEATURE = $feature

NOUN

'Noun' is the name of one of the main $word-classes, and includes words like CAT, FRED, YOU. A typical English noun has a number of characteristics, including the following:

- It has a $number (singular or plural).
- It can be used as the $complement of a $preposition, e.g. *(with) cats/Fred/you.*
- It can be used as the $object of a $verb, e.g. *(We discussed) cats/Fred/you.*
- It refers to a concrete object (a 'person, place or thing', as the traditional definition has it) – but many nouns are exceptional in this respect (e.g. SUNDAY, GRAMMAR, YOUTH).

Every language appears to have a word-class unified by properties similar to the above. In English the main subclasses of noun are $common noun, $proper noun and $pronoun.

NOUN-PHRASE

A $phrase whose $root word is a $noun – e.g. *grammatical exercises; the man in the moon; Fred; people who live in glass houses.*

NUMBER

Number is a $feature, whose possible values are 'singular' and 'plural'. So if we say that a noun must have a number, we mean that it must be classifiable as either singular or plural; and if we say that two words must $agree in number, we mean that if one is singular, the other must be too, and similarly for plural. In some languages, a third choice, 'dual' (i.e. 'two') is distinguished morphologically from both singular and plural. The contrast between 'two' and 'more than two' also applies to a handful of English words: BOTH versus ALL, EITHER versus ANY, and NEITHER versus NO.

OBJECT

One of the $functions that a $noun may have; e.g. the noun *wine* is the object in *He drinks wine every day.* A $verb may or may not allow an object, so an object is a kind of $complement. (Verbs are traditionally classified as '$transitive' or '$intransitive' according to whether or not they have an object.) One of the main distinguishing characteristics of objects in English is that they can turn into the $subject of a $passive verb: *Wine is drunk every day.* In English there are two distinct kinds of object: direct and indirect; in *She gave him that book,* the indirect object is *him* and the direct object *that book.* Both can become the subject of a passive, in at least some dialects: *He was given that book,* or *That book was given him.*

PARTICIPLE

A participle is a $form of a $verb; examples are *writing* and *written* in the following sentences:

The person *writing* this sentence is Dick Hudson.

The person who has *written* this sentence is Dick Hudson.

The sentence *written* above is about participles.

Participles are non-$finite forms, so they are always $subordinate to some other word, but they contrast with $infinitives. Traditionally three kinds of participles are distinguished (for English): present participles (*writing*), $perfect participles (*written*) and $passive participles (*written*). Although the perfect and passive participles are always identical in $shape, they are quite different in $syntax (perfect participles only occur after the $auxiliary verb HAVE, while passive participles never do, and have the characteristics of passive verbs). In syntax, passive participles are very similar to present participles – e.g. both can $modify a common noun (*the person writing this book; the book written by Dick Hudson*), and both can occur after BE (*He was writing; He was written to*). In these respects present and passive participles are similar to adjectives, whence the name 'participle' (less than obviously, it meant 'participating in more than one word-class, namely verb and adjective'). We therefore need a super-class for these two kinds of participle, which we can naturally call just 'participle'; but this means that we should find a different name for so-called perfect participles – e.g. 'perfect pseudo-participles', or simply 'perfect'.

PARTICLE

1.   A word which has no $inflections or other $morphological structure, and which doesn't fit into any general $word-class; e.g. the word *to* in *I want to go* might be called a particle. This rather traditional term is a useful dustbin in $classification, but its use is generally an admission of failure to find generalisations.

2.   In English grammar, 'particle' is used as the name of a $function and/or of the class of words that can have that function; e.g. *up* in *Fred rang Mary up*. It is one of the types

of $complement, and is the function of a fairly large class of words which are also $adverbs and/or $prepositions – UP, DOWN, IN, OUT, AWAY, OFF, ON, etc. It is the only dependent of a verb that may precede its $object even if the latter is short; e.g. *He rang up Mary*, but not *He rang yesterday Mary*. Particles are easy to confuse with true prepositions because both of them can stand between a verb and a noun-phrase; e.g. *to* in *He spoke to Mary* is a preposition, unlike *up* in *He rang up Mary*. The distinction can be shown more clearly in a diagram:

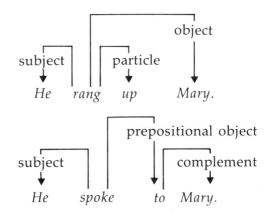

It is easy to distinguish particles from prepositions because the particle can be moved round the object (*He rang up Mary* or *He rang Mary up*) but the preposition can't follow its $complement (*He spoke to Mary* but not *He spoke Mary to*).

PART OF SPEECH

The most general $word-classes, e.g. 'noun', 'verb', are traditionally called 'parts of speech'. The term is so widely known and used that you should understand it, but the sooner it dies the better, because it is completely unhelpful and potentially misleading, as it encourages confusion between $classification and $function.

PASSIVE

Passive is one $value for the traditional $feature 'voice', and contrasts with '$active'. A passive $verb is one kind of $participle, e.g. *taken* in *The jewel was taken.*

Passive verbs differ from active ones in two respects: (a) the active $subject is 'demoted', and can either be left unexpressed (*He was appointed*) or be expressed as a $modifier introduced by BY (*He was appointed by a committee*); and (b) the passive subject would have had some function other than subject if the verb had been active; this function may be $object (*He was appointed*) but it may also be the complement of a preposition which depends on the verb (*He is depended on*; *He was made a fuss of*).

PERFECT PARTICIPLE

A $participle which is used only after HAVE, as in *He has seen her* or *Had you been to Spain?* It is called 'perfect' in the belief that the event or state referred to is finished (Latin *perfectus*) at the time of speaking, but this isn't always so as you can see from examples like *I have lived in London for 20 years, and am still there.* The name 'perfect' is therefore much less appropriate in English than in some other languages, where there are $forms called either 'perfect' or 'perfective' which do refer to events that are completed.

PERFORMANCE

Speech or writing – i.e. particular bits of behaviour or writing – produced on particular occasions. Contrasted with $competence, the knowledge of language that is necessary (but not sufficient) for this performance to take place.

PERSON

A traditional $feature of $nouns (and also, via $subject–verb agreement, of $verbs) which normally has three $values: first, second and third. First-person nouns $refer to the speaker, with or without others, so they include just the personal $pronouns ME and US; second-person nouns refer to the hearer (more precisely, the person addressed) but not the speaker, i.e. YOU; and all the rest are third-person. This feature may not be relevant to English, because it hardly applies to verbs and all the necessary distinctions among nouns can be made just as easily by referring directly to the $dictionary-words ME, US and YOU.

PHONOLOGY

The part of $grammar which deals with the structure of spoken words in terms of units such as syllables, vowels and consonants (rather than in terms of $stems and $affixes, which are handled by $morphology).

PHRASE

A group of words which are all $subordinate to one word, the $root of the phrase; for example, in *Too many people smoke*, there are three phrases: *too many* (root: *many*), *too many people* (root: *people*) and the whole sentence (root: *smoke*). The term 'phrase' is often applied to single words as well as to groups of words, because this allows rules to be more general; e.g. instead of referring to 'the phrase or word which is the subject' we can refer simply to 'the phrase which is the subject', bearing in mind that the phrase concerned may consist of nothing but its root word (e.g. *I, Fred, peanuts*).

Most phrases are part of some larger phrase, and have a specific relation to this. There are two interchangeable ways of defining this relation, using $functions such as $subject and $modifier, according to whether the function is considered to belong to the whole phrase or just to its root. For example, in *Too many people smoke* the subject of *smoke* is either the phrase *too many people* or just its root, *people*. It makes little practical difference which of these options you choose, but for theoretical purity, I favour the second system.

PLURAL

A $value for $number. A plural $noun typically $refers to a set of entities, each of which is the kind of entity to which the corresponding singular would have referred; e.g. *big dogs* refers to a set of big dogs, i.e. a set each of whose members is a big dog. Some plural nouns are irregular, and refer to a single entity; e.g. SCISSORS, BATHROOM SCALES.

POLARITY

The contrast between 'positive' and 'negative'. It may be important to be able to distinguish positive and negative $clauses, in order to deal (for example) with $tag questions, whose polarity is based on that of the preceding clause; e.g. after *They have left* we use *haven't they?* but after *They haven't left* we use *have they?*. The negativeness need not be marked on the verb, which shows that it belongs to the clause as a whole rather than to its $root verb; so we use with *Nobody has left* the tag expected after a negative clause: *have they?* not *haven't they?* However a separate kind of polarity may also apply, as a $feature, to English $tensed $auxiliary verbs, where it is marked by the presence or absence of the $suffix -*n't*: *will* versus *won't*, *was* versus *wasn't*, etc. The two contrasts are of course separate, because positive verbs can occur in negative clauses (e.g. *He has never left*).

POSSESSIVE

A possessive is a kind of $determiner, such as MY; the traditional name 'possessive adjective' misses the similarities to other determiners and the big differences from ordinary adjectives. These words can of course be used to name the possessor of some object, e.g. *my book*, but they can also be applied to semantic relations other than possession – e.g. *my departure* doesn't mean 'the departure that I possess(ed)'. The most interesting possessive, from the syntactic point of view, is the 'apostrophe *s*', as in *Fred's* or *everyone else's*. This looks like a $suffix, but is in fact a separate word (a $clitic) which, like a $preposition, is combined with a whole phrase (e.g. *the man across the road's (car)*).

PREDICATIVE COMPLEMENT

A kind of $complement which defines a 'predicate' (i.e. a fact) which is true of the $subject (or, in some cases, of the $object). In contrast, most complements define some separate entity distinct from the subject and other complements. For example, *a genius* is a predicative complement in *He seems a genius* and in *I consider him a genius*, but not in *I know a genius*. A predicative complement may be a $noun, as in these examples, but much more typical is an $adjective (e.g. *He seems sad*) or a $participle (e.g. *He kept talking*). There is no clear distinction between predicative complement and $×complement.

PREFIX

An $affix which precedes the $radical – e.g. *un-* and *pre-* in UNPREMEDITATED.

PREPOSITION

A $word-class whose members are like $verbs in that they take a $noun as their $complement, but like $adverbs in the range of $functions they can have. Examples are OF, IN, WITH, AFTER. Some sequences of words such as IN SPITE OF, IN FRONT OF, are so indivisible as to be (probably) best treated as single prepositions.

The functional similarities to adverbs are such that it may be best to consider prepositions as a subclass of adverb. This analysis would help to explain why so many words can be used either as (traditional) 'adverbs' or as prepositions; e.g. IN, in examples like *Is John in?* versus *Is John in the house?*.

Similar arguments suggest that 'preposition' should include the traditional category of $subordinating conjunction; e.g. the complement of AFTER can be either a noun (e.g. *He arrived after her*, or *He arrived after Christmas*) or a $tensed $verb (e.g. *He arrived after she left*), with a very similar meaning in each case. The similarities are easier to explain if the word belongs to the same word-class in each use, with all the difference located in the complement, than if it is a preposition in one case and a 'subordinating conjunction' in the other. Here are the $structures for these sentences, showing the functional similarities between the two uses of BEFORE:

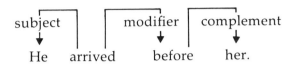

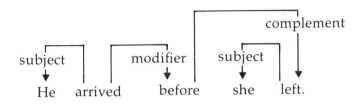

Unlike many other languages, English allows prepositions to be 'stranded' – i.e. to have their complements removed – e.g. by $passivisation (e.g. *He is thought highly of; What are you thinking about?*). Some people object strongly to stranded prepositions, on the grounds that they are not allowed in Latin, but they have been allowed in English for many centuries and are absolutely normal in everybody's speech. A stranded preposition is always the $root of a $discontinuous phrase, because its $complement has been moved to an earlier position; e.g. in *He is thought highly of*, the complement of *of* is *he*, which has been shifted into the $subject position.

PREPOSITIONAL OBJECT

A type of $complement in English, which is introduced by a $preposition; e.g. in *He depends on her*, the phrase *on her* is the prepositional object of *depends*. In a prepositional object the preposition is usually selected, more or less arbitrarily, by the verb, and therefore does not have its usual meaning (e.g. ON normally $refers to a place, but not after DEPEND). The $complement of the preposition can easily become the $subject under $passivisation: *She is depended on.*

PREPOSITIONAL PHRASE

A $phrase whose $root is a $preposition.

PRESCRIPTIVE

Grammar is 'prescriptive' if it tries to change normal behaviour, e.g. the command 'Never say *It's me!*' is prescriptive. Linguists accept that all use of language is governed by $rules, so they strongly reject any suggestion that in language 'anything goes', or that ordinary language 'has no grammar'. On the other hand, they also accept that some rules apply only in particular circumstances of use; so they accept rules like 'Don't use *ain't* when aiming at standard English' (or 'Don't use *isn't* when aiming at the local non-standard English'!), provided there is no implication that the rejected form is wrong in all circumstances.

The objections to prescriptive grammar are of four kinds: scientific, practical, political and ethical. The scientific objection is that prescriptive grammar is at best marginal, and perhaps completely irrelevant, to the aim of understanding how language works. The practical objection is that prescriptive grammar is a very crude way of getting the population to use standard forms on 'standard' occasions, and may well be counter-productive because of the resistance it engenders. The political objection is that prescriptive grammar favours the rich, as the main native speakers of Standard English, at the expense of the poor, the main users of non-standard forms. The ethical objection is that prescriptive grammar is demoralising for speakers of non-standard dialects (i.e. the majority of our population) because non-standard forms are rejected as 'slovenly', 'lazy', etc. – i.e. as morally inferior to standard forms.

PRESUPPOSITION

The meaning of a sentence may be broken down into a number of $propositions (i.e. ideas which may be true or false). For instance, the meaning of *The cat caught a mouse* contains various propositions, including (a) that there was an event of 'catching'; (b) that the 'catcher' in this event is known to the hearer. These propositions do not all have the same status, however. Some are 'asserted' (or questioned, etc.); more precisely, just one is asserted, the one expressed directly by the $sentence-root, i.e. proposition (a). The truth of the asserted one presupposes that of some of the others, which are therefore called 'presuppositions'; proposition (b) is an example, so the example presupposes the existence (at least in the hearer's mind) of some particular cat. But importantly, the presupposed propositions are still assumed true even if the asserted one is false, or negated; e.g. the existence of the cat is presupposed just as strongly in *The cat didn't catch a mouse*. In contrast, our sentence does not presuppose (in this sense) the existence of a mouse; if the sentence is true, then there must have been a mouse to be caught, but this is not true if the sentence is false.

You can see the clear difference in status between the cat and the mouse in the following:

The cat didn't catch a mouse, because there wasn't a mouse.

??The cat didn't catch a mouse, because there wasn't a cat.

The difference between *the cat* and *a mouse* is obviously related to the fact that THE is $definite and A is $indefinite. Definite nouns are generally used to $refer to entities whose existence (at least in the hearer's mind) is presupposed.

Presupposed propositions are expressed in a wide variety of syntactic structures. For example, *He knows that he's wrong* presupposes that he's wrong (as does its negation, *He doesn't know that he's wrong*), and *He has overslept again* presupposes that he has overslept at least once before (as does *He hasn't overslept again*). Notice however that some $subordinate $clauses express propositions whose truth is not presupposed; e.g. *He thinks that she's French* presupposes nothing about the truth of the proposition that she is French.

PRONOUN

A pronoun is a type of $noun which cannot combine with a $determiner, in contrast with $common and $proper nouns. Traditionally it was said to stand for (*pro-*) a (common) noun. There are several types of pronoun:

- personal: ME, YOU, HIM, HER, IT, US, THEM, (ONE);

- relative: WHO, WHICH, WHOSE, WHEN, WHERE, WHY;

- free-relative: WHAT, WHATEVER, WHOEVER, etc.;

- reflexive: MYSELF, YOURSELF/VES, HIMSELF, etc.;

- reciprocal: EACH OTHER, ONE ANOTHER;

- possessive: MINE (= *my* or *mine*), YOURS, HIS, etc.;

- demonstrative: THIS, THAT;

- partitive: SOME, ANY, EITHER, EACH, NONE (= *no* or *none*), NEITHER;

- interrogative: WHO, WHOSE, WHAT, WHICH, WHEN, WHERE, WHY, HOW;

- compound: SOMEONE, ANYONE, NO ONE, EVERYONE; SOMEBODY, SOMETHING, SOMEWHERE, SOMEHOW etc.

Pronouns are very closely related to $determiners, as most determiners can also occur as pronouns (e.g. *I bought some peanuts* versus *I bought some*, where *some* is a determiner and a pronoun respectively). Traditionally pronouns are contrasted with nouns, as one of the $parts of speech, but they occur with precisely the same range of $functions ($subject, $object, etc.) as any noun so they must be a subclass of noun.

PROPER NOUN

A sub-class of $noun which we write with a capital letter (e.g. MARY, LONDON, WEDNESDAY). A proper noun is always $countable (i.e. $refers to a single individual entity) but it is unlike a $common noun in either not needing a $determiner (e.g. LONDON, FRED), or in having to have THE (e.g. THE SEVERN, THE LEBANON). Some words may be used either as proper nouns or as common nouns; e.g. MUM (*Have you seen Mum?*, versus *Have you seen my mum?*). Some kinds of determiner are possible with some kinds of proper noun (e.g. *our Mary, that Fred*), as are some kinds of $modifier (e.g. *the London that Dickens knew*). It is possible that in such cases the proper noun has been changed into a common noun by $conversion.

PROPOSITION

A complex idea which could be expressed in ordinary language by a $clause introduced by THAT; e.g. that it's Sunday today, or that snow is white. Propositions in the $semantic structure of a sentence may or may not be $presupposed.

RADICAL

A part of a word which is not an $affix, e.g. *farm-* in *farm-er-s*. In a $compound $dictionary-word, there are two (or more) radicals, e.g. *farm-* and *-yard-* in *farm-yard-s*. Radicals are often called 'roots' but many of us use this term in an entirely different sense (see $root) so we need an alternative.

RECIPROCAL

A type of $pronoun; either EACH OTHER or ONE ANOTHER, as in *They like each other/one another.*

REFER

A word or phrase refers to the thing whose name it is; e.g. the word JOHN refers to the person John, the phrase *the book that I'm writing* refers to this book, and *nobody* in *Nobody understands me* refers to a hypothetical (and non-existent) person. This use of 'refer' should be distinguished from the more traditional use in which one word is said to refer to another

– in particular, a pronoun 'refers' to a noun (e.g. *he* refers to the word *Fred* in 'Fred said he was tired').

REFLEXIVE

A kind of $pronoun which $refers to whatever is named by some other $noun in the same sentence, and typically to the $subject of the same $verb; e.g. *Fred hurt himself, Fred showed Mary a picture of herself, The pictures of himself that Fred takes are most interesting.* The English reflexive pronouns all end in *-self* or *-selves*.

REGISTER

A register is roughly what is popularly called a 'style': a way of speaking (or writing) which is restricted to some particular kind of social context. Some examples are the registers used in sermons, in newspaper editorials, in the weather forecast, in scientific articles and in adolescent peer-group interaction. Registers are contrasted with dialects, on the grounds that the latter vary with the speaker rather than with the social context; but the contrast is not always easy to maintain – in particular, Standard English is both a dialect and a collection of registers.

RELATIVE CLAUSE

A relative clause is a $subordinate clause whose semantic effect is to identify some entity by the part it plays in the relative clause. For example, in *I carried what we had bought,* the relative clause *what we had bought* identifies a set of things by saying that we had bought them. This is an example of a 'free relative clause', one which behaves like a complete $noun-phrase. Rather more typical, though, are the more complex ones where the relative clause is linked to a $common noun by a relative $pronoun: e.g. *people who live in glass houses*, where *people* is outside the relative clause *who live in glass houses*. Here the common noun and the relative clause share the task of identifying the entity concerned: *people* says that it is a set each of whose members is a person, and the relative clause says that each of these people lives in a glass house.

Relative clauses in English can be introduced by a relative pronoun (e.g. WHO), by THAT (*people that live in glass houses*) or by no linker at all (e.g. *some people I know*); or the $root of the clause may be a $participle (e.g. *people living in this street; people chosen by the committee*) or $infinitival TO (e.g. *the people to watch; the people to do it for you*).

Another important contrast is between 'restrictive' and 'non-restrictive' relative clauses. All the examples quoted above are restrictive, which means that they help to restrict the range of things picked out by the noun-phrase (e.g. *book that I am writing* picks out a much smaller class of objects than *book* would on its own). A non-restrictive relative clause simply provides further information about the person or thing referred to by the preceding noun-phrase, as in *Mary, who runs a factory in Birmingham, is very competent*. Here the relative clause *who runs a factory in Birmingham* tells us more about Mary, but doesn't help us to identify her. Non-restrictive relative clauses are a rather literary device, and rare in casual speech. They tend to be separated by commas from the rest of the sentence.

ROOT

The root of a $phrase is the word to which all the other words are $subordinate, and which therefore provides the main link between the phrase and the rest of the sentence. For instance, in a $prepositional phrase like *in London* the root is the preposition ('*in* London') because the use of this phrase is controlled by the rules for using prepositions rather than by those for nouns; in a $clause the root is the verb ('I *like* you'); in a $noun-phrase it is the noun ('small black noisy *puppies*'). It is a matter of debate whether the root of a noun-phrase containing a $determiner is the $common noun or the $determiner (e.g. 'my left *foot*' or '*my* left foot'), but in my examples I have assumed the latter.

RULE

A fact about normal usage – e.g. 'A word (normally) precedes its $complements', 'The $object of a $verb is (normally) a $noun', 'The $subject of *am* is *I*'. All speech and writing is governed by rules, but does not always conform to the rules – sometimes we make mistakes, and sometimes we deliberately flout the rules. The rules which govern a person's use of language are the rules in that person's own $grammar, which may or may not be that of the standard language; so rules in this sense are $descriptive, not $prescriptive.

SEMANTIC ROLE

The relation between the meaning of a word and that of its $head; i.e. the contribution that the first meaning makes to the second one. For example, in *Fred snored*, the semantic role of Fred (the meaning of *Fred*) is 'snorer' in relation to the meaning of its head, *snored*; so the whole means something like 'there was a snoring in which the snorer was Fred.' It is widely assumed that semantic roles can be defined in terms of a fairly small number of very general role-types such as 'actor' (or 'agent'), 'undergoer' (or 'patient'), 'instrument' and so on.

SEMANTICS

The part of $grammar that deals with meanings. Any $phrase has a $semantic structure as well as a $syntactic one, the semantic structure being made up of the meanings of the individual words inside the phrase. These meanings combine according to $rules which can be quite complex, but in general the semantic structure is quite similar to the syntactic one. However their elements are quite distinct, because a word is quite distinct from its meaning, the thing to which it $refers; e.g. the word *Fred* consists of four letters, but its meaning, the person Fred, does not. Thus while the syntactic structure of *Fred snores* includes notions like 'FRED', 'noun', 'SNORE', 'verb', 'present tense' and 'subject', its semantic structure mentions a completely different set of notions, such as 'Fred', 'person', 'snoring', 'action', 'actor', 'time' and 'now'.

SEMANTIC STRUCTURE

A sentence has $structure on a number of $levels, one of which is the $semantic level. In this structure the elements are entities that are $referred to by the words in the sentence, which are related to each other, and to the rest of our knowledge, by $propositions and various other kinds of complex patterns (e.g. sets). For example, take the sentence *Who did you see?* The semantic structure contains propositions like the following:

- that there was an event of 'seeing';
- that this event is known to the hearer;
- that the event took place at some time before 'now';
- that the hearer was also the 'see-er' in the event;
- that the hearer, but not the speaker, knows the identity of the person seen.

In general, semantic structure is much fuller and more complex than syntactic structure (though there are a few cases of greater complexity in the syntax, such as the semantically empty words DO and THAT in *Do you know that it's bedtime?*; $idioms also add complexity in the syntax but not in the semantics). In particular, single words typically express semantic structures; e.g. *again* in *He's late again* expresses the idea that he has been late before, and *wants* in *He wants a car* means 'wants to have' – that is, the sentence could be 'unpacked' semantically as 'He wants the proposition "that he has a car" to be true.'

SEMI-COMPLEMENT

A kind of $complement of English $verbs; e.g. *there* in *Please put it there*, or *well* in *She treated him well*. These are like complements in that they are obligatory (cf. **Please put it!*, *She treated him, in the sense 'behaved towards'). But they are also like $modifiers in that they define their own semantic relations – i.e. after PUT you need an ordinary expression of place, and after TREAT an ordinary expression of manner, so any word or phrase that can be used in these positions could also be used as an ordinary place or manner modifier.

SENTENCE

A $clause containing the $sentence-root (e.g. *If you think syntax is complicated, just wait till I tell you about semantics!*), or a $coordination of such clauses (e.g. *If you tickle them, they laugh, but it's safer not to do anything*).

SENTENCE-ROOT

The $root of a sentence – i.e. the word to which all the words in the sentence are $subordinate, and which itself has no head outside the sentence. The sentence-root is normally a $finite $verb, so to all intents and purposes we can identify 'sentence-root' with the traditional 'main verb', but we should perhaps remember that some grammatical sentences contain no verb – e.g. *Off with his head!*, *What about a walk?*

SHAPE

A word's 'shape' is either how it is pronounced, or how it is written; it can be defined either as a $morphological $structure (a stem plus affixes) or as a $phonological structure.

STEM

Any word-part to which $inflectional morphology applies; to be distinguished from $radical. For instance, in *farmers*, the stem is *farmer*, but the radical is *farm-*.

STRUCTURE

In showing how one thing is made up of smaller things we reveal its structure; for example the word *cats* has one structure consisting of the four letters, and another consisting of the $stem *cat-* and the $suffix *-s*. Each linguistic structure is located at some particular $level (e.g. $phonology, $morphology, $syntax, $semantics), which decides the kind of units and relations that can be mentioned; for instance, in phonological structure the units are sound-types (classified e.g. as consonants or vowels) and syllables, but in morphological structure they are stems, suffixes and the like.

SUBJECT

One of the most important $functions in the grammar of most, if not all, languages. *He* is the subject of *was* in *He was tired* and in *Was he tired?*, and *Fred* is the subject not only in *Fred admires Mary*, but also (contrary, perhaps, to expectation) in *Fred is admired by Mary*. This function is important because it is mentioned in a lot of rules; the following is a sample of the rules for English:

- Every $tensed $verb must have a subject: *Was tired.*
- An $imperative verb normally has no subject: *Be good!*
- The subject of a verb normally precedes it: *Fred snores*, but not *Snores Fred.*
- But the subject of a tensed auxiliary verb may follow it (by $subject–auxiliary inversion): *Was he tired?*
- And the subject of any tensed verb may follow it under the circumstances that allow $subject–verb inversion: *Here comes your dad.*
- The form of a $present tense verb varies according to the $number and $person of its subject, by so-called $subject–verb agreement: *I/you/we/they snore*, but *He snores.*
- The subject of a $passive verb typically has the same $semantic role as the $active verb's $object: *He was accepted.*
- If a $participle $modifies a $noun, the noun acts as the participle's subject: *the person reading this book.*
- If a verb $refers to an action, then it is the subject that provides the actor. (NB not all verbs do refer to

actions; e.g. *John likes success* doesn't, so we must not define the subject as the actor, or 'do-er' of the action, as in traditional grammar.)

- The subject of LIKE provides the 'experiencer' of the emotion (e.g. *John likes success*); whereas the subject of PLEASE provides the 'source' or 'cause' of the emotion (e.g. *Success pleases John*) – and so on for many other individual dictionary-words.

SUBJECT–AUXILIARY INVERSION

In yes–no $interrogatives the $subject and a $tensed $auxiliary $verb are inverted, e.g. *Are you ready?* In modern English (unlike Shakespearean English, or modern German) the verb involved in this kind of inversion must be an auxiliary verb (hence the ungrammaticality of e.g. *Know you the answer?*), so when no other auxiliary is required by the meaning, we use the semantically 'empty' auxiliary DO: *Can you swim?*, but *Do you know the answer?* The same kind of inversion, governed by the same rules, is also found in other patterns:

- after initial negative phrases like *(in) no way, at no time, only once, hardly ever, hardly*: *(In) no way am I going to help her!*, *Hardly had he begun to write when he was interrupted*;
- after *so* and *nor*: *Fred has finished, and so has Bill*; and after some linking words (especially $comparative ones) in high style (e.g. *Fred ate more than did the girl he was with*);
- in 'conditional' clauses without IF: *Had I seen you I'd have stopped to help you*.

SUBJECT–VERB AGREEMENT

In some languages, a $finite verb has the features $person and $number (and sometimes also $gender), and must $agree with its $subject with respect to these features; e.g. Latin verbs typically have six different $forms for the three persons in singular and plural (e.g. *amo, amas, amat, amamus, amatis, amant,* 'I/you (etc.) love').

In English there is a much more restricted system which hardly counts as 'agreement' (as I explain more fully in the lesson at level 6). A present-tense verb (but not a past-tense verb, except the *was/were* distinction unique to BE) typically has just two distinct forms in Standard English, e.g. *know, knows.* (Some dialects have reduced these to one, which in some cases is the form with -*s,* and in others the form without it; and in Standard English the $modal verbs have the same form throughout the present tense.) The form with -*s* is used just if the subject is third-$person singular, but the other form is used with all other kinds of subject: *I/you/we/they know,* but *He knows.* Unlike Latin, there is no evidence that person and number apply to the verb, because there are too few distinct forms; which suggests that the relation between subjects and verbs in English is not really an example of 'agreement' at all.

English, more than many other languages, allows us to take account of the $semantic structure of the subject in deciding the form of the verb. This is why we can say things like *Her family are all elderly,* where *are* is used with a singular subject, *her family.* (If it had been plural it would have been *her families.*) The reason why this combination is permitted is that FAMILY $refers to a collection of people, a kind of set, and therefore has a semantic structure similar to that of a plural noun (which also refers to a set). In many languages subject–verb agreement is strictly syntactic, so this kind of syntactic 'mismatch' is ungrammatical. It is a useful facility in English, because it allows us to show whether we are referring to the individual members of the collectivity (as in the above example), or to the collectivity itself, as in *Her family is a very old and respectable one.* However it is sometimes difficult to decide precisely how much flexibility we are allowed – e.g. what about sentences like *A large number/collection of rocks is/are lying on the table?*

SUBJECT–VERB INVERSION

This is a type of sentence pattern in which the subject follows the verb, but in which (unlike $subject–auxiliary inversion) the verb need not be an auxiliary. It is found:

- in $locative inversion (e.g. *Here comes John*);
- after initial $predicative complements (e.g. *Somewhat more troublesome will be the problem of getting back again*);
- after direct speech (e.g. *'I feel tired,' said John*).

SUBORDINATING CONJUNCTION

A traditional sub-class of the $word-class $conjunction; e.g. BECAUSE, AFTER, IF, WHEN, ALTHOUGH. Some of these words can also be used as $prepositions, e.g. *He came home after the party*, or *He came home after he finished*. Moreover, the $functions that are open to these words are similar to those open to prepositions, and more generally to $adverbs – e.g. as modifiers of verbs. Because of these similarities, and others, linguists generally assume that 'subordinating conjunctions' are in fact a type of preposition (which in turn may be a type of adverb); so some prepositions take $clauses as their $complements, whereas more typical prepositions take $noun-phrases.

SUBORDINATION

One of the two basic $syntactic relations between co-occurring words, contrasting with $coordination. It is also called $dependency, but it is useful to distinguish the meanings of the terms 'subordinate' and 'dependent'. One word is normally dependent on just one other word, its $head; e.g. in *very long stories*, the word *very* is dependent on *long*, which in turn is dependent on *stories*. The meaning of *subordinate* includes that of *dependent*, so *very* is subordinate to *long*, as well as dependent on it; but *very* is also subordinate to *stories*. Thus a word is subordinate to its head, but also to its head's head, and so on. This means that every word in a sentence is subordinate to the sentence's $root, and more generally, every word in a phrase is subordinate to that phrase's root.

SUFFIX

An $affix which follows the $radical, e.g. *-er* and *-s* in *farmers*.

SYNTACTIC STRUCTURE

The $structure that a sentence has at the $level of $syntax. The units are mostly words and $phrases (though in $coordination some units are word-strings that are not phrases, e.g. *him some* in *She gave him some and me none*), and the relations are (a) $word order, (b) $subordination (i.e. $functions) or coordination. The latter relations, especially subordination, are relatively abstract and may be signalled by the word order (e.g. in English $subjects normally precede the $root verb while $objects follow it). They are also signalled by the $classification of the words concerned, including not only their $word-classes (e.g. $noun versus $verb) but also their $features (e.g. their $case).

It is very helpful – in fact, essential – to be able to present these relations diagrammatically. Different theories of syntax provide very different diagramming systems, one of which I have used in this book: the arrows showing $dependencies, as in the following example.

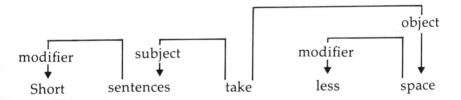

These dependency diagrams have the advantage over some of the alternatives of showing the function of each word directly, while also showing which words constitute phrases. For example, you can see that *short sentences* is a phrase, because *short* depends on *sentences* and no other word does.

SYNTAX

The part of $grammar which deals with how words are combined, in contrast with $morphology, which deals with their individual internal structures. One important part of syntax deals with the relatively concrete matter of word order, but two types of abstract between-word relations are equally important: $subordination and $coordination. If two words are in one of these relations, this generally has implications for all of the following:

- the order in which the words occur,
- the semantic relations between the words,
- the $classification of each of the words,
- the intonation.

These apparently simple facts generate a great deal of complexity, which requires a sophisticated general theory of language structure (which none of us has yet been able to produce).

TAG QUESTION

The *can't she?* in *Mary can write very well, can't she?* is a tag question, a peculiarity of English. It is an ordinary yes–no $interrogative clause whose meaning simply copies that of the clause to which it is added (its 'host'), with the exception of the $polarity and the $mood (i.e. its interrogative-ness).

In most dialects, a tag question consists of two words, a $tensed $auxiliary verb and a personal $pronoun. The verb is basically a copy of the host's root verb (e.g. *It was raining, wasn't it?*), but typically has -*n't* either added or deleted (cf. *It wasn't raining, was it?*). If the host's root verb is not itself an auxiliary verb, then the dummy auxiliary DO is used instead (e.g. *It rained, didn't it?*). The personal pronoun is based on the host's subject – a copy of this if it is a pronoun, otherwise a pronoun chosen to fit its meaning (e.g. *Mary plays football well, doesn't she?*).

There are three varieties of tag question according to the treatment of polarity (same or reversed) and of intonation (rising or falling), each communicating, a subtly different attitude:

It's a lovely day, isn't it?
(reversed polarity, falling intonation)

Let me see – your name's Mary Brown, isn't it?
(reversed polarity, rising intonation)

So, that's what you think of me, is it?
(same polarity, rising intonation)

Tag questions are excellent material for discovery-learning because they are primarily spoken rather than written, very systematic and regular, and very important in the dynamics of communication. Some non-standard varieties have additional types or uses of tag question – e.g. the invariant *isn't it* of some Welsh dialects (*You're going home now, isn't it?*), and the use of tags after facts which are unknown to the hearer (A: *Why are you late?* B: *I missed the bus, didn't I?*).

TENSE

A $feature whose values (for English) are 'past' and 'present'; e.g. *talked* versus *talk(s)*. Tense relates primarily to time; specifically, to the relation in time between the moment of speaking ('now') and the event or state which the verb describes ('before now' versus 'not before now').
There are a number of interesting deviations from the basic pattern in the ways in which we select tenses:

- A past tense in a $subordinate verb can be chosen, rather oddly, simply because this is the tense of the $sentence-root; for example, *He told me it was your birthday today.*
- A present-tense verb in a subordinate clause can refer to a future state of affairs if the main clause's verb does: *I shall come when/ if I am ready.*
- In conditionals and various other kinds of pattern, a past-tense verb can refer to a hypothetical state of

affairs, rather than to one true in the past: *If I knew the answer, I'd tell you; It's time you went to bed.*

- If a $non-finite verb is required to refer to a time in the past, this meaning can't be expressed in the usual way by an inflection, but is expressed by the use of HAVE followed by the $perfect: *Having seen Mary only yesterday, I know she's in London.*

- If a verb is required to refer to a time which is earlier than some other time which is before 'now', then the past tense of perfective HAVE is used: *He had seen her before I saw him.*

All these patterns involve just two tenses, past and present, plus a handful of dictionary-words such as WILL, SHALL and HAVE. It would be quite misleading to force English tenses into the mould of languages like Latin or French, where a much larger number of tenses are distinguished by $inflectional morphology; e.g. the Latin 'pluperfect' tense has the same meaning as the English sequence *had* + $perfect participle.

TENSED

A verb that has a tense is said to be 'tensed'. This is one value of a $feature which contrasts 'tensed' and '$imperative', the two kinds of $finite verb.

TOKEN

A token of some general $type is an example of it found in some concrete collection. For instance, in the previous sentence there are two tokens (examples) each of the word-types *of* and *some*.

TRANSITIVE

A transitive $verb is one which has an $object. The action that it expresses used to be described as 'passing over' (cf. 'transit') from the subject to the object.

TYPE

A type is an abstract category, whereas a particular manifestation or example of that category is a $token of it. For instance, in the previous sentence there are two tokens of the word-type *category*.

VALUE

A $feature has two or more possible 'values'; e.g. the feature $number has two values, singular and $plural. A noun is said to have 'a number', i.e. more precisely, a value for the feature 'number'.

VERB

A $word-class found (apparently) in every language, among whose members are dictionary-words with meanings like 'hit' and 'snore'. The importance of this word-class is shown in the etymology of the name: in Latin, *verbum* meant simply 'word'. In English verbs have the following characteristics, among many others:

- verbs inflect for $finiteness and $tense (e.g. *snoring* versus *snores* versus *snored*);
- when finite, verbs can be the $root of a sentence (e.g. *He snored*);
- the $object of a verb is a $noun (e.g. *Drink wine!*);
- when non-finite, NOT can be added before a verb (e.g. *not drinking wine*);
- a tensed verb must have a $subject (e.g. **Snores*, but *He snores*).

WORD-CLASS

A class of $dictionary-words, e.g. $noun, $pronoun, personal pronoun, which are similar in a number of respects. Some of these similarities are $syntactic (to do with how the words concerned combine with other words), but some may involve

$morphology or $semantics. Word-classes combine with $feature-values to define a word's $classification, e.g. as a plural noun.

WORD-FORMATION

(The study of) the relations between $dictionary-words which allow one dictionary-word to be considered 'derived' from one or more others. Its main branches are $lexical morphology (e.g. FARMER is derived from FARM), $conversion (e.g. the verb HAMMER is derived from the noun HAMMER) and $compounding (e.g. GRAMMAR BOOK is derived from GRAMMAR and BOOK).

WORD ORDER

The linear order in which words occur in a sentence. In English word order is relatively rigidly constrained by the rules of $syntax, based on the $functions (e.g. $subject, $modifier) of words; e.g. given that *Fred* is subject of *ate*, and *sandwiches* is its $object, the order *Fred ate sandwiches* is normal, *Sandwiches Fred ate* is abnormal though grammatical, and **Fred sandwiches ate* is ungrammatical. In some languages word order is much less closely tied to functions, so all imaginable permutations of a word and its $dependents are permitted. Such languages are said to have 'free word order'.

×COMPLEMENT

This mysterious term is the name of a particular kind of $complement, namely one whose $subject is 'external' to it (hence the 'X-'). An example is in *He kept talking*; the ×complement of *kept* is *talking*, whose subject is *he*, the subject of *kept*. The structure of this sentence is:

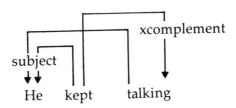

×complements are extremely common – e.g. every $auxiliary verb has one – and may be of a wide variety of $word-classes. In each of the following examples, the capitalised word is ×complement of the verb and therefore shares the latter's subject.

adjective	*He was HAPPY.*
noun	*He was a FOOL.*
preposition	*He was IN a good mood.*
present participle	*He was TALKING.*
passive participle	*He was ADMIRED.*
TO + V-	*He was TO get a medal.*

The subject of an ×complement is generally also the subject of the ×complement's $head, as in the examples so far, but some verbs allow both an ×complement and an $object, e.g. *I expect you to work hard, He kept them waiting.* In nearly all cases like this, it is the first verb's object, rather than its subject, that doubles up as the ×complement's subject.

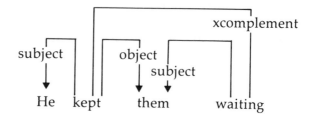

ZERO-DERIVATION = $conversion

Part V

Appendix

Grammar in the National Curriculum

The National Curriculum for English

The main stimulus for the writing of this book is the new National Curriculum for English, which came into force in 1990. (Teaching for the first stage started a year earlier, and for the other three stages is phased in between 1990 and 1992.) The relevant document is the 'Education (National Curriculum) (Attainment Targets and Programmes of Study in English) (No. 2) Order 1990', which was laid before Parliament on 6 March 1990. I shall call this just 'the National Curriculum'. Its 43 pages give quite a detailed plan for English teaching across the 11 years of compulsory education.

The National Curriculum follows closely the recommendations of a much longer document, *English for Ages 5 to 16* (Department of Education and Science and the Welsh Office, June 1988), which consists of a brief introduction by the Secretaries of State for Education and Science and for Wales, and the report of a committee chaired by Professor Brian Cox. For short we can call this 130-page book 'the Cox report'. It consists of three 'official' chapters, on oral language (speaking and listening), reading and writing, respectively, followed by 14 background chapters which explain and justify the official chapters or add details on such important matters as bilingual children. No doubt the National Curriculum will provoke some debate about how it should be interpreted, so it is important to see it in the context of the explanatory chapters of the Cox report.

In the National Curriculum the aims of the subject 'English' are grouped into a number of different 'attainment targets', each described in a separate chapter:

AT1   speaking and listening
AT2   reading
AT3   writing
AT4   spelling
AT5   handwriting
AT4/5   presentation

There are slight complications for spelling and handwriting, which merge at higher levels into 'presentation'.

Cutting across these attainment targets are the ten 'levels' which provide the basis for part II of this book. Average pupils are expected to start at level 1 when they enter primary school and to have reached level 6 or 7 when they finish compulsory secondary schooling, at age 16; but the brightest pupils will reach level 10 by this age, and the slowest ones will still be at level 3, so enormous differences in speed of progress are expected across the ability range. This complicates any attempt to devise syllabuses or teaching methods for the various levels, because for some levels the pupils could be of any age from 6 to 16!

The relation between levels and ages is shown in the figure, based on a figure in a Department of Education and Science report 'National Curriculum: task group on assessment and testing' (1987). The same system applies to all curriculum subjects, and not only to English. Each of the M's in this diagram shows the median level for the age concerned, and the X's 'represent a rough speculation about the limits within which about 80% of the pupils may be found to lie'. The levels between 7 and 10 correspond to grades F to A at GCSE.

The National Curriculum defines the curriculum partly by saying what the pupils at each level should know ('statements of attainment'), and partly by saying how they should be taught ('programmes of study'). Unfortunately the document does not have a clear structure in terms of chapters or sections, so I shall have to make up my own way of referring to its

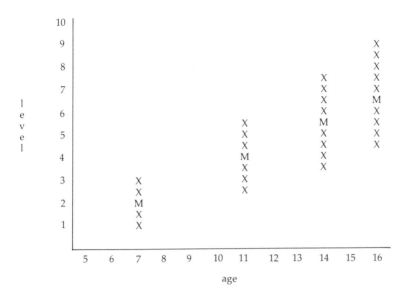

Figure 1. *Estimated relations between age and level of achievement.*

parts. I shall refer to the sections that define the attainment targets and the 'associated statements of attainment' as AT1 to AT4/5, as listed above. These are accompanied by just three 'programmes of study', for speaking/listening, reading, and writing/spelling/handwriting respectively. I shall call these PS1, PS2 and PS3. These rather complex relations are summarised below:

Attainment target	'Areas of study'	At levels	Programme of study
AT1	speaking, listening	1–10	PS1
AT2	reading	1–10	PS2
AT3	writing	1–10	PS3
AT4	spelling	1–4	PS3
AT5	handwriting	1–4	PS3
AT4/5	spelling, handwriting (presentation)	5–10	PS3

Grammar in the National Curriculum

The question that concerns us here is precisely what status grammar has in the official curriculum for English. We start with some general remarks.

The Cox committee, which developed the details of the National Curriculum for English, was explicitly asked to build on the recommendations of the Kingman committee. This is important background information, because the Kingman committee was set up to consider what children should know about language; given the broad definition of 'grammar' that I have assumed in this book, much of its work was concerned with grammar. The Kingman committee was itself set up because the question of teaching about language was the most controversial one in the general debate about the future structure of the subject 'English'. Its report was published in March 1988 (*Report of the Committee of Inquiry into the Teaching of English Language*, HMSO), and its enthusiastic support for the teaching of grammar can be seen in the following extracts.

1.12 It is arguable that . . . mastery [of the English language] might be achieved without explicit knowledge of the structure of the language or the ways it is used in society. But there is no positive advantage in such ignorance. It is just as important to teach about our language environment as about our physical environment, or about the structure of English as about the structure of the atom. And since we believe that knowledge about language, made explicit at that moment when the pupil is ready, can underpin and promote mastery as well, the argument is even stronger.

2.11 . . . If we are to help pupils function intellectually – and we take this to be a prime purpose of education – we must spend time in English classes examining words and how each contributes to the meaning of a sentence. We need to put pupils into situations where they are bound to reflect upon the complex associations of words themselves and to value words not just as currency – the small change passed between individuals in order to communicate easily – but as powerful aids to thinking.

2.27 . . . we believe that for children not to be taught anything about language is seriously to their disadvantage.

2.29 Awareness of the forms of language is an entirely natural development . . . it becomes quite natural to talk about language in classrooms. If a pupil keeps on omitting main verbs from sentences, it is inefficient to keep on drawing attention to specific omissions, when by understanding that there is a word class (i.e. verb), which functions as the nucleus of each sentence, the pupil can in future check the presence of a verb for himself. If a pupil is having difficulty with pronouns, scattering words such as *she* or *they* or *them* throughout a text, providing inadequate guidance as to what *she*, *they* or *them* refers to, it is clearly of importance that the pupil begin to apply a general rule of reference which implies the knowledge of the relationship of pronoun to noun. Since, therefore, teacher and pupil need, in discussion, a word which refers to a class of terms (i.e. pronouns) there is no good reason not to use that term. Teachers and pupils, in the process of editing and redrafting written work, will be helped by descriptive technical language to talk about it, using terms such as 'word', 'sentence' or 'paragraph'. Then it is likely that good progress will be made. Teaching language must involve talking about language, since learning without that activity is slow, inefficient and inequitable (in that it favours those whose ability enables them to generalise without tuition).

2.31 . . . one of the the school's duties is to enable children to acquire Standard English, which is their right. This is not a matter of controversy: no item of evidence received by the Committee contained disagreement with this point.

4.33 It should be the duty of all teachers to instil in their pupils a civilised respect for other languages and an understanding of the relations between other languages and English. . . . Informed and socially productive attitudes will flourish in classrooms where both children and teachers are accustomed to treat language as a fit subject for study. Pupils are most likely to acquire such attitudes and accompanying knowledge through active investigation.

The Cox committee, drawing up the National Curriculum, accepted these conclusions without reservation, as can be seen most clearly in chapter 6 of the Cox report, entitled 'Knowledge about language'. The continuity between the thinking of the two committees can be seen from paragraphs 5 and 6 of this chapter:

6.5   Despite its cogent arguments, the conclusions of the Kingman Inquiry in favour of the teaching of knowledge about language are still rejected by some. We ourselves therefore find it necessary to state a case for teaching pupils about language.

6.6   Two justifications for teaching pupils explicitly about language are, first, the positive effect on aspects of their use of language and secondly, the general value of such knowledge as an important part of their understanding of their social and cultural environment, since language has vital functions in the life of the individual and of society.

The intention of the Cox committee is therefore unambiguous: the teaching of 'knowledge about language' is an essential part of the subject 'English'. However broadly or narrowly we interpret the word 'grammar', it is included in 'knowledge of language' and therefore needs a prominent place in English teaching.

This said, however, it is important to notice that knowledge about language is not given the status of a distinct 'attainment target', so a pupil's knowledge about language is not assessed as such. Pupils are assigned to one of the levels in each of speaking/listening, reading, writing, spelling and hand-writing, but not in knowledge about language. This arrange-ment has some advantages. On the one hand it emphasises the importance of knowledge about language to all the target skills; and on the other it recognises the harsh realities of the present, in which many English teachers don't themselves know enough about language (and about grammar in particular) to cope with the demands of a separate target. But the main point to remember is that the exclusion of knowledge about language from the list of attainment targets does not suggest anything about its relative importance, because pre-cisely the same is true of the study of literature, which is universally accepted as one of the central activities of English teaching.

The Cox report's official section is divided on the basis of the three main attainment targets, as already explained, but it assumes that teaching about language permeates all of these targets, and is therefore mentioned (frequently) under all three of them. This makes it difficult to build a clear picture of what the National Curriculum expects in this area, so I have brought together the main references to knowledge about language. The Cox report does this on a more limited scale, in sections 6.22–4, but it still assumes the targets as the basis for organisation – that is, it gives separate lists of targets for speaking, reading, and writing.

In the following list I have chosen instead to classify the references according to the level of attainment, starting with level 1 and ending at level 10. It seems fair to assume that most children will be working at the same level across all the targets, though some of course may be more advanced in, say, reading than in writing. This makes it easier to think about the kind of language work that would be suitable for a group working at a particular level.

My list of extracts is also a lot fuller than the one in 6.22–4 of the Cox report, which is based entirely on the list of attainment targets. My list also includes some extracts from the programmes of study, includes references to the earlier levels (whereas the Cox report list starts at level 5), and covers skills, such as the use of Standard English and being able to consult a dictionary, which I believe presuppose some explicit teaching about language. The National Curriculum gives examples of all the attainment target items, which I have included only when they seemed helpful. Unlike the attainment target items they have no legal status.

My first extract is important enough to stand on its own. It is not tied to any particular level of achievement.

PS1:11   Pupils should be encouraged to respect their own language(s) or dialect(s) and those of others.

(The reference to *PS1:11* means the section of the National Curriculum that deals with the programmes of study for speaking and listening (PS1), paragraph 11.)

Level 1 (age 5–8, median for age 5)

[There are no relevant references specific to this level, but the following refers to the teaching of infant pupils, aged from 5 to 7.]

PS2:6   (i) Activities should ensure that pupils: . . .
        – . . . notice how words are constructed and spell-
        ed;
        – refer to . . . dictionaries . . . as a matter of course.

Level 2 (age 6–11, median for ages 7 and 8)

AT2:2   [Pupils should] demonstrate knowledge of the
        alphabet in using word books and simple diction-
        aries.
AT4:2   [*Pupils should:*]
        – recognise that spelling has patterns, and begin
        to apply their knowledge of those patterns in their
        attempts to spell a wider range of words; e.g. *coat,
        goat; feet, street.*
        – show knowledge of the names and order of the
        letters of the alphabet.

[The following applies to junior pupils, aged 7 to 11.]

PS1:13 . . . Pupils should consider the way word mean-
        ings can be played with, e.g. in riddles, puns,
        jokes, spoonerisms, word games, graffiti, adver-
        tisements, poems; the use of nonsense words and
        deliberate misspellings, e.g. in poems and adver-
        tisements.

Level 3 (age 7–16, median for ages 9 and 10)

AT4:3   (iii) [Pupils should] show a growing awareness of
        word families and their relationships; e.g. *grow,
        growth, growing, grown, grew.*

PS3:14   Pupils working towards level 3 ... should be taught to look for instances where: ...
– tenses or pronouns have been used incorrectly or inconsistently.

PS3:15   They should be taught, in the context of discussion about their own writing, grammatical terms such as sentence, verb, tense, noun, pronoun.

Level 4 (ages 8–16, median for ages 11 and 12)

AT3:4   [Pupils should] begin to use the structures of written Standard English and begin to use some sentence structures different from those of speech; e.g. begin to use subordinate clauses and expanded noun phrases.

AT4:4   [Pupils should] spell correctly, in the course of their own writing, words which display other main patterns in English spelling; e.g. words using the main prefixes and suffixes.

PS3:18   [Pupils should:]
– be introduced to some of the uses of the comma and the apostrophe;
– be taught the meaning and spelling of some common prefixes and suffixes, e.g. *un-*, *in-* (and *im-*, *il-*, *ir-*), *-able*, *-ness*, *-ful*, etc., in the context of their own writing and reading;
– be encouraged and shown how to check spellings in a dictionary or on a computer spelling checker when revising and proof-reading;
– be introduced to the complex regularity that underlies the spelling of words with inflectional endings, e.g. *bead-ing, bead-ed, bed-d-ing, bed-d-ed*, in the context of their own writing and reading.

PS3:20   ... pupils should be helped to recognise how Standard English has come to have a wide social and geographical currency and to be the form of English most frequently used on formal or public occasions. They should be helped to recognise any differences in grammar or vocabulary between the

local dialect of English and Standard English, reco-
gnising that local speech forms play an important
part in establishing a sense of group identity.

Level 5 (ages 10–16, median for ages 13 and 14)

AT1:5   [Pupils should] recognise variations in vocabulary
between different regional or social groups, and
relate this knowledge where appropriate to personal experience; e.g. talk about dialect vocabulary
and specialist terms; discuss the vocabulary used
by characters in books or on television.

AT2:5   [Pupils should] show through discussion an
awareness of a writer's choice of particular words
and phrases and the effect on the reader; e.g.
recognise puns, word-play, unconventional spellings . . . .

AT3:5   [Pupils should] show in discussion the ability to
recognise variations in vocabulary according to
purpose, topic and audience and whether language is spoken or written . . .; e.g. discuss the use
of slang in dialogue and narrative in a published
text and in their own writing and comment on its
appropriateness.

PS1:9   Teaching about language through speaking and
listening, which should have started by the time
pupils are working towards level 5, should focus
on:
– regional and social variation in English accents
and dialects and attitudes to such variations;
– the range of purposes which spoken language
serves;
– the forms and functions of spoken Standard
English.

Level 6 (ages 12–16, median for ages 14 to 16)

AT1:6   [Pupils should be able to] show in discussion
an awareness of grammatical differences between

spoken Standard English and a non-standard variety; e.g. take note of different ways in which tense and person are marked in the verb 'to be' after listening to recordings or participating in classroom improvisations.

PS1:17   Pupils should be given the opportunity to consider:
– people's sensitivity to features of pronunciation that differentiate the speech of one area from others;
– any grammatical differences between the speech of the area and spoken Standard English, e.g. in verb forms, pronoun use, prepositions.

AT2:4   [Pupils should] show in discussion of their reading an awareness that words can change in use and meaning over time and demonstrate some of the reasons why; e.g. understand that technological developments, euphemisms, contact with other languages or fashion all contribute to language change.

PS2:23   Pupils should discuss:
– examples of words and expressions which tend to undergo very rapid change in use or meaning, e.g. terms of approbation (*wicked, brill*);
– differences in the use and meanings of words used by pupils, their parents and grandparents, e.g. *wireless, radio, tranny, transistor*;
– new words that have become part of the English vocabulary during the last 50 years or so, e.g. *computer, astronaut, macho*;
– the reasons why vocabulary changes over time, e.g. contact with other languages, because of trade or political circumstances, fashion, effects of advertising, need for new euphemisms, new inventions and technology, changes in society;
– where new words come from, e.g. coinages, acronyms or borrowings from other languages (*glasnost, catamaran, chic*).

AT3:6   [Pupils should] demonstrate, through discussion

and in their writing, grammatical differences between spoken and written English; e.g. in a group, identify some of the differences between the language used in a tape recording of someone talking and a piece of writing by the same person.

AT4/5:6 [Pupils should be able to] recognise that words with related meanings may have related spellings, even though they sound different, e.g. *sign, signature, medical, medicine*; recognise that the spelling of unstressed syllables can often be deduced from the spelling of a stressed syllable in a related word, e.g. *history, historical, . . .*

PS3:25 Pupils should have opportunities to:
– learn that the writer can indicate the relationship between essential and subsidiary information if parenthetical constructions are separated by brackets or pairs of commas or dashes;
– learn other uses of the comma, e.g. around appositional constructions, and begin to use semi-colons and colons;
– learn, in the context of their own writing and reading, some of the words and roots which have been absorbed into English from other languages, so that they become familiar with the word-building processes and spelling patterns that derive from them.

PS3:28 . . . pupils should come to understand the functions of the impersonal style of writing used in academic – and particularly scientific – writing and to recognise the linguistic features, e.g. the passive, subordination, which characterise it. This should be done by reading and discussing examples.

Teaching should bring out the fact that as speech typically takes place in a situation where both speaker and listener are present, it can be accompanied by gestures and words like *this, that, here, now, you*, etc., whereas writing generally requires greater verbal explicitness. Pupils should be helped to recognise that because writers are not able to use the voice to emphasise key points in a sentence, they have to use a wide range of grammatical structure (such as the passive, or other alterations of word order) to bring about the desired emphasis. They should also recognise that writing is often more formal and more impersonal than speech; lexical and grammatical features of language both reflect and create these contrasts.

Level 7 (ages 13–16, median for age 16)

[The first excerpt is from the preamble to AT1.]

From level 7, pupils should be using Standard English, wherever appropriate, to meet the statements of attainment.

AT1:7   [Pupils should] show in discussion an awareness of the appropriate use of spoken language, according to purpose, topic and audience; e.g. analyse and reflect upon the language appropriate to a job interview, or an argument with a parent or another pupil following a presentation.

AT2:7   [pupils should:]
– show in discussion that they can recognise features of presentation which are used to inform, to regulate, to reassure or to persuade, in non-literary and media texts. e.g. . . . verbal emphasis through repetition, exclamation, or vocabulary.
– show in discussion or in writing an awareness of writers' use of sound patterns and some other literary devices and the effect on the reader; e.g. . . . rhyme, alliteration, and figures of speech such as similes, metaphors and personification.

AT3:7   [Pupils should] show in discussion and in writing an awareness of what is appropriate and inappropriate language use in written texts.

AT4/5:7   [Pupils should] spell (and understand the meaning of) common roots that have been borrowed from other languages and that play an important role in word-building, e.g. *micro-, psych-, tele-, therm-*; recognise that where words have been borrowed in the last 400 years, there are some characteristic sound-symbol relationships that reflect the word's origin; e.g. *ch-* in French words like *champagne* ... and *ch-* in Greek words like *chaos*, ..., compared with *ch-* in long-established English words like *chaff*, ...

SP3:25   Pupils should ... be enabled, through reading, listening to and talking about a wide range of texts, to use, in their own writing, those grammatical structures which are characteristic of written language and an increasingly varied and differentiated vocabulary.

Level 8 (ages 14–16)

[Pupils should be able to:]

AT1:8   – show in discussion and in writing an awareness of the contribution that facial expressions, gestures and tone of voice can make to a speaker's meaning.

AT2:8   – talk and write about literature and other texts, giving evidence of personal response and showing an understanding of the devices and structures used by the writers, with appropriate reference to details; e.g. write essays commenting upon points of style, character or plot in comparison with other texts; show how or why a dramatist or novelist used questions and/or repetition to build up emotion ...

– discuss and write about changes in the grammar of English over time, encountered in the course of their reading; e.g. ... pronouns (from *thou* and *thee* to *you*), verb forms, negatives.

AT3:8   – demonstrate knowledge of organisational differences between spoken and written English; e.g.

... the fact that speech is interactive, spontaneous and informal while writing is more tightly planned.

PS2:26   – recognise authorial viewpoint and . . . persuasive or rhetorical techniques in a range of texts.

[The following also applies to the age range from 14 to 16, though it is not tied to any specified level.]

PS3:31   Pupils should have opportunities to . . . learn, for example by presenting the same material for different purposes or audiences, or in different forms, how they can achieve different stylistic effects in their writing by a conscious control of grammatical structures and lexical choice.

Level 9 (ages 15–16)

[Pupils should be able to:]

AT1:9   – show in discussion and in writing an awareness of the ways in which language varies between different types of spoken communication; e.g. describe how different kinds of language use, such as jokes, anecdote, conversation, commentary, lecture, could be explained to a foreign visitor.

AT2:9   – demonstrate some understanding of the use of lexical and grammatical effects in the language of literature; e.g. the repetition of words or structures, dialect forms, archaisms, etc.

AT3:9   – make an assured and selective use of a wide range of grammatical constructions which are appropriate for topic, purpose and audience, demonstrating awareness of the means whereby a writer may choose to achieve a desired emphasis . . .; e.g. vary sentence beginnings; alter word order; use lexical or structural repetition, passive constructions, adverbial connectives, elliptical constructions, non-finite subordinate clauses and choose varied and appropriate vocabulary such as colloquial, formal, technical, poetic or figurative.

– demonstrate in discussion and in writing knowledge of ways in which language varies between different types of written text; e.g. ... personal letters, formal letters, printed instructions, reports in different newspapers, playscripts or films.

PS3:35 ... pupils should be taught:

– how to recognise and describe some of the lexical, grammatical and organisational characteristics of different types of written texts; e.g. letters, tabloid and broadsheet newspapers, teenage magazines, specialist hobby periodicals, holiday brochures, travel books, instructions, playscripts;

– about the nature and purpose of impersonal styles of writing, and the vocabulary and grammar characteristic of those styles, e.g. the use of the passive voice and of other ways of depersonalising text – such as not using pronouns.

Level 10 (age 16)

[Pupils should be able to:]

AT1:10 – show in discussion and in writing an awareness of some of the factors that influence people's attitudes to the way other people speak.

AT2:10 – demonstrate in discussion and in writing some understanding of attitudes in society towards language change and of ideas about appropriateness and correctness in language use; e.g. comment on the arguments, attitudes and styles displayed in a running correspondence, on an issue of language usage or performance, in a newspaper or weekly periodical.

AT3:10 – demonstrate, in discussion and in writing, knowledge of criteria by which different types of written language can be judged; e.g. ... clarity, coherence, accuracy, appropriateness, effectiveness, vigour, and awareness of purpose and audience.

These subtargets for knowledge about language appear to be sensible and reasonably coherent, with a steady progression from concrete to abstract and from particular to general. No doubt some of the details are debatable – for example, it seems odd that attitudes to language varieties are not discussed until level 5, a level which some pupils will never reach; whereas grammatical terms like 'verb' and 'tense' are introduced at level 3. However there is no point in picking over the details of the regulations, and especially not at this early stage.

What will be much more important in deciding the success or failure of the National Curriculum is how it is implemented: how individual teachers interpret general phrases such as 'show in discussion an awareness of grammatical differences between spoken Standard English and a non-standard variety.' The aim of this book is to try to help teachers to teach about language in a way that they and their pupils find intellectually satisfying, rather than lurching from one half-understood point or activity to the next.

References

Ahlberg, Janet and Ahlberg, Allan 1982: *The Ha Ha Bonk Joke Book.* Harmondsworth: Puffin.

Aitchison, Jean 1976: *The Articulate Mammal: An Introduction to Psycholinguistics.* London: Hutchinson.

Aitchison, Jean 1978: *Teach Yourself Linguistics.* London: Hodder and Stoughton.

Aitchison, Jean 1981: *Language Change: Progress or Decay?* London: Fontana.

Aitchison, Jean 1987: *Words in the Mind: An Introduction to the Mental Lexicon.* Oxford: Blackwell.

Anderson, L. and Trudgill, P. 1990: *Bad Language.* Oxford: Blackwell.

Andrews, Avery 1985: The major functions of the noun-phrase. In T. Shopen (ed.), *Language Typology and Syntactic Description I,* Cambridge: Cambridge University Press, 62–154.

Bawden, Nina 1987: *The Finding.* Harmondsworth: Puffin.

Bolinger, Dwight 1980: *Language. The Loaded Weapon: The Use and Abuse of Language Today.* London: Longman.

Bolinger, Dwight and Sears, D. A. 1981: *Aspects of Language,* 3rd edn. New York: Harcourt, Brace.

Brontë, Charlotte 1847: *Jane Eyre.* 1975 edn. Oxford: Oxford University Press.

Brown, K. 1984: *Linguistics Today.* London: Fontana.

Bruner, Jerome 1965: Some elements of discovery. Cited by Cox from *The Relevance of Education,* Harmonsworth: Penguin, 1974.

Burton-Roberts, Noel 1986: *Analysing Sentences: An Introduction to English Syntax.* Harlow: Longman.

Cameron, Debbie 1985: *Feminism and Linguistic Theory.* New York: St Martin's.

Cheshire, Jenny and Trudgill, P. 1989: Dialect and education in the United Kingdom. In Cheshire et al. 1989, 94–112.

Cheshire, Jenny, Edwards, V., Münstermann, H. and Weltens, B. 1989: *Dialect and Education: Some European Perspectives.* Clevedon: Multilingual Matters.

Comrie, B. 1989: *Language Universals and Linguistic Typology* 2nd edn. Oxford: Blackwell.

Cox Report: contained in *English for Ages 5 to 6*, with an introduction by the Secretaries of State for Education and Science and for Wales. DES and the Welsh Office, June 1988.

Coupland, N. (ed.) 1990: *English in Wales*. Clevedon: Multilingual Matters.

Crack-a-Joke Book, collected by children for Oxfam, 1978. Harmondsworth: Penguin.

Crystal, David 1987: *The Cambridge Encyclopedia of Language*. Cambridge: Cambridge University Press.

Crystal, David 1988: *The English Language*. Harmondsworth: Penguin.

Edwards, Viv and Cheshire, J. 1989: The survey of British dialect grammar. In Cheshire et al. 1989, 200–215.

Fawcett, Robin and Perkins, M. 1980: *Child Language Transcripts 6–12*. Pontypridd: Polytechnic of Wales.

Freeborn, Dennis, French, Peter and Langford, David 1986: *Varieties of English: An Introduction to the Study of Language*. London: Macmillan.

Fromkin, V. and Rodman, R. 1988: *An Introduction to Language* 4th edn). New York: Holt, Rinehart and Winston.

Goody, J. and Watt, I. 1962: The consequences of literacy. *Comparative Studies in Society and History*, 5: 304–45. Reprinted in P. Giglioli (ed.), *Language and Social Context*, Harmondsworth: Penguin, 1972, 311–57.

Greenbaum, Sidney 1991: *An Introduction to English Grammar*. London: Longman.

Hawkins, E. 1987: *Awareness of Language: An introduction*. Cambridge: Cambridge University Press.

Huddleston, Rodney 1984: *An Introduction to the Grammar of English*. Cambridge: Cambridge University Press.

Huddleston, Rodney 1988: *English Grammar: An outline*. Cambridge: Cambridge University Press.

Hudson, Richard 1980: *Sociolinguistics*. Cambridge: Cambridge University Press.

Hudson, Richard 1981: Some issues on which linguists can agree. *Journal of Linguistics*, 17: 333–44.

Hudson, Richard 1984: *An Invitation to Linguistics*. Oxford: Blackwell.

Hughes, Arthur and Trudgill, P. 1987: *English Accents and Dialects*. London: Arnold.

Kingman Committee 1988: Report of the Committee of Inquiry into the Teaching of English Language. London: HMSO.

Leech, Geoffrey 1989: *An A–Z of English Grammar*. London: Arnold.

Leech, Geoffrey, Deuchar, M. and Hoogenraad, R. 1982: *English Grammar for Today: A New Introduction*. London: Macmillan.

Longworth, I. and Cherry, J. (eds) 1986: *Archaeology in Britain since 1945*. London: British Museum Publications.

Milroy, James and Milroy, Lesley (eds) 1985a: Regional variation in British English syntax. London: Economic and Social Research Council.

Milroy, James and Milroy, Lesley 1985b: *Authority in Language: Investigating Language Prescription and Standardisation*. London: Routledge.

National Curriculum: Education (National Curriculum) (Attainment Targets and Programmes of Study in English) (No. 2) Order 1990. Laid before Parliament 6 March 1990.

Ong, Walter 1982: *Orality and Literacy: The Technologizing of the Word*. London: Methuen.

Palmer, Frank 1971: *Grammar*. Harmondsworth: Penguin.

Perera, Katherine 1984. *Children's Writing and Reading: Analysing Classroom Language*. Oxford: Blackwell.

Phythian, B. A. 1980: *Teach Yourself English Grammar*. London: Hodder and Stoughton.

Quirk, Randolph and Stein, G. 1990: *English in Use*. London: Longman.

Quirk, Randolph, Greenbaum, S., Leech, G. and Svartvik, J. 1985: *A Comprehensive Grammar of the English Language*. London: Longman.

Radford, Andrew. 1988: *Transformational Grammar: A First Course*. Cambridge: Cambridge University Press.

Romaine, Suzanne 1984: *The Language of Children and Adolescents: The Acquisition of Communicative Competence*. Oxford: Blackwell.

Smith, Neil and Wilson, D. 1979: *Modern Linguistics: The Results of Chomsky's Revolution*. Harmondsworth: Penguin.

Spender, Dale 1980: *Man Made Language*. London: Routledge.

Stubbs, Michael 1986: *Educational Linguistics*. Oxford: Blackwell.

Trudgill, Peter 1974: *Sociolinguistics: An Introduction*. Harmondsworth: Penguin.

Trudgill, Peter 1975: *Accent, Dialect and the School*. London: Arnold.

Trudgill, Peter 1990: *The Dialects of England*. Oxford: Blackwell.

Upton, Clive, Sanderson, S. and Widdowson, J. 1987: *Word Maps: A Dialect Atlas of England*. London: Croom Helm.

Walmsley, John 1984: The uselessness of 'formal grammar'. Committee for Linguistics in Education working paper, obtainable from Tom Bloor, Modern Languages Department, Aston University, Birmingham B4 7ET, enclosing self-addressed, stamped envelope suitable for A5 pamphlet. Price £1.

Wenham, E. J., Dorling, J. A. N., Snell, J. A. N. and Taylor, B. 1972: *Physics: Concepts and Models*. London: Addison-Wesley.

Williams, Ann 1989: Dialect in school written work. In Cheshire et al. 1989, 182–9.

Index

Note: This index does not cover the 'encyclopedia of grammar' in Part IV, which serves as its own index. Words which are listed in the encyclopedia are marked in this index by '$'.